D0267610

FROM BIPLANE TO SPITFIRE

THE LIFE OF AIR CHIEF MARSHAL SIR GEOFFREY SALMOND
KCB KCMG DSO

by

ANNE BAKER

LEO COOPER

First Published in Great Britain 2003 by
LEO COOPER
an imprint of Pen & Sword Books
47 Church Street
Barnsley, S. Yorkshire, S70 2AS

ISBN 0 85052 980 8

A CIP record for this book is available from the British Library

Typeset in 10/12.5pt Plantin by
Phoenix Typesetting, Auldgirth, Dumfriesshire.

Printed in England by
CPI UK

DEDICATION

To Penelope
David, Peter, Rose, Chris
and Julian

CONTENTS

FOREWORD

Bryan Watkins

Great in the field, in the air and in the council chamber, his character was so fine, his personality so lovable. His is indeed an irreparable loss.

Sir Philip Sassoon

Every student of the history of the war of 1914-18 knows that General Allenby's last great advance, which crushed the Turkish Army, was made possible by the Royal Flying Corps, inspired by Geoffrey Salmond and directed by his brilliant staff work. But everybody does not know how much British Aviation, in every activity, owes to his knowledge, energy and foresight since that war . . . By the death of Geoffrey Salmond we have lost a great leader of men, a great organiser, a true statesman, and a fine technician. But above and beyond that, many have lost a very dear friend.

From an obituary by C.G. Grey

History is chary of awarding the accolade of greatness to any man. Indeed, such an award is all to often open to challenge as the years go by. However, there can be no challenging the fact that both Air Chief Marshal Sir Geoffrey Salmond KCB KCMG DSO and Bar and his younger brother Jack, Marshal of the Royal Air Force Sir John Salmond GCB CMG CVO DSO, were the only brothers to hold the supreme appointment of Chief of Air Staff in succession.

Whilst Jack's considerable achievements have been recorded for history by Dr John Laffin in his biography, *Swifter than Eagles*, no such records exist of those of his brother. Since Geoffrey's tragically early death in 1933, they seem almost to have become lost in the mists of time. Yet it is to Geoffrey's vision and wisdom that we owe so much that is now great in British Aviation. His early understanding of the possibilities of aviation has had a profound effect on the development of military airpower and the growth of international air travel. His daughter, Anne Baker, has written a book that redresses this imbalance; not only does she recount the historical impact of this remarkable officer, she also provides an insight into the man behind the admired leader.

Geoffrey Salmond's importance is not confined to his achievements during his lifetime but extends to the depth and breadth of his vision of the future of both military and civil aviation. That vision is clearly reflected in his pioneering work on long-range transport and on spurring the pace of aircraft development through an enthusiasm that could not fail to infect others. Perhaps his most important legacy was the impact that he and Jack made on the spirit of their infant service, right from the earliest days in France. Their gallantry and natural gift of leadership, combined with their outstanding professional skills and their deep concern for the welfare of all under their command, made a major contribution to the very identity, and indeed, the traditions, of the Royal Air Force as they exist today.

The biography of her father that Anne Baker has given us is a vivid story of a family committed to the life and early development of the RAF. It is fitting that it should have been written by Geoffrey Salmond's own daughter since she was part of that story for the first eighteen years of her life. This story embraces the fortunes of both brothers, for to write a biography of Geoffrey without writing about her uncle, Jack, was impossible; the two men were inseparable friends and their professional lives were closely intertwined.

The brothers were among the leading pioneers of the Royal Flying Corps, qualifying, in the dawn of military flying, as pilots on the first two courses held at the Central Flying School at Upavon. Geoffrey had already attended the Military Staff College at Camberley as an officer in the Royal Artillery. There he had developed his controversial ideas about the use of aircraft in the context of the tactics and military strategy of the day. That experience stood him in good stead during his years in command of the RFC in Egypt and the Middle East, years that would see him rise from Acting Lieutenant Colonel to a very highly regarded Major General with a CB, two DSOs and numerous Mentions in Despatches, in addition to the Egyptian Government's Order of the Nile.

As the title of this biography indicates, it is the constant flow of Geoffrey's letters home to his wife Peggy that constitutes the main source of information upon which this book is based. In addition, Jack's unpublished diaries of the fighting in France also provide a vivid picture of the work of the RFC in that theatre.

Geoffrey's letters to Peggy describe the initial landing of the advance party of Headquarters RFC in France, of which he was a member, and the rush to set up the very rudimentary airfields from which the squadrons would have to operate during the hectic early days which lead up to the Retreat from Mons;

his brilliant invention of a grid system to co-ordinate target identification between the RFC pilots and the artillerymen they were supporting; life in the headquarters; his successful tour of command of the legendary No. 1 Squadron, which was to lead to his promotion and selection to command No. 5 Wing, earmarked to go to Egypt in November 1915, to guard the Canal; the problems which confronted him on arrival, not least being the indifference of the Army to their new offspring, the RFC; the important role of the Wing in winning the war with the Senussi, so creating a new realization within the minds of the Army of what the RFC could do for them.

The book covers the growth in power and influence of the RFC in Egypt. Geoffrey established a Training Brigade for pilots and groundcrew, not only for the Middle East but also for the BEF in France. It was a project which grew and grew. Sited at Ismailia, Geoff called it his 'Little City by the Sea'. He even built an aircraft factory there.

In 1917, when General Allenby arrived as Commander-in-Chief, the RFC in Egypt and Palestine was in a position to provide the whole range of air support that he was going to need in his major offensive against the Turks. By September 1918 Geoffrey Salmond's air force had gained complete superiority over the Germans. Anne Baker gives us an insight into Allenby's offensive to take Damascus, when air power effectively demolished the Turkish 7th Army, as well as Geoff's long-term friendship with T.E. Lawrence, including the support he gave him for his Arab guerrilla operations.

The war over, the ink was scarcely dry on the terms of the Armistice when he made the first flight from Cairo to Baghdad, and thence on to Karachi and Delhi, in a Handley Page 0/400 bomber. His idea of an Imperial Air Transport Company was to be fulfilled much later by the launch of Imperial Airways.

The book also describes the birth of the significant concept of air control when, in 1920, Geoff launched an air-based campaign to bring the 'Mad Mullah' in Somaliland to book. It was extremely successful and led to the assumption of policing responsibility throughout Iraq by the Royal Air Force.

In March 1921, as soon as the Cairo Conference on the future of the Middle East had settled the pattern of control of the area, Geoff put his hand to a masterpiece – driving a furrow across the face of the Iraqi desert to serve as a navigation aid for the new RAF air route to Baghdad. Within three months, the route, with its supplementary dumps of fuel and emergency landing strips, was ready. For many years this proved a life-saver for those airmen who had no navigation aids other than a compass. Traces can even be seen from the air to this day – a legacy to Geoffrey's ability to initiate a simple, logical and highly effective solution to an important problem of the time.

In 1922 he returned to England to take up a new post as Air Member for Supply and Research (AMSR), one in which he would play a significant role in the development of the aeroplane as a fighting machine and in the RAF's support for a struggling British Aircraft Industry.

By putting measures and studies in hand to ensure that future aircraft construction would be based upon the use of metal for airframes and by the creation of the High Speed Flight, he set the Service on the path which would ultimately bring in such aircraft as the Hurricane and the Spitfire, without which the Battle of Britain would not have been won.

From this highly significant tour of duty, Geoff then flew out on the first through flight from London to Delhi to take over command as Air Officer Commanding, India. We get an appreciation of the growing influence of aviation in that continent including the dramatic air evacuation of women and children from the Legations from Kabul in 1928. Pilots who had never flown over 10,000 feet before coaxed their laden Vickers Victorias over the snow-capped mountains of the Hindu Kush to safety.

Peggy had been with him for much of his time in India and they returned to England in 1931 on his appointment as AOC-in-C Air Defence of Great Britain, a post he took over from Jack. Geoff took up his new duties just in time to see his brainchild, the High Speed Flight, win the Schneider Trophy outright for Britain. The forerunner to the Spitfire was born!

There were, at that time, dangerous pressures to disarm. When Geoff attended the World Disarmament Conference in Geneva he and Jack may have changed the course of the history of the Second World War when they prevented the Royal Air Force from becoming emasculated. Geoff's influence on the future of our country is again demonstrated by his fighting speech at the dinner of the RAF Association's Old Comrades, when he spelt out the dangers which were threatening the Royal Air Force. This undoubtedly awoke a slumbering British public. There was mayhem in the House of Commons, but so stoutly was Geoff defended by his good friend Sir Philip Sassoon that those Members who were baying for his blood were duly silenced.

Geoffrey Salmond's career was crowned by his appointment on 1 April 1933 to succeed Jack as Chief of Air Staff. His tenure of office was eagerly awaited throughout the Service and by British Aviation. His death from cancer, only 27 days after he assumed office, was a tragedy beyond belief.

The service of the Crown has traditionally been something of a family business and for brothers both to rise to high rank is not uncommon, but no two brothers in the history of any Service have made the combined level of contribution made by Geoffrey and John Salmond. Their like will not be seen again.

PREFACE

Although my father died when I was only eighteen, I and my sisters and brother always felt with him, that we were part of the Royal Flying Corps and of the very early days of the Royal Air Force.

From our earliest childhood we were surrounded by aeroplanes, aeroplanes dropping message bags on our ship when we left Egypt, aeroplanes flying in fantastic manoeuvres at the first Air Displays at Hendon, and then we were all in India when my father organized the evacuation of 500 men, women and children from Kabul, the capital of Afghanistan. As the Victorias flew over the snow-capped mountains of the Hindu Kush we all held our breath hoping they would survive.

When I was writing about this rescue in *Wings over Kabul* I felt that I should ask the late Lord Trenchard if I might read his father's letters to my father at the time. I was quite nervous of meeting him but was greatly reassured by his generosity and kindness. He said I could read what I liked as I was "part of the family". These generous words stayed in my mind and inspired me to write the story of the very early days of the Royal Flying Corps, when the world seemed young and full of adventure to those soldiers who decided to join the newly formed service and later, when war came, to take their fragile aeroplanes to France. My father and his brother were among those early fliers, and I hope that from their letters and diaries I have been able to recapture what they and so many of their friends felt at the time. Many of these airmen were to lose their lives in the first war, whilst others like my father and his brother were lucky enough to live on to put their hearts and lives into the Royal Air Force.

ACKNOWLEDGEMENTS

My grateful thanks are due to P.J.V. Elliott of the Royal Air Force Museum for permission to read the Trenchard Salmond letters which are reproduced with permission of the Controller of Her Majesty's Stationery Office. To Dennis Bateman and the Historical Branch of the Ministry of Defence for their research. Also thanks are due to the Public Records Office, the National Army Museum, Chelsea, the Imperial War Museum, Captain Alexander Swann, Mike Goodall for his History of Brooklands, and the late Air Chief Marshal Sir Ronald Ivelaw Chapman for their invaluable help and cooperation. Thanks also to Diana Athill for her great help, Roger Elliott for his brilliant photography and my sisters Joyce and Penelope for their patient help and encouragement. Most of all I must thank all my children, especially Julian, for his untiring help, and I would like to pay a tribute to my mother the late Lady Salmond, who encouraged and inspired me to write this book.

1

THE FASCINATION OF FLIGHT—
LOVE, LINEN AND PIANO WIRE

In the spring of 1910 two brothers, young Army officers, met at Brooklands racing track. Most of the track was reserved for racing cars, but along the grassy verge stood a line of recently-constructed small wooden huts with tin roofs. Beside them on the grass was a row of extraordinary machines: powered heavier-than-air aircraft in all shapes and sizes which were rapidly replacing balloons and kites in the hearts of inventors bent on conquering the sky. Most of these machines were French, including the Henri Farman owned by the writer Mrs Maurice Hewlett and the biplane on which the brilliant French aviator Louis Paulhan was working.

The first British aviators were either very rich or very eccentric (or both!), for the British government frowned on the aeroplane. In March 1909 it announced that 'The War Office is not disposed to enter into relations at present with any manufacturers of aeroplanes'. A good deal of self-confidence was needed to be one of the men who gathered at Brooklands clad in overalls, or sometimes, in summer, in their pyjamas, to top up their Antoinette or Gnome engines with castor oil or to dope their aeroplanes' wings, the fragile wooden frames of which might well be held together with piano wire or string and covered with brown paper. It was the owners themselves who tested the aeroplanes here, the flying test likely to involve rising only a few feet from the ground. Topping the trees at the end of the 'runway' and avoiding the sewage farm beyond them was seen as a considerable achievement.

The Army was no more enthusiastic than the Government about flying, its opinion in general, most forcibly expressed by the Cavalry, being that aeroplanes would be no good in war and could only 'frighten the horses'.

In spite of this disheartening forecast, the brothers Geoffrey and John Salmond found it impossible to ignore the fascination of the air, the dream of flying which had bred the legend of Icarus and had haunted inventors ever since

Leonardo da Vinci had designed his prototype of a flying machine. On that spring day they were more serious than usual, understanding each other's response to the scene before them better than anyone else could. Their careers hitherto had been similar: both had joined the Army at the age of nineteen, Geoffrey being commissioned into the Royal Artillery after graduating from Woolwich, John the King's Own Royal Lancashire Regiment after Sandhurst, and both had seen service in the South African War of 1899 to 1901. Geoffrey, the elder by three years, had been awarded the Queen's Medal with seven clasps. Now he was 'cramming' for the Staff College, while John was stationed with his regiment in Jersey.

On the track in front of them, Colonel Cody and his two sons were at work on the first model of his latest machine, the vast 'Cathedral', of which the third model was to win the Military Competition on Salisbury Plain two years later, in the summer of 1912. Although it would fulfil all the requirements of the competition it would never be adopted by the Army, or be used at all in the air, proving disappointing in performance owing to its size and unwieldiness.

Jack Salmond was to write: 'Sitting on a mound, we watched the gallant Cody make an unsuccessful attempt to get his 'Cathedral' off the ground, and a French ace starting on a cross-country flight.' This was Louis Paulhan, who was probably practising for the London to Manchester race, which he would win that April, gaining the *Daily Mail* prize of £1,000. 'Seeing that fast-disappearing speck in the sky, and realising that it was controlled by one man, whose life depended utterly on his individual skill, was an inspiring and thrilling sight. I definitely made up my mind that somehow or other I was going to fly.' Geoff was no less elated, but for him the decision was less simple. He was not only in the midst of the Staff College examination, but was also engaged to be married.

From childhood the brothers had always been the closest friends. Their father, Major General Sir William Salmond, was a dedicated soldier and had been knighted in 1902 for his part in the South African War. Geoff, the elder, was born in Dover Castle, where his father was serving, but the two brothers and their three sisters were mostly brought up in Victorian London. Their mother was artistic and beautiful, and Jack wrote in his memoirs, 'I have always thought my father a very lucky man because he married one of the most beautiful and sweetest of women.'

Both boys went to a preparatory school in Yorkshire, Aysgarth, from where Geoffrey won a scholarship to Wellington College where he was later joined by Jack. Both were made College prefects and there seemed no other career for them in those days than to follow their father into the Army. Geoff was full of youthful enthusiasm. He was always light-hearted and full of fun, very like his younger brother in his dark good looks, but with a tremendous capacity for 'seeing the funny side of things' and a great capacity for friendship. Jack, on the other hand, was taller and very good-looking. His languid charm hid a capacity for leadership which was to be of vital importance in the years ahead. He wrote of Geoff, while at Wellington:

> I was fortunate in having my brother, Geoff, who was a prefect, behind me. Although he was three years older, which at school is a gulf as wide as the Seven Seas, this made no difference to our mutual exchanges of confidence when, occasionally, we were together. My regard for him was unbounded, and that affection which should be the birthright of all brothers and which in our case was particularly strong, remained constant and at call despite the gap in seniority between us.

Although the brothers would have heard of the early experiments in gliding, perhaps of Sir George Cayley or Lilienthal and Pilcher, it still seemed impossible at that time to fly a heavier-than-air machine from the ground, and the Army seemed to hold out the best opportunity for an adventurous career.

Geoffrey graduated from Woolwich into the Royal Artillery and at the age of nineteen set sail for South Africa. Almost at once his longing for adventure was rewarded, for the ship, which was also carrying troops from the 10th Hussars and their horses, struck a rock just outside Cape Town. Volunteers were called upon to unloose the horses in the hold before the ship sank, so that they would have a chance to swim to safety. Geoff volunteered and worked feverishly with a subaltern of the Hussars, until the beams overhead began to crack. All the horses were released and he was particularly proud of his own charger, a clever old campaigner, who with pricked ears swerved aside from the dangerous rocks between the ship and the shore, and, swimming farther down the coast, managed to land unharmed on a beach, where Geoff recovered him safely. Once on shore the 10th Hussars invited Geoffrey to a special dinner in which he was thanked for his help.

Geoff's regiment now joined General Buller's force at Estcourt in preparation for an attack. Many photographs taken by him with an early camera survive. The long lines of horses and guns, and all the details of camp life are shown. Perhaps the most interesting are those of men in their thick khaki uniforms riding their horses through the Tugela river and across the wide hot plains, dragging their guns and equipment. At one point the CO decided it was necessary to blow up a bridge across the river before the enemy reached it. There were many bushes and branches floating down the river, and Geoff, a strong swimmer, offered to swim downstream under water disguised as a bush to lay the charges. His Commanding Officer rather crushingly replied, 'What would your mother say?' which must have infuriated him.

Observation balloons were used in the South African war and were fairly successful in 'seeing the other side of the hill', as General Swinton said. There were, however, drawbacks. The balloons could not be used in winds of more than twenty mph and had also to be packed for transport in cumbersome wagons, hauled by steam engines. Nevertheless they were a notable example of observation from the air, as opposed to the Cavalry, in wartime.

Geoffrey took part in the operations on the Tugela Heights and also in the relief of Ladysmith. He was later to say that on one occasion he gave a lift to a young reporter who had just escaped, and found it was the young Winston Churchill. Geoffrey was awarded the Queen's Medal with seven clasps for his part in the campaign.

After a brief posting to China to take part in the suppression of the Boxer rising, Geoff came home to find that his brother had already left for Durban with his regiment. After leave, Geoff was sent out to the Transvaal. The brothers did their best to meet whilst on leave when they were in Africa. On one occasion when Jack was with him Geoffrey had heard that there was a fortune teller in the district, of quite unusual clairvoyance. The brothers decided to test her powers and went together to see her, saying they were great friends and asking if they could possibly be related to one another. She looked at them severely and, no doubt noting their different regimental uniforms, told them there was no relationship whatever. They could hardly leave her tent without laughing.

Soon afterwards the Boer War came to an end, but both brothers still longed for action. Jack was seconded to West Africa as soon as he was twenty-one to join the West African Frontier Force. Geoffrey travelled to Liverpool with him and saw him off. It was to prove a very exacting and testing time for Jack, for he was often alone with a few men in the jungle where he had to make quick decisions which affected the whole future, and often the lives, of his small company, as well as his own.

Meanwhile, Geoffrey was serving at home with his regiment. However, only a year later he set sail for Africa once more, this time on a 'special assignment' in the Secret Service. He was to go out as a civilian and was not able to tell his brother of his arrival. It was only by chance that Jack, then on his way home on sick leave, met a visitor at Lokoja who recognized the photograph on Jack's desk. He wrote later:

> I heard from a new arrival that he had seen my brother Geoffrey on one of the West Coast ships, dressed as a civilian and asserting that he was now a journalist. I was puzzled at this, and the more I thought of it the more apprehensive I became. Evidently he had left the Army, but what could be the reason? The conclusion I ultimately reached was that his usual luck in racing must have disastrously broken and he had had to resign his commission. I waited a week to hear more news, and then left. It later transpired he was on Government Secret Service, which explained everything.

Jack immediately transferred his whole bank account into Geoffrey's account in London, but did not mention this in his Memoirs. The 'special assignment' did involve danger. Once, in a train, Geoffrey felt he was being watched. On some excuse he left the carriage, and when the train slowed down he flung himself out, rolling down a steep bank and escaping into woods nearby. Later he became desperately ill, but at length managed to return to England and safety. He rejoined his regiment and, still restless for adventure, volunteered to go to Japan to train as an interpreter.

It was while both the brothers were still in Africa that a wave of interest in gliding, in kites and in balloons had spread through Europe. This was especially true in England, although there was little encouragement from the Army or from the Government. Perhaps public enthusiasm was largely due to the impact of Colonel Cody, a larger-than-life showman who had come over from America and at first produced a wild west show, wearing a huge Stetson over his flowing hair and cowboy boots, together with a richly saddled white horse. After a time Cody turned his attention to balloons and kites.

For a hundred years the Army had favoured captive balloons for reconnaissance, but Cody saw that to watch enemy movements in wartime it would be simpler and less costly to lift a man into the air with a large kite. He designed a completely successful man-lifting kite and his success gained him a job in the balloon factory at Farnborough, where with his enthusiasm and confidence he became, in 1906, Chief Kiting Instructor to the Army. His courage in testing the kites himself earned him tremendous admiration, but still the Generals were doubtful of his flamboyant and unconventional approach, making them even more sceptical of anything to do with flying machines, for Cody had begun to build a heavier-than-air machine in his spare time.

Meanwhile, in 1903, rumours of the very first powered flight by Orville and Wilbur Wright in far away Kitty Hawk in North Carolina intrigued and inspired those who felt it could be possible for a heavier-than-air machine to fly. Until 1900 the engines, based on motor car engines, had all been too heavy, but the Wright brothers had modified a Pope Toledo car engine in their own bicycle workshop and achieved what had seemed impossible. Their first flight had been for twelve seconds, Orville lying full length on one wing to balance the engine, but their last flight was for 59 seconds. There had been only about a dozen witnesses, but their father had contacted the local paper.

In England, Colonel Capper, the head of the Balloon Unit, decided to visit America to see if the Wright brothers would come to England and demonstrate their machine, but the War Office blocked the plan, eventually telling the Wright brothers that they had 'no plans to buy an aeroplane'. Thus a very valuable chance to advance flying in the United Kingdom was lost.

News of the Wrights' success could not help having an effect on all those young officers in the Army, who, like Geoff and Jack, were longing for adventure. Flying seemed the latest and most thrilling possibility. However, as the Army gave it no encouragement, the two brothers in 1906 were still devoted to their regiments. That summer they met on leave in Norfolk, Jack recovering from bouts of malaria and Geoff just home from Japan. Their father, Sir William Salmond, who had just retired, had taken a charming house some thirteen miles from Norwich, close by the River Waveney and the village of Ditchingham. The brothers and their sisters were soon absorbed in tennis parties, river picnics and dances. Jack, tall, good-looking and dashing, was soon to break many hearts, but Geoff, who arrived a few days later, was so full of fun and jokes that he soon became as popular as his brother. Nobody, however, could have foreseen what effect a chance meeting would have on the family.

At one tennis party, on the lawn of neighbouring Ditchingham Hall, the brothers met the two elder grandchildren. Peggy and Joyce Carr were seventeen and eighteen. Peggy, the eldest daughter of William Carr's five children, was very pretty, with blue eyes and curling chestnut hair and had a light-hearted attitude to life which at once appealed to Geoff. He wrote, however, that that first meeting 'meant nothing to me' but a few days later there was a small dance at which Peggy wore a white frock and blue sash. After just one dance she and Geoff sat out together. Later he wrote: 'From the start it seemed that whatever I thought she thought too, and whatever I said seemed quite natural to her. It was as if I had such a lot to say to her from the beginning.' Soon he was desperately in love. Peggy felt just as he did, but her parents were dismayed. William Carr was a barrister and his wife the daughter of the Master of University College in Oxford where she had been brought up. They had formed the hope, unusual at the time, that their eldest daughter should go to one of the new ladies' colleges, perhaps Lady Margaret Hall. Even if she did not follow this plan, they felt she was far too young to become engaged. And even if she did become engaged so young, surely this remarkably dashing young man, just back from Japan, who had seen service in South Africa and China, belonged to a world too wide for their daughter? Before they could become engaged William Carr decided to send Peggy to France to complete her education, making it a condition of their marriage that Geoff should first pass the Staff College entrance exam.

In those days parents carried great weight and in spite of Geoff and Peggy's devotion to each other, they followed his wishes, but decided to write to each other every day. Letters flew from Deepcut and Farnborough, where Geoffrey was stationed to 60, Rue Bosnières at Caen in Normandy, and then to Norfolk when Peggy returned. Each letter was numbered and the total reached over 200 in the year of their engagement. Geoffrey did not often mention his passion for flying, but in one letter, dated 1908, after hearing that Wilbur Wright himself was coming over to France, he wrote:

> My darling, I have got an idea, Peggy, of going to France and seeing
> Wilbur Wright and his aeroplanes, because our Army will take them up

very strongly soon, and if they did it would be a great thing to be one of the first in the field. We might get my £650 a year quicker that way. I have always been awfully keen on aeroplanes, ever since Mother told me when I was quite a wee thing how she had been to see Sir Hiram Maxim's plane and seen his machine run along rails and rise half an inch, to be dashed to pieces ultimately. I think if I could get Jack to come I would put off some of the bills and go, as when I had seen it I would have some right to see the fellow who runs the Government factory here and get him to take me, if I thought it good enough. In that case, I would look on that trip as an investment. The more I put it off the more chance there is of someone else forestalling me. All the same, I am not going to let the Staff College work stop for all this. There are certain times when one's opportunity does come and sometimes I have the feeling very very strong, and when I have had it, up to now, it has always turned up trumps because I seized it. I am beginning to feel it now, but not quite convincingly yet.

His opportunity was to come – but not for some months.

Meanwhile Wilbur Wright had landed in France, and was demonstrating his aeroplane near Paris. He had made a breathtaking display. He and his brother Orville had spent the last few years perfecting their aeroplane after the first flight at Kitty Hawk in North Carolina and the French aviators had had to develop machines without any comparison with the Wright aeroplanes. The French owed their expertise directly to Lilienthal, whose gliding had also inspired the Wright brothers, and to his disciple, Captain Ferber. Ferber had written, 'To design a flying machine is nothing, to build one is not much, to try it in the air is everything.' They were in advance of those struggling to design aircraft in England. Already Captain Ferber had designed his own aeroplane and fitted it with wheels instead of the skids used by the Wright brothers, thus enabling him to land at will, wherever he wished and he had also joined with a motor racer, M. Levasseur, in producing the famous Antoinette engine, named after their benefactor's daughter. Gabriel and Charles Voisin also built box-kites and aeroplanes at their new factory in Paris, and had towed their gliders in a motor boat along the Seine. In France, even before the 'Champagne meeting' at Rheims, there was a passionate interest in flight.

At home the Army was still sceptical of any help the aeroplane could give them. Geoffrey took rooms at Shrewton near Salisbury in order to concentrate on his exam. It must have been agony to him to be so near to Larkhill and Brooklands and yet unable to fly. Whenever possible he would bicycle over to Larkhill to watch the attempts of Army officers and enthusiasts to get their aeroplanes off the ground.

It was the same atmosphere at Brooklands. Already, in 1907, A.V. Roe had completed his first aircraft and taken it to the motor racing track. The Antoinette engine had not yet arrived from France, and sympathetic motorists rallied round to tow it for him. When, however, the engine arrived he was able to make a first flight. It was June 8th 1908. He actually claimed to have flown sixty yards two feet from the ground, but there was some doubt as to whether it was a true 'flight'. It was usual for 'watchers' to lie flat on the grass in order to make sure that the aeroplane was, in fact, airborne.

Roe was not allowed to sleep in the shed with his aeroplane and such was the official prejudice against flying that he was ordered to leave Brooklands soon afterwards. His request to park beside Cody on Laffin's Plain was also refused, and so it was not until 13 July 1909 that the first official flight by an Englishman in a British aeroplane took place on Lea Marshes.

Perhaps it was the summer of 1909 which was at length to alter the British Government's attitude, for on 25 July, a misty early morning, a small aircraft appeared over the sea near Dover Castle. It landed quite inconspicuously in a field, and the French pilot, Louis Blériot, stepped out to the amazement of a few farm workers who were standing nearby. The £1,000 offer by the *Daily Mail* for the first airborne crossing of the Channel had been won. Jack wrote in his hitherto unpublished diary, 'One day, out of the clouds, a little aeroplane had gently dipped to earth on Dover Cliffs, and England ceased to be an island. It was the herald of vanishing isolation and security for the United Kingdom and all her Empire – but no one realised it at the time.'

Back in Jersey, after his meeting with Geoff at Brooklands in 1910, Jack wrote:

> I began to read all I could lay hands on of the chequered and painful road the pioneers had trodden and to think of the effects this young science might have in war. When the time came to write an obligatory annual essay I chose 'Airships and Aeroplanes in War' as my subject. It had a success and was forwarded to the War Office and, later, predisposed my Colonel to look kindly on my application to join the Royal Flying Corps.

When he was next on leave from Jersey, Jack went to the new airfield at Hendon, hoping to be taken up. He wrote that when he arrived at Hendon he was told that the wind was too gusty. He was just turning away when Grahame-White appeared, brushed the objections aside, ordered out the machine and climbed into the pilot's seat. 'To see the earth rushing smoothly backwards and to realise that I was airborne remains one of my red-letter moments,' Jack wrote. 'We landed on the far side of the aerodrome, taxied round and returned. Price two guineas, but I would have paid a King's ransom.'

Meanwhile Geoff's dreaded Staff College exam was drawing nearer. He wrote despondently to Peggy: 'So many gunners are in for it. Gunners must do awfully well to get in.' However, he did pass the examination and his promise to William Carr had been fulfilled. He could now marry Peggy.

At the Staff College there were official 'calls' to be made, which Peggy dreaded, and dances and parties which she loved. It was, on the whole, an amusing life, but there was a thread of seriousness running through it: Geoff's growing passion for flight and obsession with the unknown future of the aeroplane. At every spare moment he would travel to Weybridge and Brooklands, often taking Peggy with him. Brooklands was now firmly established as an experimental ground for the aircraft industry – Bristol, A.V. Roe and Grahame-White all began building huts and flying there. Surrounding the race track were many sheds belonging to the young enthusiasts. Several flying clubs had opened already and more were planned. Minor crashes were very common, but as the speed was slow and the wing-loading low there were not many serious injuries, although the fragile aircraft were often completely smashed.

It was still considered a great thrill to be able to fly at all in 1910, and those lucky enough to own an aeroplane were looked upon with the greatest respect and admiration. The Hon Alan Boyle wrote at the time:

> I partitioned off a corner of my shed and slept in a hammock so that I was able to take advantage of the still hours of the early morning . . . We were all learners in those days, in fact no one except Grahame-White and A.V.Roe knew anything about it at all, and they did not know much. I remember quite well, after I had been out walking along my wheel tracks and examining them, being fearfully pleased when I saw them disappear for a yard or two.

Box kites and Blériots

Walter Raleigh, the author of the first official history of the Royal Flying Corps, describes the years from 1908 to 1912 as ferment. After the early struggles by such gallant pioneers as Fulton at Larkhill and A.V. Roe at Brooklands, there was suddenly an upsurge of interest and encouragement for everything to do with the air. Bleriot's flight across the Channel in his fragile monoplane, without map or compass, had caught the public imagination and the Aeroplane Meeting at Rheims had been followed by meetings at Blackpool and Bournemouth. Encouragement came from Lord Northcliffe of the *Daily Mail*, who offered prizes for the first round-England flight and the first flight from London to Manchester. There was the realization of danger, too, and the shock of the deaths in flying accidents of the Hon. C.S. Rolls at Bournemouth and later, in 1913, of the magnificent Cody. The public realized that, in spite of all their training, the pilots took their lives in their hands each time they flew. Peggy wrote:

> We had often been to Brooklands to watch Cody flying and saw the start of the round-England race, Cody flying unsteadily over the trees which

surrounded the airfield then, and I think he completed the course while others had forced landings and one bumped back to land as he had forgotten his map.

Meanwhile, exciting events had been taking place in Scotland. In spite of the attitude of many of the Generals, Lord Haldane, then Minister for War in the Asquith government, had encouraged Lieutenant Dunne and Sir Hiram Maxim to take part in experiments in aeroplane construction, especially in stabilising them, and persuaded the Duke of Atholl to allow them to carry out secret trials on his estate at Blair Atholl. These experiments were not entirely successful, and in March 1909 Lieutenant Dunne was informed that the cost had proved too great. It had only amounted to £2,000. At the time Germany was spending no less than £400,000 on 'Military Aeronautics'. Lord Haldane, however, was still interested and himself went to Scotland. After seeing Lieutenant Dunne's latest aircraft, which had backward sloping wings, performing the function of a stabilizing tail, he was so impressed that in May 1909 he had decided to announce in the House of Commons that he would arrange for a sub-committee to study the possibility of military aircraft. This decision led to the formation of the Advisory Committee for Aeronautics, which was presided over by Lord Raleigh of the National Physics Laboratory, and gave an opportunity for the Navy as well as the Army to pool their knowledge of aviation. On 10 October the War Office announced that the scope of the Balloon Factory at Farnborough should include 'aeroplaning' as well as ballooning. This recognition of the value of aircraft as a means of reconnaissance was a great step forward. The studies of the Advisory Committee led quite naturally, on 1 April 1911, to the formation of the Air Battalion. The enthusiasm with which this development was greeted was reflected by the forty volunteers who immediately applied to join. There were to be two divisions in the Battalion. The Balloon Factory, which Mr. Mervyn O'Gorman had taken over as Superintendent in 1909, became the Army Aircraft Factory, while the rest of the Air Battalion was to be trained in all aspects of flight at Larkhill on Salisbury Plain. The creation of this Air Battalion would lead directly to the formation of the Royal Flying Corps in May of the following year.

On 4 March 1912 Colonel Seely, Under-Secretary of State for War, announced that he had appointed Lord Haldane as chairman of a committee to set up a Royal Flying Corps. Nobody would hold executive rank unless he was an expert flyer. The Air Battalion would be absorbed into the new Corps, the Headquarters of which would be at Netheravon on Salisbury Plain. To join the RFC, officers would need the consent of the military authorities, be medically fit and obtain a Royal Aero Club Certificate. The cost of the Certificate, some £75, would have to be borne by each officer, but would be refunded on acceptance into the RFC. The Royal Flying Corps was constituted by Royal Warrant on 13 May 1912.

Peggy wrote of Geoff at this time:

'It was while we were at the Staff College that Geoff became obsessed with flying. He would rush off to Brooklands and Salisbury Plain to watch flying whenever he could.' Jack had also decided to become a pilot. He wrote: 'There was now, in 1911, talk of a Flying Corps being formed, as the continental nations were far ahead of us in numbers of aircraft and in organisation.' He decided to learn to fly with Grahame-White, who had now started his own Flying School at Hendon, before joining the new Central Flying School at Upavon, which was to start the first course of military flying in August.

I was then working for the entrance exam to the Staff College, but the prospect of becoming a military pilot was infinitely more attractive. So, with my books numbering fifty at least, I transferred to lodgings over a greengrocer in Colindale Avenue, a featureless little street running directly to the main entrance of Hendon airfield. It was a good-sized room with a bed, a chair and a diminutive table, so those books never left the carpetless floor on which they were thrown higgledy-piggledy the first day.

There were only two instructors to cope with a dozen pupils, and they deserve medals for their good temper. We ceaselessly demanded flying which was impossible to provide. As tuition was barred if there was the slightest wind, it was necessary to get it in between dawn and about nine o'clock in the morning, or late evening when the air was calm. Frequently at 3.30 in the morning I threw stones at the window of one or other of the instructors, but it was always a sleepy but smiling face that appeared, and very soon he would be on the aerodrome with a cheerful 'Good morning gentlemen, now whose turn is it to go first?' and out would come a well-thumbed note-book. Grahame-White, the proprietor, put in a few appearances, but his free decisive invigorating personality definitely made them occasions.

At last I was told I was about to begin instruction and that B.C. Hicks was to be my instructor. Now he was not normally an instructor of miserable pupils but a very fine flyer of considerable reputation. Consequently I was very pleased indeed. But my pleasure was short-lived, because as he was about to start on what was then considered a long-distance flight, my lesson merely consisted of sitting in the cockpit of his monoplane in the hangar and his saying, 'You do this and that with the stick and this and that with the rudder', after which he breezed off with an apology. And that was all the instruction I had before embarking on my first solo flight – this was in August 1912. The aeroplane I was given for this longed-for adventure was an Anzani-engined monoplane which I had seen the previous day running red-hot on the ground and spouting oil over its pilot. I climbed into the cockpit with an uncomfortable sinking feeling. The engine of the oil-bath started at the first swing of the propeller and I very gingerly raised the machine off the ground and at once felt like the Angel Gabriel. We landed at the far end of the aerodrome, taxied round and returned without mishap.

This sort of luck could not last indefinitely and later on, after a bump, I pulled the stick back, the machine reared its nose into the blue and at the top of its climb the engine stopped. We hit the ground at an acute angle, the engine parted company with the rest of the machine in a cartwheel over the grass, and I stepped out of the remains with only a bruise on my head. Before taking my 'ticket' I had some dual instruction with one of the instructors on a Boxkite. This dual instruction consisted of sitting on a bar immediately behind and a little above him, leaning over his back and feeling with my hands what he was doing with the stick. These machines (biplanes) had 50 hp Gnome engines and were sluggish and underpowered and much inclined to stall on a turn to starboard unless you put the nose well down. The loss of height was particularly awkward [when] flying for one's Certificate, which consisted of several figures of eight and landing on a mark. I well remember the 13th August when I took my ticket, as my wing scraped the long grass on my last turn, but was either not noticed or was ignored by the kindly official. I was allotted Certificate No. 272.

One can imagine what the news of Jack's flying adventures meant to Geoff, still working at the Staff College, but flying was considered terribly dangerous, and foolhardy for a married man. Their first child, a daughter, Joyce Margaret, had arrived on 5 December, making him feel even more responsible.

In the summer of 1912 Geoff was once again in camp at Amesbury on Salisbury Plain, attached to the 8th Hussars, while Peggy and the baby were at Ditchingham. It seemed to him an ideal time to watch the flying at Larkhill, and perhaps have the great thrill of persuading one of the aviators to take him up. He had to rise very early, as most flying took place at dawn when there was very little wind around. He would bicycle over to the airfield, and return to the Hussars Mess in time for breakfast.

At this time tests were being made for aircraft to land on ploughed land. In those early days when, with engine failure or other emergency, an aircraft might well come down in a ploughed field, it would have been disastrous to land across the furrows, and so tests were being made to see how they could land safely.

On 23 August Geoff wrote to Peggy:

My darling, today I have had the grandest experience I have ever had. I flew two hours three minutes in an Avro biplane. We went up to 5,000 feet, disappeared in clouds and did no end of things.

I got up at 4.30 this morning and went up to Larkhill but did not succeed in getting a flight. Then Sykes, the Commandant of the Military Wing, asked me to help him to do some tests of aeroplanes on plough. We had to watch the aeroplanes do the tests. I thought it might help me to get a flight, so I went and he incidentally told me the Avro was going out to do its three hours' duration test today at 10 a.m., so I at once said, 'Has he got an observer?' and he said, 'No, would you like to go?' I accepted at once and got leave from my regiment, and was up there at 9.30.

The wind had been getting up all the time and I was afraid the flight wouldn't come off. However, the little chap who was to drive the aeroplane does not know fear and didn't think of not going. It was sunny and so he meant to go, whatever the wind did. He is a Naval Officer, by some wonderful means employed by the Avro Company. I was weighed and put on a helmet and thick jacket and given a barograph, an aneroid and a stop watch. I sat in front of the pilot in a very tight little seat, and at 10.12 we started. It seemed only a second before we sort of sprang into the air, and after that we simply climbed. We were up at 1,000 feet in nine minutes. I soon got used to the whirl of the propeller and the occasional wobbles. I had to hold the aneroid over my right shoulder for the pilot to see how we were climbing. It got quite cold and sometimes we disappeared entirely into clouds. It was glorious and grand – magnificent. The Avro is a specially built machine in which passenger and pilot are quite boxed in, so that you see nothing at all in your immediate front, only out to the sides, and a little forward. You are kept entirely free from wind, etc. It felt just as if I was in an express train. We had been going splendidly for two hours when suddenly the engine began to knock and so we had to come down. We volplaned 2,000 feet down, and made a beautiful landing. It was a wonderful experience. They all tell me, considering the wind, it was the best performance down here. The wind was sometimes blowing 32 miles an hour. I must be off and dress now. Ever and ever, Your Geoff.

Peggy, reading the letter on the terrace at Ditchingham, overlooking the quiet park, must have needed all her courage to support Geoff. The words 'when suddenly the engine began to knock' must have especially frightened her, but she loyally accepted his passion for flying without question.

Geoff managed to get one or two more flights as an observer over the next few days and also watched the flying with Captain Gerrard, one of the first instructors at Upavon, where Jack had started his military flying course. He went over to see him, still undecided as to what he should do. Meanwhile, he was umpiring manoeuvres for the Army. He wrote: 'I am umpiring tomorrow and I am also going to do some official observation of Avro tests for speed, in the early morning. That means I shall be in the Avro aeroplane observing. It ought to take an hour, from 6 to 7. I have to be up there at 5.30, which means getting up at 5 a.m. at the latest.' These tests were still carried out in the very early morning, when there was scarcely any wind.

While serving with the 8th Hussars, Geoffrey was very involved with the manoeuvres which took place in Norfolk at the end of the summer. Aircraft were being used for reconnaissance, almost for the first time. Lieutenant Longmore and Major Trenchard from Upavon were flying over the Thetford to Newmarket road when they saw the 'enemy' quite clearly and reported their position to the generals, landing in a field near them. Geoffrey wrote:

> On Monday we did very little fighting. The aeroplanes did wonders. Of course the weather was very favourable, but they found out everything. What generally takes an awful lot of fighting to find out was discovered in a few hours. The result was that the big battle took place much sooner than was expected, and the manoeuvres came to an end last night.

In another letter he wrote: 'Yesterday the General-in-Chief, Allenby, was captured, and the whole show rather collapsed.' It was at the end of these manoeuvres that General Grierson remarked grumpily, 'The aeroplanes completely spoilt the war.'

Jack had arrived at the Central Flying School at Upavon just before those manoeuvres. He reached the isolated wind-swept Station not far from Salisbury to take part in the first official course which was to start in August. He described his arrival at Upavon in unforgettable terms:

> It was a very wet day, with wind and rain scurrying over the Downs and making the windows of the wooden Mess rattle when I entered. There were several people there, and it is interesting to realise how a strong personality will leap across and hit one immediately. For in the corner, sitting rather apart, was a dark glowering man with a parchment coloured face, and a light behind his eyes, whom I was soon to know as Trenchard, and it was not long before I knew what that fire meant.

A Naval officer, Godfrey Paine, was running the School and Trenchard was soon to become his Adjutant, while Jack, half-way through the first course, joined Arthur Longmore, another Naval officer, as an instructor.

Perhaps it was a visit to Upavon to see Jack which helped Geoff decide. He wrote:

> My darling, such news. I shall come down to you on Saturday. Won't that be splendid? I went over to Upavon on the bike to see Jack instead. I found him this time. It was ripping seeing him again. The course they

go through is a very mild affair. They fly, if the weather is absolutely calm in the morning and evening, and have lectures during the day. It is not a bit strenuous and after Jack had been there a fortnight nearly he had only flown five times I think. The country round there is lovely. General Henderson at the War Office, who is running the Army Air show, has got his certificate and he is a married man. Darling, I don't really think it is such an awful thing to do. When you get used to it the awful risks which one reads about in the papers disappear to a great extent. My own idea is that I should take out my certificate and join the Special Reserve. They may want me for a few months' course at Upavon, but that is nothing very dreadful, and the village of Upavon is simply ripping. And we could get a little house. After that I would rejoin the Regiment. There is a course starting in January sometime. Also by taking out your certificate you would, to a certain extent, pull yourself out of the ruck, and that is one of the things to do, especially in our Army. I expect you will make me explain all this to your Father. I hope he won't be too severe. I am so looking forward to Saturday next, darling. Ever and ever and ever, Your Geoff.

Peggy's father was not too severe. She wrote later: 'At last, on a holiday, Geoff announced that he was going to fly and get his flying certificate. Of course I did not like it very much but nothing could be done about it and I was established with the baby at Ditchingham while he went off to Brooklands.'

Thomas Octavius Sopwith, who had started the famous Sopwith School of Flying at Brooklands, was a colourful figure who had been a racing driver, a yachtsman and even a balloonist, flying over London in his balloon 'The Padsop' before becoming fascinated by flight in heavier-than-air machines. Tom was lucky enough to have a private income and so was able to purchase his first aeroplane from Howard Wright even before he had learnt to fly. He passed his Aero Club test within one month at the age of twenty-two.

While Geoffrey was at the Staff College, Sopwith was in America on a very successful tour, but early in 1912, he returned and started the Sopwith School of Flying.

There were four aeroplanes on the original course, described in the advertisement as 'four entirely different types of aeroplane'. C.S. Grey, the aeronautical journalist, wrote:

His school machines will comprise his old Howard Wright biplane... his American Wright (Burgess Wright) biplane, a school Bleriot and a Howard Wright monoplane. The two biplanes will be fitted with dual controls, so that the pupil can learn the controls in the air. Mr. Sopwith will also have his 70 hp. tandem Bleriot for his own use, and will probably have a Martyn-Handyside to fly as well.

In May a Henri Farman biplane was added. The Blériot had been fitted with a covered-in fuselage and the wings had been re-covered and doped. It was tested on 7 June. C.S. Grey ended his description: 'To the man who wishes to become a really good all-round flyer the Sopwith School appeals at once.'

When Geoffrey arrived at the school he wrote to Peggy: 'My darling, here I am. I have decided. I have taken a room. At the Blue Bird. Sorry, sorry, sorry, but it is so convenient.'

His next letter ran:

> I got up at 5.25 this morning and went to the ground, but they said it was too windy. To me there seemed no wind at all, but it shows how careful they are. I am very disappointed . . . all this motor racing goes on during Thursday afternoons and you cannot be taught till quite late. There are any amount of soldiers here, all with the Bristol. They are an unruly lot. They pulled out the Bristol biplane themselves this morning, before the Instructor arrived, and flew it on their own. One of them broke a stay and they all got sat upon when he arrived. It would have been all right if the tell-tale stay had not been there, but I should have liked to have seen the Instructor's face when he came on the ground and found one of his aeroplanes in mid-air. There are two gunners, one of whom I know, with the Bristol people. There is only one other pupil at Sopwith's whom I know.

With the Bristol school, unknown to Geoffrey at the time, was a young man who was to become a great friend in later life – young Joubert de la Ferté, whose father's house was at Weybridge. Joubert wrote of his first solo flight:

> After a quick meal of coffee and rolls and a scrambled toilet I was away on my motor bicycle to Brooklands airfield. There was something quite unforgettable about the English countryside on that fine morning. Birdsong was almost deafeningly loud and the blended scent of flowers, wet grass and, at the time when tar macadam was confined to trunk roads, the musty smell of warm dust in the lane left an impression that has stayed through the years. I have never felt so utterly alone and helpless as the rickety old kite trundled faster and faster over the ground and finally lifted a few feet into the air. The far boundary of the airfield came rushing to meet me and with a prodigious sigh of relief I switched off, wiggled the joystick hopefully but ineffectually and finally bumped to a stop without breaking anything. The seat itself was set most insecurely in a rack, rather like that used in a rowing boat, and as such adjustable to the pilot's length of leg. Rarely was there fitted a belt, or any form of screw to prevent the seat from being jerked out of the rack by a sudden shock.

Naturally, Geoffrey played down these hazards in his letters to Peggy. He wrote diplomatically: 'It is very dull here indeed, but it will be so lovely when you come, darling.'

When Geoff changed his lodgings he wrote: 'I see the Gamma, the airship I went up in, has made a bad landing and wrecked the car part of it. I am sure, in war, that they will never stand the weather.'

It is fascinating to think that Geoff had actually flown in the Gamma. Airships had had rather more success than aircraft at the beginning of the century. Produced by the Balloon Factory in 1907, the Nulli Secundus was a cylindrical semi-rigid airship with external keel and hemispherical bow and stern. In October 1907 it had established a record by flying from Farnborough to London and circling the Crystal Palace. It was followed by the Beta in 1909, and next by the similar but larger Gamma, in 1912. Geoff's words, about their vulnerability in bad weather, were almost prophetic.

His letters now began describing his first flying lessons. The weather was growing colder, so that flying without warm clothing, perched behind the pilot in the Maurice Farman, which was entirely open to the air, was a bit of an ordeal, but Geoff soon managed to buy some really thick woollen gloves and a warm jacket. In September he was very concerned about two accidents which had made the public nervous about monoplanes. He wrote:

> I am so sorry about this fresh disaster. I knew Bettingham quite well – we trekked together in South Africa and he lived with us – it is very sad. It is the same thing, I believe, that caused the accidents, the cowl over the rotary engine getting hit by a loose part. I don't think the monoplane is good enough yet.

It was these two accidents, following so closely on one another, which convinced the military authorities that the monoplane was not safe. It was decided that no more monoplanes were to be flown by the RFC, an almost disastrous decision, for it put Great Britain behind the Continent in the development of fast, light aircraft. Not until Sopwith designed his machines during the war were monoplanes accepted once more.

In the next letter Geoff was writing:

> I had two flights this morning. I was only a passenger, but I had my hand on the lever.

And two days later:

> This morning I went up and was taken twice round by the School's first pilot, a man called Perry. It was rather windy, so he would not teach me much. Of course he would not have let me go up if I had been alone,

besides I wouldn't have wanted to – I quite see that in this show you must go slow and not be in a hurry. It requires lots of patience, but that is good for one.

Until recently, Copeland Perry had been the chief test pilot at the Royal Aircraft Factory at Farnborough. He had succeeded Raynham as Tommy Sopwith's senior instructor and had taught Major Hugh Trenchard to fly in August. Trenchard had been awarded Certificate No.270 only a few days before his 40th birthday.

Geoff wrote again: 'This morning was a grand day for flying. I went up half a dozen times behind the instructor. He is teaching me how to land and how to rise.' On Sunday 13 October Sopwith's new Wright biplane made its debut. It was a modification of his old Burgess-Wright biplane with innovations designed by Sopwith and incorporated by Sigrist. A few days later Harry Hawker, a young Australian trained at the school, tested it and gained a new British duration record, flying over Brooklands for 8 hours and 23 minutes.

It must have been a great thrill when Geoff flew solo on the Henri Farman on 6 October. It would seem that Tommy Sopwith closed down his school soon after this and the pupils transferred to the Vickers School. Sopwith had taken over a converted ice-skating rink at Kingston and was building his own aircraft there, supported by Sigrist and Harry Hawker, now his test pilot. Later they formed the famous Sopwith Aviation Company. At the Vickers School Geoff had three lessons on 9,10 and 12 December, his tutor being A. Knight.

Geoffrey saw that he would not be able to 'take his ticket' before Christmas. However, he was allowed to proceed to the Central Flying School in January and complete his flying lessons there.

Afterwards Peggy wrote of those early days: 'I joined Geoff at Brooklands and watched him bump, bump, bump and land, very white and bruised, after an unsteady flip round. Flights were far between as they were only allowed when there was no breath of wind.' She stayed once or twice with him in his lodgings, leaving the baby at Ditchingham with her grandparents and nurse. Years later Geoff was to tell his daughters, 'Your mother is as brave as a lion.' Perhaps he was remembering that small, lonely figure standing on the cold damp airfield in the early morning, watching him return from one of his first erratic flights.

In January, 1913 after Christmas spent at Ditchingham with Peggy and Joyce, Geoff joined the second course of the Central Flying School at Upavon. With his clothes packed in his father's holdall he caught the train and, as he said, 'swaggered about like a Colonel in consequence'. Jack was by this time an instructor, having been promoted halfway through the first course, and Major Hugh Trenchard was Adjutant. There were about twenty officers and thirty-five non-commissioned officers on the second course. They were all wearing their distinctive uniforms; some were Naval officers, including the

Commandant, Captain Godfrey Paine, who had been especially selected by Winston Churchill, Major Fulton of the Royal Horse Artillery, members of the Royal Engineers, members of the Indian Navy and Captain Gerrard of the Royal Marines. Those who already possessed aircraft were originally asked to bring them to Upavon. Captain Gerrard had brought his 50 hp Nieuport. However, after the monoplane disasters, he parted with it. Major Fulton, after attempting to build a Blériot-type aeroplane himself, had then taught himself to fly at Larkhill and had been awarded the very first Aero Club certificate.

Perhaps it was at Upavon that the unifying spirit of the RFC was first felt. The air historian, Walter Raleigh, was to write later:

> The great achievements of the Royal Flying Corps during the War may seem to make its early history and early efforts a trivial thing in comparison. But the spirit was there, as some of the merits of the later performances may be detected in the tedious and imperfect rehearsals, the long hours of duty flights and experiments, demanding that three o'clock-in-the-morning kind of courage which is willing to face danger in the midst of a world at ease.

This courage was demonstrated by the mechanics and all those who helped to keep the machines in the air, as well as by the flyers. Only those of independent spirit chose to leave the old ways and to tread an entirely new path into the future. The Warrant Officers, Non-Commissioned Officers and men, all of whom had originally been drawn from the Royal Engineers in the early days, were as important as the pilots and observers themselves and with their expertise and interest in the aeroplanes a close comradeship grew up in all departments of the Service, which was to prove of inestimable value during the vital years ahead.

Geoffrey was thrilled with the Maurice Farman and Henri Farman aircraft on the course. He wrote: 'I had a fly this morning. It was ripping. I went up behind. A Naval Lieutenant was my instructor. Everyone thinks flying a most ordinary affair here. The machines are simply splendid affairs – the very best that there are.' The Maurice Farmans which Geoffrey admired so much were 'pusher' aircraft and were to continue to be used as training machines at Upavon for many months. The four longerons (or tail booms) ran out behind the centre section to the box rail, which had two rudders. In front of the aeroplane was a pair of giant skids which formed the undercarriage and carried four wheels. The elevator was between their upper tips. The nacelle (or long shoe) rested on the lower main plane, where a 70 hp Renault engine pushed behind, while two passengers sat in tandem in the front. There were pedals for rudders, a stick for the elevator and a pair of handlebars which worked the ailerons. It was normally held together with piano wire. The Maurice Farman Shorthorn was a modified version, with no skids, and the elevator was forward. It was powered by a 100 hp. Renault engine. But, in spite of Geoffrey's enthusiasm, the Farman machines were not entirely reliable. In the Henri Farman a lack of balance in the 50 hp Gnome engine could cause trouble, while the Maurice Farmans, though more reliable, could suffer from engine failure and vibration.

There were four flight instructors on Geoff's course: Major Fulton with his Avros, Lieutenant Arthur Longmore (Geoff's instructor, later Air Chief Marshal Sir Arthur Longmore) with Maurice Farmans and BEs, Major Gerrard with Henri Farmans and Boxkites, and Jack Salmond on BE8s. Bristol Boxkites and two Short tractor aircraft had been removed in favour of Maurice Farmans with Renault engines.

Geoff wrote: 'Jack and I walked down to Upavon yesterday to try and find rooms.' The Antelope Inn was full up and they could not find suitable lodgings for Peggy in the village. Geoff suggested that she should meet him in town at a weekend. Later he described his day:

> Flying early at 8.45, then work in the sheds, workshops or a lecture till the evening when flying was possible again. I had a game of golf this morning with Trenchard, the Staff Officer here. I like him very much, which is a good thing . . . I have just come from the shops where I have been putting together an old aeroplane they have there. It is great fun, only three of us are there. There was practically no flying today, it was too windy. One of our instructors was flying a machine over from Farnborough and had to come down at Whitchurch as some petrol connection was leaking. He got a local blacksmith to repair it and got away before a car we sent out from here reached him. He is awfully pleased about it. Then he had all sorts of fellows to try and start him up because, of course, unless you know it, a propeller is rather a ticklish thing to start. I think the local blacksmith should join the Flying Corps.

In February the weather became much colder. Flying in the open cockpit without a really thick flying suit and with perhaps only woollen gloves became really hard. Luckily, if it was windy they worked indoors on an old Bristol biplane and Geoff wrote, 'It began to snow last night and this morning there was a thin layer of snow on the ground.' It seemed, however, that even before his examination Geoff was allowed to fly solo, for he wrote a few days later:

> After working all day, flying began at 4.15 p.m. and I was detailed to take a machine round to Jack's sheds, which are some distance from ours. It was to be handed over to Jack's flight, as we are giving it up. I did about 10 miles and then brought it back to Jack and handed it over. It was rather fun. The ripping part of it was landing on ground I had not landed on before, as you selected your landing place as you were coming down. They are such ripping machines, these Maurice Farmans.

Peggy, knowing how cold the weather had become, arranged to send him a really warm waistcoat. He wrote, 'Next week we are starting before breakfast, so it will be splendid' and added, 'I saw Jack's name in the *Gazette* as having been at the Levée.' He also wrote: 'They have a wonderful new decoration which they wear over their medals, which means they are efficient pilots in the RFC.' This was the very first mention of the RFC Wings. Those Wings, which all members of the Royal Flying Corps were so proud to wear throughout the First World War are, of course, equally proudly worn by the RAF today. On 15 February, Geoff again wrote:

These Maurice Farmans certainly are wonderful machines. The story goes that Maurice Farman himself does not know why his machines fly so well, he does not know the secret. The French Government want him to make them capable of going faster than 60 miles an hour, but they say he won't do it, because he thinks they might not fly so well. He seems to have hit on the secret by accident somehow, for they certainly are wonderful. But I daresay it is only a story.

A few days later, Geoff was writing:

My own darling, I am so sorry I told you nothing much about the Certificate. I don't tell you on purpose because you see you imagine it all yourself, and then you get alarmed or worried and so on, but that is why. I really think it's best not to, but I will make an exception over the Certificate, as it is an event. Well, I hadn't the least idea on Monday morning that they would propose my going for it. But it was a good day and Longmore, my instructor, told me to go up alone and practise landing on a mark. So I did. I landed the first time right across the mark and every other time quite close. Then he told me not to go into the lecture that morning, and that at 12 noon I was to go for my certificate. The right hand turn in the Maurice Farman is quite the same as a left hand turn, because it has a stationary Renault engine and not a rotary Gnome engine. I did my five figures of eight all right, but wasn't certain whether I had done five until I saw the observers waving handkerchiefs, and so I turned to go for my mark. That, of course, was the most anxious time, and unless you land within 50 yards you have to do it all again. What you have to do is to shut off your engine before you touch the ground and then when you have finished rolling you must be within 50 yards. Well, as I turned I saw another aeroplane in the way, so I had to turn round and fly round and then come back again. I landed 39 yards from the mark. The second time I was baulked again by other aeroplanes, but when I did have my shot I landed within five yards. So it was done, and everyone congratulated me.

Certificate No. 41

ROYAL FLYING CORPS.

(Flying Certificate—Officers.)

CENTRAL FLYING SCHOOL,

UPAVON,

6th March 1913.

THIS IS TO CERTIFY that Captain W.G.H Salmond, Royal Field Artillery.

has graduated at the Central Flying School, and is qualified as a flyer in the Royal Flying Corps.

He is recommended for duty in* First Reserve for Military Duty.

Capstain R.N.
Commandant.

*Here insert "Naval Wing," "Military Wing," "First Reserve, for Naval duty," or "First Reserve, for Military duty."

W 2557—2015 500 8/12 H W V   G. 12
                                    664

On 28 February he was writing:

> I got up early and flew Jack's Maurice Farman this morning. It was lucky
> I did, as I did not get another flight today. I wonder what you think of
> everything now you have got my letter about jobs?

He was obviously worried, now that he had passed his Certificate, about the
future. Brigadier General Sir David Henderson had been down to see the
members of the course, and Geoffrey knew he might be chosen for some special
job, as so few of the pilots had also passed the Staff College exam. He wrote:
'It is blowing hard tonight so doesn't look much like flying tomorrow. They
are experimenting here with wireless on an aeroplane and got some small
results today.'

Next day he wrote:

> I caught a cold out flying in Jack's machine as I forgot to do up the collar
> round my neck and I felt the cold morning air rushing past it, and tried
> to close it while flying but I couldn't. It was the top button of the collar
> which was left undone. This morning I did it up well and had quite a
> good fly. It is blowing great guns now, but of course it doesn't matter as
> everyone is away. I am dining with the Commandant tonight.

There was a possibility of a job in Colchester and they nearly bought a house
there, but on 12 April, 1913 Geoffrey received a letter from the War Office. It
ran:

> Dear Salmond, We are arranging for an officer to assist temporarily in
> aviation work at the War Office. The pay will be regimental emoluments
> plus 10/- a day, and the appointment will probably last two months.
> Would you be prepared to accept this?

Geoffrey's career in the RFC had begun.

The RFC earns its Wings

The year 1913 was to prove a very happy one for Peggy and Geoff. He had
accepted the job in the War Office and they were able to rent a flat in Grenville
Place, in London. The months of separation and indecision were now over.
That summer Jack, who was still an Instructor at Upavon, was also able to
enjoy great happiness. He wrote:

> In 1913 I went to Scotland to marry the girl I had met some years previ-
> ously, Joy Lumsden, daughter of James Forbes Lumsden of Rubislaw,

Aberdeen. I brought her south to the Manor House, Upavon Village, at the foot of the hill about a mile from the aerodrome at the top. Here was all we wanted, a charming old place in a fold of the Downs, a small garden and a trout stream running past it, and we were very happy.

Joy matched his own high spirits. One day he took her for a flight, strictly against rules, disguised as an air mechanic, to find the Commandant on the tarmac when he returned. He called him aside and said, 'What the devil . . .' to which Jack replied 'Sir, it was no use asking you first, because I knew you would refuse.' The Commandant warned him that he could be sacked for that, a sentiment with which Jack could only agree, but no action was taken. 'A good Commander is never unreasonable' said Jack later.

That year at Upavon, just before the First World War began, was probably their happiest. Meanwhile, the public was becoming more and more anxious about our air defences. In October 1912 an unidentified airship was seen flying above Sheerness and it was suddenly realized how vulnerable our coastline was, and also that the air forces of France and Germany were far superior to our own, both in numbers of machines and the quality of their engines. It was only too obvious that, in spite of the enterprise and élan of such men as Tommy Sopwith, Grahame-White and A.V. Roe, Britain was still far behind in aircraft development. Most of the aircraft of all types were French, and the Aircraft Factory at Farnborough, now under O'Gorman, was not receiving enough Government support.

Things came to a head in a rumpus in the House of Commons. A young MP, Joynson Hicks, had questioned the official estimate of the number of aeroplanes fit for military service. He asked, early in March, if the Secretary of State for War would confirm that the total effective strength of the RFC was only 'two biplanes and three Maurice Farmans at Montrose (No. 2 Squadron); one B biplane and two Maurice Farmans at Larkhill (No. 3 Squadron); two Breguet biplanes and two other biplanes at Farnborough (No. 4 Squadron).' The Minister denied this, saying there were 101 aircraft in the RFC. The House was, however, sceptical and Joynson Hicks himself visited all the military airfields and found that although there were certainly 101 aircraft, most were unserviceable and several others quite unfitted for military use. This outcry led to more orders being placed with British firms, and also in the estimates for aeronautics being almost doubled in 1914, from £520,000 in 1913 to £1,000,000 the next year.

Geoff, in London, was working on the Staff under General Sir David Henderson, who was now Director of Military Aeronautics at the War Office, doing battle for money and resources, and Major Sefton Brancker, who had joined them after qualifying as a pilot. General Henderson, a quiet, sympathetic and intelligent commander, was beloved by all who served under him, which contributed much to Geoff's – and therefore to Peggy's – happiness.

is everyone nice?

In spite of difficulties, it was a year of rapid development, not only in the Military Wing but also in the Naval Wing. Winston Churchill, who had become First Sea Lord in 1911, realized the great potential of the aeroplane and himself qualified as a pilot early in 1913. He was well aware of the need for a stronger RFC, and it was he who had appointed Captain Paine to run the Central Flying School at Upavon. The Naval training establishment at Eastchurch soon developed into the most important school for Naval officers learning to fly, and already experiments with floatplanes had been taking place at Barrow-in-Furness. As early as 1911, Howard Pixton, Avro's test pilot, was testing their Type D, a tractor biplane, at Brooklands. He approved of it, saying that if it stalled, it would flutter down like a leaf. Pixton had many adventures with it, once even mending a rudder post with a broom handle, but unfortunately in May that year it crashed. Soon afterwards Commander Oliver Swann inspected the wreckage. He decided to buy the rebuilt aeroplane for £700 of his own money, and had it transported to Barrow-in-Furness, where he was stationed. Captain Sueter, then in charge of the airship HMA R1, gave permission for him to build a small hangar beside the Cavendish Dock, and here Swann worked on his Avro. Floats were lashed to the skids of the machine, and modifications were kept to a minimum. His first experiments led to a capsize, when he was heard to shout, 'Save the damned aeroplane – I can look after myself.' After much trial and error, improved floats were once more tried on 18 November 1911. *The Aeroplane* published an eye-witness account:

> The machine left the water several times, just rising clear, so that Commander Masterman saw daylight under the floats. He computes the distance travelled to be 50 or 60 yards in these skips. Commander Swann said that he felt the machine strike the water each time, between skips.

Unfortunately the plane capsized. This experiment was the very first in attempting to create a floatplane. Commander Swann was later to become a qualified pilot and a great friend of Geoffrey Salmond. He was described by Trenchard as an aviator of great distinction.

★   ★   ★

Gradually, and without the consent of Parliament, the Admiralty decided to take over their own flying organization. In June 1914 the 'Naval Wing' became quite naturally the Royal Naval Air Service, a service separate from the RFC. The two branches of the Air Service were not to be united again until 1918.

During 1913 there were also enormous advances in experiments in air-to-ground signalling, for it was realised that reconnaissance could not provide real-time intelligence without swift communication with the ground forces.

Klaxon horns, flags and Very lights were all tried, but none proved satisfactory, and the study of wireless was still in its infancy.

In April 1913 Lieutenant Cholmondeley of 3 Squadron attempted a night flight from Larkhill to Upavon and back. He guided his machine by the light of the moon, but found as he neared the ground to land that there was a dark shadow over the runway. He next landed by the light coming from the open hangar doors. Later, petrol flares were used, which were so successful that they were still in use in 1917. In addition, records in height and distance were being broken. Longcroft set out from Farnborough on 21 May to fly to Montrose, covering 550 miles in almost six hours, and reaching a height of between 5,000 and 6,000 feet. On 13 December Jack Salmond took up a B.E. and recorded a height of 13,140 feet, a new British altitude record.

When Geoff and Peggy went to the Aero show in 1913 they would have seen a small biplane with a pusher-type propeller at the rear, its front cockpit occupied by an observer who had an uninterrupted field of fire forwards. It was a private venture, but from this machine the Vickers FB5 Gun Bus was to evolve during the first few months of the war. The air-cooled Lewis gun was chosen as most suitable for aerial needs, although no action was taken until September 1914.

At this time Peggy also remembered Colonel Hugh Trenchard coming to dinner with them at their flat in London: a tall, dark, serious young man, who talked till late at night with Geoffrey on the future of the RFC.

Perhaps the most important event occurred during the next summer. Lieutenant Colonel Sykes, the head of the Military Wing, himself an immensely brave aviator and a brilliant organizer, persuaded the War Office to hold a mock mobilization of the whole of the RFC at Netheravon, on Salisbury Plain, in June 1914. The programme of training devised by Sykes was a plan to unite the Squadrons and to iron out their individual problems. On 26 June the complete Military Wing was reviewed by Mr Asquith, the Prime Minister. The spirit of the men in the RFC could not have been higher. The Corps had earned its Wings.

2

THE WAR IN FRANCE

The Retreat From Mons

Through the summer of 1914 life went on as usual. There were tennis parties at Ditchingham and river picnics on the Thames and at Oxford. Peggy's brother Billy, who was now thirteen, would be starting at Eton in the autumn and their pleasant life seemed likely to go on for ever. There was some anxiety, it is true, over the Irish question, which had rocked the Cabinet, but nobody worried a great deal about that. In London, at Grenville Place, Peggy's second child arrived in May. The baby was a girl, a determined child from the first, with a glint of red hair. Geoff and Peggy had rather hoped for a boy, but they were too happy to dwell on disappointment for long.

It was, however, true that no one working at the War Office could remain unaware of the dark shadow hanging over the future. Geoff knew that Germany was increasing her military strength all the time and that war was possible, even inevitable. But whereas we, looking back, know how long that would last when it came, and have been shown the misery and agony of long trench warfare, few soldiers at that time had any idea of what it would be like. When at the Staff College in 1911, Geoffrey had written an essay saying he thought that the next war, if it came, would be fought from trenches on both sides and was severely reprimanded for thinking of anything so contrary to military theory. In the summer of 1914 most soldiers felt, light-heartedly, that if war came it would be over by Christmas, and longed to be on active service, delighting in the chance of action and adventure. To Geoff and Jack, who had stepped out of line and, with the other young aviators, were facing war in the air for the first time, it must have needed all their courage and confidence to face the unknown future.

In June the Archduke Ferdinand of Austria and his wife were murdered in the street at Sarajevo and the crisis had arrived. Austria accused Serbia;

Germany pushed Austria into making unreasonable demands on Serbia; Serbia called on Russia for help; Russia was tied by a treaty to France. Soon it was obvious that German forces were massing on the frontiers of Belgium.

In the last weeks of June and July General Henderson's staff, led by Major Sefton Brancker and which included Geoffrey Salmond, worked day and night to keep the squadrons up to strength. Every suitable civilian aircraft was pressed into service, and Brancker ordered two of his officers to go over to France and to buy up all spares and equipment possible. The £1,000,000 ordered for aviation during the year was rapidly running out, but Sir Charles Harris, to whom Brancker applied for help, said: 'Well, it's hell with the lid off now! Go and order what you think is necessary.' There were still those in the Cabinet who advised caution but, with the news that German forces were advancing towards Belgium, the feeling in the country was rising. It was unthinkable that we should not help our ally, France, when she was in such danger. A member of the staff at the War Office wrote:

> We knew the French Army relied on us absolutely – some of us could hardly contain our rage and shame. There were several officers on the General Staff who were seriously thinking of resigning their commissions and joining the French Army, and pilots in the Royal Flying Corps who were talking of flying quietly across the Channel, without orders, to help our French friends in the air.

On 4 August the German Army marched into neutral Belgium. The British Government sent an ultimatum, and by midnight Britain was at war.

During July sixty-three aircraft, 105 officers and ninety-five transport vehicles were available for the RFC. 2, 3, 4 and 5 Squadrons were ready for action, 1 Squadron was being converted from balloons, and 7 Squadron, commanded by Captain John Salmond, was almost complete at Farnborough. As soon as war broke out he was ordered to command 3 Squadron on Salisbury Plain. On the evening of 9 August, Geoffrey came home to Grenville Place to pack his things for France. Joyce was only two and a half, but all her life she has remembered the scene – her father packing hurriedly, and kissing her mother and new baby sister goodbye. It was dark and a car was waiting outside for him. Soon he was gone. Peggy wrote afterwards:

> Geoff still had khaki uniform. A few days after War was declared, Geoff came home and told me he was going over to France to establish the RFC Headquarters. He got out his uniform and packed his bag, and when it was dark a War Office car drove up and fetched him.

She did not know when she would see him again.

He was driven to Queen Anne Street where, for the first time, he met the charming, intelligent and, at that time, totally unmilitary Maurice Baring, who was to become one of his greatest friends over the next few months. Only a few days previously Baring had asked his friend General Sir David Henderson if he could join the RFC. He was a linguist who knew seven languages, had been a correspondent for *The Times* and a member of the Diplomatic Service. Sir David realized that it would be a great boon to have him at his side when in France with his tongue-tied staff, and Baring heard only the day before that he was to report for duty. He wrote: 'Major Salmond came to fetch me, after dinner at nine o'clock at Queen Anne's Gate, and we started in a motor to Farnborough. We slept in the Queen's Hotel, in a billiard room which was full of officers.' They slept with their valises on the billiard table. He wrote on the next day, 10 August:

> Rose at 5.30 and went into a remote and secluded part of the country to put on my puttees at my leisure. After breakfast Captain Longcroft arrived and we three started off as an advance party to make arrangements for the arrival of the Flying Corps in France. But at that time I knew nothing. I did not know where we were going or what we were going to do. Colonel Sykes came to see us off at Farnborough.

Years later, Maurice Baring, remembering those hectic days, paid a tribute to Geoffrey:

> There can have been rarely a closer intimacy than that which bound those who formed part of a unit of three during the first four days of the Great War and of a Mess of seven during the retreat and the advance. During those first four days we shared the same billiard table, railway carriage, field, tin hut and barn, and later the same billet in garden, farm, hotel, convent, road and château. From the very first evening when we drove to Farnborough together and slept where we could in an over-crowded billiard room, I never saw Geoffrey Salmond vary; nothing ruffled his imperturbable good humour; nothing escaped his unostentatious sense of humour. As we left Farnborough Station his canvas bath was said by an officer seeing us off to be in excess of what one could take to war, and he threw it out of the window with a wistful laugh . . . Others have appreciated and will appreciate his activities in wider and further fields; among more important tributes there is perhaps room for the testimony of an eye witness who saw him throughout those early, anxious days, unafraid of responsibility, never despondent, always ready to help and to act, indescribably kind, and never failing to see the funny side of the most distracting situation. The conversation was Greek to me – Longcroft and Salmond talked the whole time of bumps, pancakes, stalling and taxi-ing, and I did not dare ask a question . . . I went into the town (Redhill) and

bought a pair of gaiters to use instead of puttees, but Longcroft and Salmond said they would never do, they disapproved of both the cut and colour, so I had to keep my excruciating puttees.

They arrived at Newhaven at one o'clock, and found the boat not yet ready to sail for Port B (the code name for Boulogne) and so they decided to bathe in the sea at Seaford. Baring wrote: 'We bathed in the dazzling sea, the last bathe and the last piece of real leisure for a long time.' They slept in the railway station and on the next day, 11 August, after inspecting the arrival of many stores, they embarked at 3.30 pm and sailed for France with a party of mechanics. They reached Boulogne in darkness and slept on board ship.

On 12 August Baring recorded his first, unusual impression of France.

> We woke the next morning in France, early, between four and five, all became aware of a startling new impression. All the nightmare cloud which had hung over the last few days in London seemed to have been blown away. Everybody was brisk, cheerful and optimistic. This was so throughout the war . . . Whenever one came back to France from England one seemed to step from a dark room into a bright one.

Perhaps it was the feeling that they were at last in action, helping the War effort, which gave them the light-hearted feeling after all the anxiety and strain at home.

Baring, Longcroft and Geoff rose at five, and started at seven o'clock by train for Amiens. The train was crowded with soldiers, and with French people who shouted *'Vive l'Angleterre'* and threw flowers and fruit at them. Baring continued:

> In the railway carriage with us there was an elderly Frenchman. When he heard that Salmond and Longcroft belonged to the Flying Corps, he said: *'Ah, les aviateurs, ils n'ont pas besoin d'aller a la guider, pour se faire casser la guerre ceux la.'*

On arrival they found a great deal to arrange – an airfield for the squadrons, pegs for the aeroplanes, water carts, a consignment of oil, food for the aircrew and billets. Geoffrey wrote to Peggy that night:

> My darling, this must be a very short note as I am using my electric light and it is very precious. We arrived here this morning, at about 12 and have had to do practically everything. I have wired to the War Office to say that all is ready for the machines to come tomorrow. It is a strenuous time. I will write more when I have time. I am so glad to think you are at Ditchingham now. Days fly past, there is so much to do. The French are

enthusiastic over us, and so of course we are inclined to think them charming in consequence. They are very quiet but full of confidence. We are out in the open field tonight – it is very warm and jolly. I am just going to bed now, and I think of you darling, happier now you are no longer alone. The machines should come tomorrow. Ever and ever, Geoff.

Mercifully, it was still hot and one perfect summer day followed another. That night it was no hardship to sleep outside and Geoff and Maurice Baring slept in the grass in their sleeping bags on the airfield. Baring wrote: 'We awoke in the dawn, and bathed in the dew. A small crowd watched this operation, and cheered.' Amiens was bedecked with flags and everywhere they were greeted by welcoming crowds.

On 13 August the first three squadrons arrived. The first pilot to land in France was Harvey Kelly, in his BE2a. Five days later the Aircraft Park, without its aircraft, landed at Boulogne. A rather desperate officer wired to Headquarters: 'An unnumbered unit without aeroplanes which calls itself an Aircraft Park has arrived. What do we do with it?' It was, in fact, to become the nucleus of the supply and maintenance of all the British aircraft in France.

Meanwhile, in England, Peggy remembered seeing young men crowding the recruiting stations, some even still carrying tennis racquets. They were light-hearted, as everyone felt sure the war would soon be over.

At Upavon Jack was desperately busy getting 3 Squadron ready to move to France. Robert Brooke-Popham, who had commanded the squadron before-hand, was now to be DAA & QMG in charge of transport. Jack wrote:

> This meant my working in double quick time, drawing stores, collecting transport and, most important of all, getting to know the qualities of the officers and men of the squadron. Our machines were Blériots and Henri Farmans; each would have to fly with pilot, mechanic, tools and kits of both, overseas. The weight of those was pure guesswork, and many were the cuts I made in personal baggage.

One Blériot crashed on take-off, but all the others flew safely over the Channel to Amiens. Before they left Dover each pilot had been issued with what seems to have been a motor car tyre inner tube which he was instructed to blow up and wear round his waist in case he fell into the 'drink' on the way to France. One light-hearted young pilot spent a little time trying to drop his inner tube like a quoit on the top of Cap Gris Nez lighthouse.

Meanwhile Jack felt that, as transport was the weakest link in the chain, he should travel with it to Southampton. It was composed of a medley of vehicles which would have done justice to a travelling circus in its diversity. Its brightest feature was a large commercial van, with Maple and Co. painted on both sides in large letters. It was packed to the brim with all the stores and spares necessary, until the arrival of the Aircraft Park – itself an unknown quantity. There were also several motor-cars, including a Daimler, which had been donated to the RFC at a rally in Hyde Park in July.

Jack remembered his father's experience in the Egyptian Campaign of 1881, when the rudders of some ships had been packed in a ship which sank, while hulls were in another, so he refused to allow the stores to travel in separate ships. He wrote: 'This caused a commotion and I was told to put my refusal in writing.' However, soon all was well and

the whole of us were decanted into one ship, and on the high seas. Now was the moment when, by instruction, I could open a sealed envelope which contained the name of our destination. Boulogne was hot favourite, and so it was. Arriving there, the ship was quickly unloaded and then there was a hiatus; there were no orders for a forward move awaiting us. I could get none from the several offices I visited. At last someone suggested I should look up Major (later Lord) Ironside as he usually knew everything and anyhow got a move on if he didn't. My confidence at once revived, as I knew him and the punch he usually applied to everything he did. It was not misplaced. Although our movement orders did not appear to be his business, he at once undertook to find out and promised I should get them before evening, which I did. That night we slept anywhere on the quayside; early morning saw us well on the way through dust and cheering villages to Amiens. Here I was relieved to find the squadron had arrived intact except one machine that turned up a few days later. So now, with the transport halted along the edge of the aerodrome, we were a complete unit, ready for any call. That evening I had to go to Headquarters and went to the Hotel du Rhin. There I found my brother Geoffrey, who had come to France ahead of us as one of the advance party of Royal Flying Corps staff officers. We had dinner and then went to his room where we talked far into the night on what was to be the outcome of this first introduction to war of a new arm, working in an element which had only recently been partially conquered. Armies and Navies had tradition and experience behind them, but what had we? Behind us nothing, but before us an absolute confidence that soon we should prove indispensable to both and, some day, decisive for Victory.

It was on 9 August, two days before Captain Geoffrey Salmond, Maurice Baring and Captain Longcroft had left for France, that the original British Expeditionary Force, under the command of Field Marshal Sir John French, began to embark. By the 20th it was concentrated in an area between Maubeuge and Le Cateau. The Expeditionary Force consisted of the First Army Corps under Lieutenant General Sir Douglas Haig; the second Army Corps under General Sir James Grierson, who died soon after landing and was succeeded by General Sir Horace Smith-Dorrien; and the Cavalry Division under Major General Allenby. The German generals seem to have made no attempt to prevent their landing; they were confident that they could surround and annihilate the small British force, so small in numbers compared to their vast army. But they had reckoned without the toughness and resilience of the BEF, which left with such high hopes for France, and which was so soon to be fighting for its life at Mons. On 14 August Sir John French himself arrived to inspect the RFC squadrons, and on the following day they were ordered to leave for Maubeuge, much nearer the front line, in the first of many hectic moves. Maurice Baring described the journey:

> 4.30. Set off for our next destination in a car with Brooke-Popham and Captain Buchanan. We drove along a straight road through acres of deserted country [with] rich cornfields all ready to be reaped but nobody to reap them. Everything was silent and deserted. Women and children came to look at us, but no men were to be seen anywhere.

The French authorities were most helpful, providing blankets and straw for the men, and it was from Maubeuge that the first air reconnaissance of enemy positions was made. Finding that the aircraft were being fired on, by our own guns as well as the enemy, the aircrews were up all night painting large Union Jacks on the undersides of the aircraft wings.

Lieutenant Barrington-Kennett was the Adjutant and the colourful and gallant Prince Murat was French Liaison Officer. Geoff was to write: 'Barrington-Kennett is such fun, he makes me roar with laughter.' Maurice Baring, with his talent for languages, was soon arranging for billets, food for the men and fodder for the horses, which he obtained through the generosity of the French Headquarters.

On the 17th, news came that the garrison at Liège had fallen, and that the German Army was sweeping across Belgium. Jack Salmond was to write later: 'My squadron did many useful reconnaissances. During this time Captain Joubert de la Ferté, flying a Blériot in company with an aircraft of 4 Squadron, was the first pilot to cross the line in our history.' Joubert himself wrote later:

> On 19 August Lieutenant Gilbert Mapplebeck and I did the first recon-naissance from Maubeuge. It was a sunny day with about three-tenths cloud. Mapplebeck was sent off in the direction of Louvain and I was told to go to Waterloo. Flying for the first time on 1/1,000,000 maps, both of us went adrift. Gilbert lost himself on the way back to Maubeuge, and I spent most of the day flying round parts of Belgium to which I had not been instructed to go. After getting lost over the coal-mining area of Mons, I finally decided to land at a large town where the houses still seemed to be flying the Belgian flag. This was Tournai, where my aircraft

was refuelled and I was given lunch by the Commandant of the place. From there I took off again, lost myself once more, also running out of fuel, landed near Courtrai. Here my reception was not at all friendly. It had not occurred to the War Office to provide us with identification papers and a good many of us were to experience difficulty owing to this lack of forethought. I was on my way to prison in Courtrai when I was saved by the intervention of a little Belfast linen manufacturer. He was in the crowd around the aircraft and, hearing me swear very heartily, rushed forward shouting, 'Och, sure, and he's an Englishman,' and taking from his pocket a small Union Jack (which is still one of my treasured possessions), hung it on the aircraft. Immediately the atmosphere changed. My aircraft was refuelled and I was given directions on how to reach Waterloo, over which I finally did my reconnaissance and, tired but thankful, regained Maubeuge, having long ago been given up as dead. Both reconnaissances were negative, but at least they showed that the defence of Liège had held up the German advance.

On the 22nd there was the sound of heavy firing. It was thought that Namur was being shelled and later reports by Captain Joubert de la Ferté showed heavy fighting around Charleroi, where he reported that he saw lines of German troops sweeping round to the west and the French in retreat. Henderson himself took the news to British Army Headquarters and Sir John French took the matter very seriously. After a conference next day at Le Cateau, he decided to call off the offensive he had planned and to retreat. The pilot's report had saved many lives, and prevented the British Expeditionary Force from being surrounded.

Jack was to write:

> The clash was not long in coming: on the day after we arrived Liège fell, and within a week the British Army was fighting for its life at Mons. But the flood which began rolling towards us was spotted and reported by the Royal Flying Corps, first on the right, then in front, and then on the left, sweeping round on our left flank. This latter was Von Kluck's great enveloping movement to annihilate the British Army. It was seen early and its progress reported to the Commander-in-Chief. The retreat began, and the octopus arm, which the German Supreme Command had designed to strangle us, closed without its victim. The Royal Flying Corps had won its spurs.

Led by Maurice Baring, the Staff, ordered to retreat, set out in an unusual assortment of vehicles which they had been able to collect at the rally in Hyde Park, mentioned by Jack, in which many cars and vans had been donated. Geoffrey could hardly find time to write to Peggy but a few letters in pencil survive. 'A German aeroplane has just passed over, and everyone has been firing, trying to bring it down, but they are hard things to hit. This is only to tell you that I am well, and not a letter. Jack is all right too. All letters are censored, so I cannot tell you anything of interest.'

They arrived at Le Cateau in the evening and an airfield was established outside the town. Baring wrote: 'I had nothing to eat all day. We slept, dozens of pilots fully dressed, in a barn in and under an enormous load of straw. Everybody cheerful, especially the pilots.' It was at Le Cateau that there was the first exchange of shots in the air. Lieutenant Harvey-Kelly, of 2 Squadron, with Lieutenant Mansfield as observer, gave chase to a German aircraft and forced it to land. Not wanting to let it escape, they landed close by and pursued the German aircrew on foot into a wood. Harvey-Kelly and his observer then returned to the aircraft, set it on fire and flew back in triumph to Le Cateau. At that time the only weapons carried by aircrews were rifles and revolvers for their own protection, as reconnaissance was still considered the only *raison d'être* of the RFC. Fighting in the air was still foreseen only by the few. Pilots flew over enemy lines with only a compass and map to guide them.

On 25 August the battle of Le Cateau developed and von Moltke tried to crush the Expeditionary Force once more. Geoffrey wrote: 'We are still in front of this wretched position; it is horribly strong by now, but of course we can't stay here for ever. That is the comforting fact.' On the 26th they were again in retreat. The pilots were told that after a sortie they must always inspect the airfield before they landed, as it might well be in German hands – in which case they must fly further back. The van, brightly painted and marked HP Sauce, was always a good landmark!

In the anxiety of the retreat, General Henderson was always calm. Jack wrote: 'Our General, David Henderson, has been wonderful throughout, never hasty, though he must have been anxious and often very tired, never downcast, though he must have accurately known the situation.' Maurice Baring also wrote of General Henderson at that time: 'He never showed the slightest sign of anxiety for a single moment. Some of the pilots reported columns of Germans miles long, and said their maps were black with lines showing columns of German troops.' Baring was driving with Barrington-Kennett, who said he was intensely depressed, as he thought the Guards had been defeated. 'This has never happened in history,' he said. 'They have never been beaten.' Next day the RFC was again in retreat and halted outside La Fère along the road.

Several messages sent by General Henderson to GHQ on 27 August which survive among the Salmond family papers make clear the importance of air reconnaissance. That day General Henderson wrote:

> Reference orders received this morning by Captain Baring, ADC. The RFC has moved to landing ground south of La Fère. I am sending on to

try to assist retiring troops but think there are not many on this road south of St. Quentin. Reconnaissance report I Army columns not yet returned. Reserve supply Park at La Frette near here. I can send forward supplies by motor wagons if required. Am erecting wireless and will communicate if necessary by that, as I cannot get you on the telephone. La Fère 27 August David Henderson Com. RFC.

In a message to GHQ at 9.10 am he had written:

Reconnaissance reports one of our columns, head at Guise, tail at Etreux, about 7.30 am Another column tail at Essigny, head at crossroads half way between Essigny and Ham. I am sending ten good officers to St. Quentin by motor to help reorganise troops there. Shall I send some food to Ham. Am reconnoitring further behind our column. David Henderson. La Fère 9.10 am.

Another message read:

27/8/14. GHQ 1/A. Aeroplane pilot reports long column moving south-west on road from Le Cateau to near Catelet. Observer landed with 1st Corps to report above to General Haig. (Signed) GOC RFC.

In the evening Henderson sent a further message:

General Wilson's order received. RFC transport will move early by Laon and Soissons. Aeroplanes will fly direct and an officer will report arrival and take any orders for reconnaissance. GOC RFC. La Fère. 6.30 pm 27/8/1914.

Meanwhile, a broken Division arrived at La Fère and were given food by the RFC transport officers. Maurice Baring wrote: 'These men arrived in a state of the greatest exhaustion, but it was curious how quickly they recovered.' He added:

A machine crashed in a turnip field . . . That morning we realised the full seriousness of the situation. Rumours were flying about that the whole of the British Army had been surrounded. Up to half past ten, I expected to see German helmets coming over the edge of the turnip field every moment. Towards mid-day more reassuring news came – I know not where from.

At this time the pilots were flying from dawn till dusk over the enemy lines, bringing back reports which were analysed by Colonel Sykes and Geoffrey

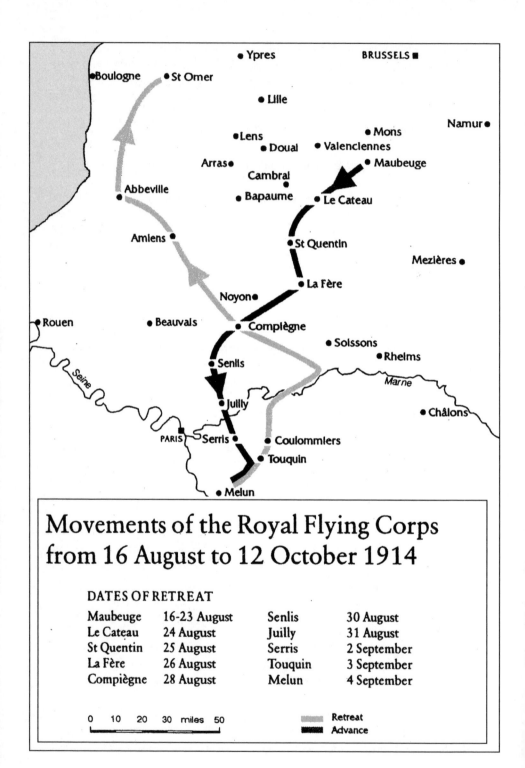

Movements of the Royal Flying Corps from 16 August to 12 October 1914

DATES OF RETREAT

Maubeuge	16-23 August	Senlis	30 August
Le Cateau	24 August	Juilly	31 August
St Quentin	25 August	Serris	2 September
La Fère	26 August	Touquin	3 September
Compiègne	28 August	Melun	4 September

0   10   20   30   miles   50

Retreat
Advance

Salmond and relayed as fast as possible to Army Headquarters. The RFC was constantly moving and the Headquarters would move nine times over the next ten days.

A telegram from Colonel Sykes two days earlier concerning the Aircraft Park survives:

> O.C. Aircraft Park. Please pack up all Aircraft Park and move to Havre. Those aeroplanes fit to fly and for which you have pilots should proceed to Havre by air, except two Sopwiths. Cholmondeley and Spratt to fly those to St Quentin tomorrow and land on our new ground there, if it is quite obvious that we are there. They should fly high, as the French shoot at nearly every aeroplane seen. Those machines unfit to fly to Le Havre and those for which you have no pilots – first remove engines and pack up and despatch to Havre. Then pick up those machines for which you have packing cases and send to Havre. Remove in fact all you can to Havre as soon as possible. 2 pm Frederick Sykes 25/8/14 GS RFC.

Although the Union Jack had been clearly marked on the wings of the aircraft on arrival at Maubeuge it was still obvious that the French could not distinguish it. A telegram survives from the War Office at this time. It runs:

> WO Aitken War Office 4.40 Aircraft Commander General Headquarters Expeditionary Force. Have you adopted any recognition marks on aeroplanes and from available experience do you think recognition marks desirable and practical? 5.10 pm 29 August General Headquarters 1914.

Later, during September, roundels in red, white and blue were painted on the wings in preference to the Union Jack. They are the RAF's symbol to this day.

Peggy wrote later of this time:

> In the first few days Geoff said they had not decided whether to retreat to the coast or on to Paris. Geoff found himself at some crossroads directing the poor fatigued soldiers retreating in long lines – many walking or riding in their sleep – as they had had no sleep for many days.

On 30 August Geoff wrote:

> I see by the papers that you have our news. Let's hope you will have more welcome news soon, but it will take time, and don't let anyone be in a hurry. We are in a pretty place here, simply perfect if it wasn't for war. Well done, with the Red Cross. It is splendid. Mrs. Segrave is distributing milk or something in London. God bless you, dear Peg . . . I think

everyone is getting used to the war out here, and the novelty is wearing off. I think our men tune up to war quicker probably than other nations. They have such stout hearts, and I sort of feel they can stand up to the hurly burly of it all. Jack is looking very well, and Barrington-Kennett [BK] is a very nice chap. You must not be depressed at home. All my aeroplanes flew off this morning at 4 am!

Jack wrote afterwards:

If the retreat, during the ten days that followed, was trying for the Royal Flying Corps, our hardship was nothing compared to the Infantry. Those haggard, dogged men, with sunken eyes and bent heads, sleepless from endless fighting and marching, trudged rearward with little food and without complaint – a nightmare army of heroes, who saved England. Thus I saw them after the rearguard battle of Le Cateau, where the 5th Division stood against overwhelming odds, and suffered very greatly, disciplined, patient, gaunt.

Several officers, of whom Jack Salmond was one, who had left their Regiments to join the Royal Flying Corps, found the suffering of their comrades almost too much to bear, and, with General Henderson's permission, they offered themselves to Sir Charles Ferguson, who was in command. Jack wrote:

We found him, after some difficulty, almost alone on some rising ground, and I delivered my General's message. He looked tired, but very calm, and, after pondering for a moment, turned to me and said, 'Thank David will you, but tell him I think I have almost more officers left than men.'

Meanwhile the retreat continued. From Compiègne they were nearing Senlis. In the evening, Baring wrote: 'It was dark and a large moon rose over the misty fields. The poplars looked spectral and the landscape had the silver witchery of a Corot picture.' They arrived at Senlis at 8.30 pm and Baring went to a small hotel (burned two days later by the Germans) and had supper with Harvey-Kelly and Corballis, two young pilots. A lady asked one of them (a French pilot) *'Dis donc, Hubert, as-tu des aventures en aeroplane?'* Baring was afterwards often called 'Hubert' by Corballis.

On 31 August they arrived at Juilly, where, in the evening, a crisis arose. It was rumoured that long lines of German troops were advancing on the field in which the aeroplanes were parked. They could not of course fly at night in those days. Baring wrote:

The question was, what was going to happen to the Flying Corps? The pilots would never leave their aeroplanes. Finally, a troop of Irish Horse was sent to look after us, and some French territorials. The aerodrome was in a field by some crossroads. Troops were deployed to defend it. On one road Murat's car was placed. He put on his helmet, which he only did on great occasions. He stood next to it all night, armed to the teeth. We lay down by some stones in the road. We were armed to the teeth also. I had a revolver, but no rifle, but Barrington-Kennett said, 'I will defend you'. Some of the North Irish Horse kept on champing up and down the road all night and treading on me. Uhlans were supposed to be about three miles off [but] no Germans appeared in the night. The German cavalry, as it turned out afterwards, were themselves cut off. When dawn came we looked rather bedraggled and Salmond's face was white with chalk from the dust which he had gathered sleeping on the road.

Jack was also with them that night. He wrote: 'Prince Murat in shining silver helmet stood guard all night on the highway. A lonely and romantic figure. We flew off in the half-light of early dawn.' All this time the words, *'Réculer pour mieux sauter'* were ringing in his head, and they proved to be true, for on 6 September, when the Headquarters had reached Melun, quite suddenly the long pursuit came to an end. Three days earlier, when the pressure on the British Forces had begun to ease slightly, Captain Joubert de la Ferté and Lieutenant D. L. Allen were sent out in a B.E.2a to see if they could locate Von Kluck's cavalry, which had been 'missing' for two days. On the right of the Expeditionary Force they saw groups of German infantry moving south-wards. Dusk was approaching and, in the half-light, they could see many thousands of twinkling bivouac fires. They realized that the main German advance had changed to the east – groups of horses were being watered at streams and ponds, showing that the cavalry had changed direction. They reported to Headquarters immediately and Sir John French was at once informed. German High Command, unable to defeat the British Expeditionary Force, had turned its attention to the French, and decided on a fatal left wheel across the British front. On 5 September Geoff wrote to Peggy: 'We are on the eve of great things.' On the next day the Battle of the Marne was fought. It would change the whole history of the war.

From 6 to 11 September, the Allied forces pushed the extended German line back, and it was not until the 13th that the enemy managed to make a stand along the River Aisne. The battle of the Aisne lasted until 25 September and then a series of movements to the north-west began as both armies tried to outflank each other and reach the Channel coast.

The Tide Turns

On 3 September the Governor of Paris, General Gallieni, had suddenly appeared at British Headquarters demanding to see Sir John French. Only Archibald Murray, his Chief of Staff, was present and Gallieni, bespectacled and intense, had explained to him his brilliant plan of ordering Manouri's army to march eastwards and to strike at the German flank. Two days later, after some hesitation, General Joffre was persuaded to obtain the co-operation of the British and, while it was too late to reverse the British retreat that day, early on 6 September, the British Expeditionary Force was ordered by French to turn and advance. At the same time, at 1.30 am on 6 September, Foch had received Joffre's famous 'about turn' order. Quite fortuitously, Napoleon's strategy at Sedan had once again been implemented. The Germans marched into a trap between the 5th and 6th French Armies, and the battle of the Marne, although fought by tired and exhausted soldiers, was to prove the Allies' first great victory.

Due to the genius of Gallieni, six hundred Paris taxicabs were commandeered on 6 September to transport three thousand troops to the front, and all were inspired to join in the deliverance of Paris. It was on 9 September that the retreat of the German Army began. Next day, after the great battle had been won, Geoffrey was able to write to Peggy and a letter in faint pencil survives:

> The Germans are retreating. It is hard to know exactly why, but it is probable that they thought their right flank was in danger of being enveloped. Anyhow we are following them up and making things as unpleasant as we can! The Flying Corps has done very well indeed, wonderfully well. I believe they have surpassed all expectations in the eyes of the great ones. I wish the Germans would see the futility of this war. Eric Segrave is going to be Brigade Major of the 12th Brigade. He is awfully pleased and so is dear J. The only thing he is worried about is that Mrs. Segrave will get anxious as of course it means being right up. It is splendid, this retirement, as it means that the whole of the big offensive plan of the Germans has come to an end – anyhow for the present.

Meanwhile Maurice Baring had to go to Paris for extra supplies, where he found the whole staff of the Embassy had disappeared, having burnt many documents. Only the chauffeur had refused to leave. It seemed to everyone a miracle that the Prussian forces could have been deflected at the last moment from reaching Paris. During the battle, Sir John French sent this despatch to London on 7 September:

> I wish particularly to bring to your Lordships' notice the admirable work done by the Royal Flying Corps under Sir David Henderson. Their skill,

energy and perseverance have been beyond all praise. They have furnished me with complete and accurate information which has been of incalculable value in the conduct of operations. Fired at constantly by friend and foe, not hesitating to work in every kind of weather, they have remained undaunted throughout. Further, by actually fighting in the air, they have succeeded in destroying five of the enemy's machines.

The weather had been splendid for flying during the first few days of the battle, but on 9 September, when the German retreat began, and when RFC Headquarters had moved to Coulommiers, a storm broke, and for the next few days it was impossible to carry out many reconnaissances. On the 12th Jack wrote:

We settled down at Fère-en-Tardenois, but a very violent storm on the first day carried away a large number of our aircraft, before the transport could arrive with picketing pegs and ropes. Some of my Henri Farmans were blown into the air and landed upside down with their backs broken. The genius of Brooke-Popham at supplying all our needs soon put this right and it was not long before we had our full complement again.

Next day Geoff wrote to Peggy:

I am so sorry you have had such an anxious time. Never mind, the tide has turned and it is the Germans' turn to clear out. The Kaiser must be sick that his whole show is turning out wrong – at least we think it is. Our men are so splendid, and fight so well, not a scrap of deterioration about them. I have just read Sir John's despatch. I was so glad he has given Smith-Dorrien such praise – he deserves it all, and is deserving more every day. The town we are billeted in had everything turned upside-down out of sheer wantonness. Jack is very well, and so is everyone. It has poured with rain the last two days, but the pursuit has gone on just the same, and the more rain the worse it is for the Germans, in retreat – much worse than for us.

Meanwhile, at Fère-en-Tardenois, where they were to stay for a whole month, the billets had been left in such a disgraceful state by the hastily retreating Germans that the pilots preferred to sleep in the fields outside the town, burrowing in haystacks, or under the wings of their aircraft. Once the storm was over, one can imagine the long shadows of the early autumn evenings spreading over the misty fields, succeeded by the peaceful starry September nights, contrasting so vividly with the hectic days, when the pilots and observers flew over the enemy lines, flinging themselves into the heat and danger of battle.

Of that time Jack wrote:

> The value of air reconnaissance to the Army was proving itself, and now
> Corps Commanders were asking for aircraft to be specifically allotted for
> their own use. Up to this time all four squadrons had moved and worked
> with General Headquarters as one command under General Henderson.
> The Commander-in-Chief decided that this, the first step in decentral-
> isation, was advisable and I was ordered to detach a flight daily to report
> to Sir Horace Smith-Dorrien, commanding the Second Corps, and this
> flight returned home every evening. This worked so well that it was made
> permanent, and it was thus that the Corps Squadrons were born, which
> later worked with every Corps along the Front.

This was a great step forward. Soon Sir Horace Smith-Dorrien was writing:

> My great admiration for the splendid work the Royal Flying Corps is
> doing for my Corps every day. Nothing prevents them from obtaining the
> required information and they frequently return with rifle or shrapnel
> bullets through the aeroplanes or even their clothing, without considering
> such, to them, ordinary incidents worth mentioning. Today I watched
> for a long time an aeroplane observing for the six-inch howitzers for the
> Third Division. It was, at times, smothered with hostile anti-aircraft guns,
> but nothing daunted, it continued for hours through a wireless installa-
> tion to observe the fire, and indeed to control the Battery with the most
> satisfactory results.

Spotting and reporting the positions of hostile batteries became an operation
of the first importance after Maubeuge had fallen, as the Germans had
brought down their siege artillery to the Aisne, and the British guns were
outranged and actually outnumbered. On the Aisne those aircraft which
carried wireless were of the utmost importance. During the month at La
Fère, the two B.E.2 aircraft earmarked for wireless telegraphy became very
popular with the Army. The two pilots, Donald Swain Lewis and Baron
Trevener James, were often overworked and exhausted, as the artillery
constantly asked for a wireless machine, not only as a reconnaissance aircraft
but also for artillery observation. The two aircraft themselves were worn and
the wing fabric was often patched, but Lieutenants Lewis and James never
spared themselves. Early in 1914, under Major Muspratt, they had evolved a
heavy wireless set, weighing 75 lbs. which entirely filled the observer's
cockpit, but which sent back very satisfactory messages. In the retreat from
Mons, however, the set had proved too cumbersome, and it was only at Fère-
en-Tardenois that a lighter and more satisfactory wireless set was created. In
September the Headquarters Wireless Telegraphy Unit was formed under the

command of Major Muspratt and in December it became 9 Squadron. Even so, Jack wrote that a very high officer had told him that wireless could never be of any operational value. But he wrote, 'My brother Geoffrey and I most thoroughly believed in its future in the air and were not perturbed when this very wise man condemned it.'

Both Jack and Geoffrey also saw the huge possibilities of photography from the air. Five rather blurred photographs taken by Lieutenant George Pretyman of 3 Squadron were developed and taken by John Salmond to Headquarters. They showed how an improved photograph could help in the identification of enemy emplacements. At first there had been little encouragement on the part of the Army, although 3 Squadron had taken detailed photographs of the Isle of Wight before the war. It was only because many of the pilots had brought their own cameras to France that photography from the air had started, the pilots strapping their cameras to the outside of the aircraft and changing the plates by hand during flights. One can imagine the difficulty of leaning from the open cockpit to do this, wearing thick flying gloves and often in freezing cold and windy weather. Members of 3 Squadron were, however, tireless in taking and developing their own photographs, and over the next few months C. C. Darley was to improve the art of photography from the air out of all recognition.

Geoffrey wrote home on 21 September:

> I hear the most extravagant things said about the Flying Corps, all in praise. Everyone's eyes have been opened, but although the RFC has been splendid, our soldiers, the infantry and cavalry, have done wonders. Indeed, what a glorious outcome of all the doubts and dark forebodings as to what would happen if England were ever involved in war. Jack is very well and flourishing. The German method of war as regards the inhabitants seem to make them quite unpopular. Rheims Cathedral was set on fire by shell-fire, the roof fell in, and they say fell on a heap of German wounded, but I don't know that for certain yet. Many of the villagers tell us the Germans pay for a certain amount of stuff they take. I think the majority are all right. I don't find anything to convince me they are barbarians yet. Of course the burning of Louvain was appalling, but it must have been the act of an absolutely mad General. I am so glad my letter cheered you up. I wrote to Mother and it did the same. I thought you all might feel depressed. You should see everyone out here. At the worst time our men were ready to laugh, and never looked depressed. They are wonders. Also, it is worse to read, probably. Love darling, ever so much. Ever your loving Geoff.

★ ★ ★

While the Army was fighting for its life in France, Trenchard was creating new squadrons at home, not just replacements for those in the field, but the first foundations of a fighting force. At the very start of hostilities he had commandeered Brooklands with all its civilian aeroplanes and equipment, and with that as a nucleus, he had created new training schools all over England.

On 22 September Geoff received a long letter from Sefton Brancker vividly describing the problems at home:

My dear Salmond, Very many thanks for your most interesting letter; I wish I could tell you anything worth hearing. The Flying Corps have done magnificently and no mistake – the papers have been all over it, but it has amazed me not a little that they have almost entirely omitted mention of B.E.2 and quite forgotten O'Gorman – one or two actually claim the honour of making the RFC what it is for themselves and their futile attacks of the past! I am going to have your letter typed and passed round; it will be interesting and instructive to everyone – and please continue re spares and transport as you say you will. Trenchard is doing magnificently as he naturally would. He has got a move on at Farnborough which it has never seen before, and already from the chaotic remnants which you left behind, there are the beginnings of three Squadrons, one of which, No. 6, I hope will go to join you before the end of October. What we want most is more senior officers, and these you have refused to send us so far. The first batch of twelve from the CFS have come out after six weeks training, and some of them have done 24 hours in the air, which gives you some idea of how Paine and the instructors have worked. I want to get a stream flowing through the school staff. They are having a very strenuous and depressing time, and some of your flight commanders (newly promoted or otherwise) and flying officers should by degrees replace MacLean and Co. at Upavon. We are having lots of trouble with new machines; BE8 won't climb, but we are improving her. The reports about her instability were tosh, and probably arose from one BE8 not being properly tuned up. FE2 has been wrongly designed and will be delayed. The Monosoupape Gnome has not done well so far, but I have hopes, and with it B.E.8 should be a fizzer. The latest 8a Gnomes are only giving 62 on the bench and we are having to investigate them. We can't really try the Vickers Fighter because of the Monosoupape's delinquencies. We have lots of 70 Renault R.A.F.ls and 80 Gnomes on order in England, but the Lord knows whether they will go round when made. We have been pretty reckless one way and another in our endeavours to push things but we have been d-d [sic] lucky. We have had quite six accidents, which with our luck of last March would have been fatal, but no-one has been seriously hurt, although Holt is away after being very much shaken up after having been dived straight into the ground by a clumsy pupil. The office is beginning to adjust itself; I have an excellent fellow, M . . . , (gunner of course) as GSO2 in Bertie Fisher's place; the latter is doing B.M. to a new Cavalry brigade which goes out next month. The next change I am contemplating is that Paine shall become DGHA in my place. I think it would be an excellent precedent to have a sailor in the WO and he would run the show very well. But I know if I suggested it, Winston would want him to command a Dreadnought! Well this is enough; I envy you very much. Both Trenchard and I have given ourselves up as damned – anyway so far as the RFC is concerned. If he is wanted to command his regiment though, I propose to let him go. My love to all; Sefton Brancker.

★   ★   ★

By September the wounded were pouring home and hospitals and convalescent homes were becoming overcrowded. Peggy's aunt, Mary Carr, who lived in a beautiful Elizabethan house in the next village to Ditchingham, had converted it into a hospital for wounded soldiers. Peggy had joined the Red Cross and was nursing there every day, leaving the babies across the park with their nanny at Ditchingham Hall. Casualty lists were coming out, and there was always the dread of a telegram. Joy, Jack's wife, and Peggy wrote to each other, wondering what warm gloves or flying coats they could send out to Jack and Geoff. At this time Geoff managed to write a long letter to Peggy, explaining why the Germans had retreated and what he felt their future plans would be:

> They had begun to retreat before they had had a general engagement. They retreated because they had made a gigantic strategic error in turning SE and having the British Army (UNBEATEN, they thought it was) and a French Army on their right flank. They realised their mistake and commenced their retreat, no doubt with the idea of throwing back the right wing and of course we were on them like a knife, because a retreat is the very hardest thing in war to carry out successfully. During the retreat they lost heavily but they did it very well and at once stood when they got to the Aisne. They will have to retreat again and again. They will lose heavily. This time they will have to retreat because they can't help it – not because they have made an error. This big battle must be wearing them out, but it is hard to say how long the war will last. They probably have arranged by this time all sorts of places in their rear where they can stand again, so that it is no good being too sanguine. The papers seem to get almost hysterical in their accounts of the war, especially when the first retreat began. This time when they retreat it will be after this very big battle – no doubt they will find it harder than their first one. Nowadays

with aeroplanes, it is extraordinarily hard for a side that wants to retreat to get away. Formerly it was done in the night and during the next day, and the other side took several days before it knew for certain that the enemy had evacuated their position – now all that is changed, and if the weather holds good, we know it at once. The result is the battle never ceases and if the Germans retreat we shall be after them at once – so that this 18 day battle will go on and on – so there you are, darling, the odds are that the war should not last a very long time. . . . The weekly *Times* is coming out all right – I think I have thanked you for your parcels. The socks fit beautifully dear darling, it was sweet of you to make them, and such a surprise. You have been one long glorious joy. I do so love that photograph that you sent me. You are both too ripping for words. I always give them my last look before I go to sleep. Yes, all this is just a nasty dream, that is just what it is. Ever and ever and ever Your Geoff. [PS] Jack has just come in to the rest room with some reports, so I must stop. I am 12 miles from the Front here, so you can be happy, dear one.

Later Maurice Baring wrote about that autumn to a friend, Ethel Smythe:

Never was there a finer autumn. And the French landscape . . . seemed to bask in the richness and tints of that fine September. The little gardens were laden with fruits, and the reaped fields were bathed in a calm light. How, one used to wonder, were they reaped, and by whom? The country seemed deserted; in the distance you saw brown ricks, and great long shadows played over the plain. I remember the heat of the stubble on Saponay aerodrome, pilots lying about on the straw, some just back from a reconnaissance, some just starting, some asleep, some talking of what they would do after the war; the blazing farmhouses where we used to buy eggs and chickens and, once, a goose. The smell of cider, and the courtesy of an old farmer's wife.

In the church Mass used to be said to a congregation huddled in the chancel, while the aisle was full of wounded. Maurice Baring continued:

I remember the clicking of typewriters in our little improvised office, and a soldier singing 'Abide with me' at the top of his voice in the kitchen. And then the beauty of the Henri Farmans sailing through the clear evening – 'the evening broken by homing wings', and the moonlight vision over the stubble of the aerodrome, and a few camp fires glowing in the mist, and the noise of the men singing songs of home.

B. K. and Saint Omer

In early October, while RFC Headquarters was still at Fère-en-Tardenois, Colonel Sykes sent Geoffrey Salmond to study French methods of aerial photography. Geoffrey visited the French Corps Headquarters and found that their photographic organization was highly centralised, and also that they appeared to have more technical expertise than the RFC possessed. In his report he recommended the concentration of all photographic personnel into sections, one for each flying Wing. Sir David Henderson at once formed an experimental section, which he was to send in January to 1st Wing Headquarters. The Section was to consist of Lieutenant J. T. C. Moore-Brabazon, Sergeant Lewis and Lieutenant Campbell. They had to report on the best form of organization and the best camera for air photography. Colonel Trenchard was the first to encourage them. Meanwhile, Darley of 3 Squadron had fixed up a darkroom in the stable of the Château de Werpes and developed his own plates. He showed his photographs to his Commanding Officer, Jack Salmond, who, realizing the significance of their quality, took them to his Corps Headquarters. By the end of January, the whole front had been photographed and a long German Sap was revealed. As a result the plan of attack was modified, and General Joffre was so impressed that he asked for copies. In March, Geoffrey's plan of setting up a photographic section at each Wing was recommended by Brabazon and Campbell and was subsequently adopted.

While visiting French Headquarters, Geoffrey had also had time to study their method of control of artillery from the air. As long ago as 1911, the French had produced maps divided into geometrical squares so that a pair of numbers would identify a position within a score or so of yards. These maps had been duplicated and given to their pilots and also to the Commanding Officers of their Batteries. At first the system of signalling was primitive, but with the development of wireless there were endless possibilities which Geoffrey was not slow to appreciate. Lieutenant Lewis of 'the Wireless Machine' had also invented a rough squared map. He had ruled the squares and marked them in ink and had shown it to Geoff, who was so impressed that he took it to a Major Jack of the Topographical Section, who soon produced a specimen sheet. Described as 'pin-pointing', these squared maps were in use by October 1914 on the 1st Corps front and were so successful that all the other Corps were clamouring for more of them. Geoffrey himself worked out a system of artillery-to-air cooperation based on the squared map, which later in June was to be adopted throughout the RFC in France and was headed 'Major Salmond's System'. Meanwhile it became desperately urgent, especially after the fall of Antwerp, that the Expeditionary Force should return to protect the Channel ports. This operation has often been called 'The Race for the Sea' but was, in fact, a series of attempts by both armies to outflank each other. Finally, the

Germans tried to outflank the Allied line with their 6th Army, but were halted by the timely arrival of the French 1st Army. Again the enemy tried a great cavalry sweep round our flank, and again it was countered by the gallant French cavalry and a newly arrived Army Corps. All of which was, of course, faithfully reported by the RFC.

The Headquarters moved by way of Abbeville to St Omer. When they left Fère-en-Tardenois 'BK' was determined to leave the office and all billets in the town immaculate. He stayed behind with Maurice Baring, cleaning the billets himself, even leaving newspapers folded on the table. As they drove away by car, they had a puncture which Barrington-Kennett mended. At the next town they were so hungry that they stopped for dinner, but when another crisis arose BK immediately left his meal and went to help. He was, indeed, a man who set the highest standard of duty and was always an inspiration to his colleagues. They arrived at St Omer on 12 October, two days after the fall of Antwerp. The opposing armies now faced each other from the Swiss frontier to within 30 miles of the North Sea.

On a clear day it was now possible to see the white cliffs of Dover from the air, and to marvel at the narrowness of the gulf between those peaceful cliffs and the struggle developing in France. A year later, a youthful pilot, Cecil Lewis, described one of his first flights at St Omer:

> There to the North was the coastline – an unmistakable landmark – Boulogne, Calais, Dunkerque. Beneath were the straight French roads, with their avenues of poplars. Calais itself nestled under the right wing-tip, compact and cosy, one tall church spire and ten thousand chimneys, breathing a vague bluish vapour which hung pensive in the sky. Beyond the harbour was the leave boat starting for England, two white furrows and a penn'orth of smoke. An escort of destroyers flanked her, and beyond the steel-grey sea, almost hidden in the evening haze, was the outline of the Dover cliffs – white beyond the water. It seemed a different world.

Soon pilots were mapping the country and reporting gun emplacements and the arrival of German reinforcements to the Corps and RFC Headquarters, now established in a château at St Omer. They were tireless in their support of the Army.

Maurice Baring described the small château at St. Omer which, though they did not know it, would be the Headquarters of the RFC in France for the next two years. It was a modern stucco building, red and white. Sir David Henderson had a small office and bedroom upstairs, Geoffrey Salmond, Barrington-Kennett and Maurice Baring all shared another room, while Prince Murat had a third. The office downstairs was very primitive. Barrington-Kennett used to sit at a card table, Salmond at another rickety piece of furniture, and Brooke-Popham had a second card table for his work, which soon became littered with paper. The Sergeant-Major sat on a box in front of other boxes. 'A bevy of clerks filled the room,' said Baring. 'Each clerk had a typewriter and each clerk's box had about a dozen candles stuck on to it, burning and guttering. The atmosphere was quite solid.' They slept on the floor in their valises [sleeping-bags]. Soon, their routine after the hectic and long day's work was to brew tea in a small kettle on going to bed, to talk till late, and in the morning to sing songs while dressing. Maurice Baring had already decided to read Dante before going to sleep. Geoff, not to be outdone, wrote to Peggy asking for one of Dickens' books. The songs in the morning were sure to have been inspired by Geoff, whose good humour was always at its best when surrounded by his friends. One of the songs most popular at that time was the music-hall song 'Archibald, certainly not!' Lieutenant Borton, with his observer Thompson, in avoiding some anti-aircraft fire burst into this song. 'We sang it,' he explained later, 'because it seemed to sum up our attitude towards anti-aircraft guns at that time.' Soon the other young pilots began to sing it too, and every anti-aircraft gun was christened 'Archie', a name which stuck until the end of the war.

Antwerp had fallen on 10 October, two days before the arrival of the RFC at St. Omer. Geoff wrote, hoping to encourage the family, on 18 October:

> Darling, you should not be disheartened because Antwerp has fallen. It is no earthly good to the Germans unless they want to violate Dutch neutrality, and Holland and the Scheldt. It makes no difference to us whatsoever, except that it releases a certain amount of troops to concentrate against us. But, as I said before, don't think that will make any difference, as we are good enough for them any day.

A few days later he was writing:

> I hope you are getting accustomed to the proximity of the Germans to England. It will be so lovely when it is all over. The Germans certainly did well to get Antwerp and Ostend, but it is rather like a lion bullying and then eating a mouse – and that is really all they have to boast of . . . I am writing this now in bed, with candlelight to help me. Let my love come to you at all times of the day, and make you happy dear.

Geoff also begged Peggy not to allow anyone to be afraid of a Zeppelin raid, saying:

> Be quite quite happy and make other people the same. Laugh at their fears and tell them that if the Germans did do it, they would get absolutely smashed and would only help our army in France. We are bang full of

confidence here and don't honestly care a single rap about Antwerp. . . . I am writing this at 11 pm whilst a long message is being dictated in cipher. Then I have to take it down to the signals officer. I have a car waiting for me. Brancker has been out with me for a couple of days and has returned now.

All through October the terrible battle known as the First Battle of Ypres was waged. The victory belonged to the spirit and courage of the British and French soldiers and their magnificent stand against the German Army, which was constantly being supported by further reinforcements. The RFC could do little but bring back reconnaissance reports, report gun positions and map the country as they watched the terrible trench warfare from the skies. Then, on 25 October King Albert of the Belgians ordered the locks at Nieuport to be opened, thus flooding the country between the Yser and the railway embankment. Three days later Belgian engineers succeeded in letting in the sea. The Germans were forced to retreat, but it was not until 11 November, after much fierce fighting, that the crisis of First Ypres finally passed.

Casualties in the battle had been terrible. The First Brigade, which met the Prussian spearhead, had gone into battle 4500 strong. By 12 November the First Battalion Scots Guards had no officers and only one hundred and fifty men but they had held the line and the battle had been won at a fearful cost. Geoffrey could not describe the battle as his letters were heavily censored, but he managed to write in pencil on 4 November:

I think it looks as if we have won the battle. It has been terrific – not for me, but for everyone at the very front. Unfortunately today, of all days, a thick fog has covered the whole of our front, so that we have been able to see nothing. They [the Germans] are indeed fortunate. Perhaps tomorrow may clear the weather up. You see how terribly important aircraft information is. I have had such dear regular letters that I am almost ashamed at not having written for so long, but I have been hard at it from morning till evening. All telegrams etc. come to me at night, so that I am constantly having things brought up to me; if they are not important I am asleep again the very next minute, and they seldom are, luckily, at that time of night.

There was still almost no night flying and all reconnaissance and artillery spotting had to take place between dawn and dusk. He added:

I heard last night that I had been promoted Major along with a host of others in the Regiment. The great speculation is whether Germany will dare to come to terms after the battle, or whether she will still stick to the bare chance of snatching a victory through some mistake we make.

More light-heartedly, on 12 November Geoff wrote:

> In your last letter, you do not know, you write, whether I am a Major or not – I wonder when you did find out for certain? I shall certainly expect a letter next time addressed to Major Salmond. I don't like the 'Major' much – it sounds 'fat'. Still, the next rank is Colonel and the next after that is General, so it is [all] in the right direction, I suppose. Love and love ever your Geoff.

And on 23 November:

> My dearest, another scrawl. This goes by Hilaire Belloc who is staying a night with us. It is very cold. We are all right, but the fellows in front must be wretched. Jack is well and so am I.

At the end of November General Henderson was asked to take over the command of the 1st Division, replacing General Lomax, who had been severely wounded when at Hoogen. He could not refuse – and Colonel Sykes was left in command of the RFC in France. Before Sir David Henderson left, he divided his Squadrons into Wings. The first Wing, comprising 2 and 3 Squadrons, was to be under Major Trenchard, who was to be brought out to France to command it; the second, under Lieutenant Colonel Burke, comprised 5 and 6 Squadrons. The 1st Wing was to work with the Indian Corps and the Fourth Army, the 2nd with the Second and Third Army Corps. It was a great step forward in the decentralization of the RFC, bringing them more and more into contact with the Army Corps and leading to the realization by the Army Commanders of the great potential of aircraft.

Jack wrote that as the weather grew colder he was determined that his Squadron should be well housed. It was at first difficult to find a suitable landing-ground near Corps Headquarters, but he eventually found a root field by the Château de Werpes and his men marched up and down to flatten the surface. Jack himself flew in in a small single-seater Scout – the only one in the RFC – and the whole Squadron followed safely. The airfield was kept serviceable in spite of the rain and mud of the first winter, by a supply of cinders from the local gasworks. These were laid by the Squadron and then trampled in.

Meanwhile, Maurice Baring wrote an amusing account of his first meeting with Trenchard, whom he went to meet at Boulogne:

> The boat came in about half past four. Standing quite by himself on the deck of the boat was a tall man, with a small head and a Scots Fusilier cap on. That, I said to myself, must be Colonel Trenchard – it was. On the way to St. Omer Colonel Trenchard asked me a great many pertinent

questions, few of which I could answer. A certain intuition warned me after a time that we were going the wrong way, and when we came to a barrier where there were some French soldiers I got out and asked the way, and it turned out we were going swiftly and directly in the opposite direction to St. Omer. We didn't arrive at HQ till 8 o'clock. Colonel Trenchard slept on the floor of the Guest Room.

Baring wrote that the Headquarters was expanding 'and was growing apace in the way of clerks. Our office was fuller than ever, and the number of candles, for we still had neither lamps nor electric light, would have done honour to a Cathedral.'

When General Henderson left for the 1st Division he asked Baring if he would go with him as Intelligence Officer, to which the reply was 'I should like nothing better.' He later wrote:

> My main recollection of the first period at St. Omer is a stuffy office, full of clerks and candles and a deafening noise of typewriters. A constant stream of pilots arriving in the evening with Burberrys and maps, talking over reconnaissance. A perpetual stream of guests and crowds of people sleeping on the floor, a weekly struggle, sometimes successful, sometimes not, to get a bath in the town, where there was always a seething crowd of supplicants and a charming, capable lady in charge who used to call one *'Mon très cher Monsieur'*. Hours spent on the aerodrome, which were generally misty. Then a few expeditions along abominable roads to Bailleul, Poperinghe, and Hazebrouk, and occasional visits to Boulogne and Dunkirk, and a tense feeling the whole time that the situation was not satisfactory but that it would somehow or other come all right in the end.

Although Geoffrey never mentioned it in his letters, or Jack in his memoirs, it was no secret that there was no love lost between Trenchard and Sykes. It was a sad clash of personalities which both men bitterly regretted, and which was to influence the careers of both. Trenchard, on finding that Sir David Henderson had left the Headquarters, offered to resign and go back to his Regiment, the Royal Scots Fusiliers, but Lord Kitchener himself, who had so much appreciated Trenchard's organization at home, would not allow him to do so. He recalled Sir David to RFC Headquarters in December, and in January Trenchard was promoted to Brevet Lieutenant Colonel. The Headquarters Staff remained as before, while Colonel Trenchard was in command of the 1st Wing. The atmosphere was not, however, so relaxed and comfortable as it had been before, and both 'BK' and Geoffrey felt the strain. Maurice Baring, on the other hand, was delighted to be back. Although completely devoted to Sir David Henderson, he wrote: 'I suffered the whole time from RFC sickness.' He had missed the light-hearted spirit of the RFC, the daring young pilots and possibly, too, the companionship of Barrington-Kennett and Geoffrey Salmond.

Meanwhile Geoffrey, in such close touch with his brother and the pilots, secretly longed to be in command of a squadron, but realized that the work he was doing was vital, if not so glamorous. He had written in October:

> I am rather distressed because I think you may be disappointed because my name is not mentioned in despatches. I could hardly expect to be because my job is very unexciting with practically no chance of doing anything except the War Diary and suggesting reconnaissances. The only thing is to be philosophical about it, and not discontented. Dear old Jack is mentioned and richly deserves it. BK and I call ourselves the 'complete Babus'. Babu is an Indian name for clerk. You see we write orders in our different spheres and check any chance of misunderstanding between the Staff and the squadrons. All very important no doubt, but not calculated to give one much scope. I just get very discontented at times because of this, but in a show like this everyone has to give up self and do one's job, however dull it is. Now here come some air reports, just arrived, so I must stop.

Geoff could write this to Peggy, but his natural good humour and sense of fun usually prevailed. On 27 November he wrote:

> Two of our fellows captured a German aeroplane the other day. They fought them in the air, and frightened them so that the enemy's pilot lost his head and came down in our lines. The day before another German machine came down and was captured with its two officers. Their engine went wrong and as there was a very strong wind blowing from the Germans towards us, they couldn't get back. I am writing this past eleven at night. Hurrah! The Russians have had a victory, but we all hear of a terrible explosion in a battleship . . . Always something to spoil our joy. Dear, I do hope this horrible German invasion doesn't come off, but if they do no doubt they will find they have miscalculated. I should say the Russian victory will make them more inclined to try a fleet action soon. Sometime before the end of the year.

Both Barrington-Kennett and Geoffrey Salmond were feeling that they could no longer stay so far from the front line. Every day pilots came in to the Headquarters with their reports, often having faced death many times. Acts of courage and self-sacrifice were reported daily, and Geoffrey felt it impossible to remain at Headquarters while others, including Jack, were at the front.

On 30 December he wrote a heartfelt letter, very different from his usual encouraging messages. After asking Peggy to take great care of herself, he wrote:

> It is like a firework show at the Crystal Palace. First comes the illuminations, a wonderful rocket, and everyone says 'Oh, isn't it tremendous'. Then the advance on Paris suddenly sparked up, and everyone trembled, not knowing whether it would spread to them. Then that fizzled out, and something went wrong, and everyone said, 'What a show, we'll start fireworks ourselves, and let them see what we can do.' But suddenly there was a tremendous crackling all along the line, the sky got red and great clouds of smoke belched forth, and in the glare you, who were looking on, could quite distinctly see the Cathedral at Ypres all silhouetted against the sky amidst the crash of what sounded like so many million rifles, whilst at the foot of the Cathedral and stretching onwards and backwards, you could see things moving and as you strained your eyes they looked like men struggling – such heroes all. Then suddenly the thunder grew fainter till only distant rumbling was heard and all was still. The people who were near you held their breath, and someone said, 'What next?', and even as he said it, far away you saw another flame shoot into the sky, the whole landscape was all lit up, but it seemed far, far away, the noise increased, and as you looked you could see masses of men marching towards the flames, all soldiers and splendid soldiers too, in perfect order, towards the flames. As they reached it they spread out fanwise and then the tumult increased, bombs fell from the sky, and even you could hear the clash of steel. It was terrible to watch, until at last the lights grew familiar, the last shreds of the conflagration sputtered out and the audience held their breath again. Then someone muttered, 'WHAT NEXT?' This, of course, is all jaw, but I am in that mood darling, so please forgive me.

General Henderson understood Geoffrey's feelings, perhaps even better than he did himself, and only a few days later Geoffrey was writing to Peggy:

> Darling one, the General asked me the night before last whether I would take a squadron. I have considered it a lot and wish I had not been asked but had been ordered. He told me to think it over, and so I took a good many peoples' advice and I have now told him that I will. Now you must not worry, dearest. The General's question to me was practically an order and if I refused I would not really be doing the thing that he hoped I would do, otherwise he would never have asked me. Then I hope it will not be for long, and that I will get a Wing in time, but he said nothing about that. There is no command I would like better to have than a Wing,

and I would not really be capable of it unless I had a squadron first. I told him that I would prefer to have one out here and he said he could not promise that, but that anyhow a number of squadrons would be coming out soon. I have that to comfort me and if I come home I will have you, dearest, for a time anyhow. As he said, it is no good staying in an office all your time, and he is quite right. There are two things that one ought to do. One is to have Staff service and the other is to have command and apparently I am to have that now. Also, in a way, unless the General thought I was worth it he would not have asked me, as no one has been made a Squadron Commander who has not had all the experience before. If he had offered me a Wing I would have jumped at it, but at the same time I would have felt that I had not the inner knowledge that I ought to have. As for flying, Trenchard has forbidden Jack to fly – as a rule Squadron Commanders do very little. Anyhow dearest, there is no way that I know where you can do more to help the country in this war than by having a real good squadron.

On 9 January he again wrote:

This letter goes by the King's Messenger, who in this case is the Duke of Marlborough. I have heard nothing further about the squadron, and as I have a great many things to do I daresay I shan't for some time . . . It was sweet of you to try and stay up for New Year's Eve and pray to stop the war, darling . . . I rather gather that some of your wounded have got frost-bite, as you suddenly say, 'I hope their toes won't come off.' . . . I thought that raid on Cuxhaven was a splendid thing. Really good. What I thought so striking was that the flyers started on board ship, then flew in the air, dropped bombs etc. then returned to the place and landed on the open sea, when suddenly out from the sea appeared a submarine. In they got, (they lost their machine, that couldn't be helped) and down they went and reappeared that night at Dover (say). That is the part I think so wonderful. I don't think the papers made half enough of that side of it.

In his next letter, on 11 January, he wrote:

The General is in Paris and goes to England tomorrow – he may fix up something when he goes home. I am really extremely excited about it all, because it may mean I can come home and see you, darling, and however much you may disagree with the idea, that is something worth looking forward to. In a way, I shall be sorry to leave this job, as I revel in putting up new developments, which must come in time, but it is a dog's life, always scribbling and then just dashing off to some command in a car. I saw Trenchard the other day, and he said the General had told him about me and a squadron. I thought of your poor frostbitten soldiers as I saw any amount of ambulances coming in from the front with soldiers with their feet all tied up. I wonder what the old Germans are going to do next.

As Geoff had surmised, the General returned from England with the news that he was to go home almost at once to take over a Squadron.

The days with Maurice Baring and BK and the charming Prince Murat were over. They had shared so much together – from the early days of the hectic rush of the Advance Party setting up the reception for the first Squadrons and the new Headquarters, through the unforgettable days of the retreat from Mons, 'the turn of the tide' and the race for the sea and the comradeship of the days in the château at St Omer in their shared, crowded room, where they brewed their evening tea by candlelight after the hectic day was past.

Just before he left St Omer, Geoffrey heard that he had been mentioned in a despatch from Field Marshal Sir John French himself, 'for gallant and distinguished service in the Field' – the first of seven 'mentions' that he would earn in the war.

Soon after Geoffrey left, Barrington-Kennett developed pneumonia and Baring saw him off on leave, still insisting on carrying his own bag. He would never return to the RFC for he had learnt of the plight of his own Regiment and now was to rejoin the Guards. Prince Murat also became ill and left the Headquarters in March, leaving Maurice Baring to stay loyally at General Henderson's side, quietly supporting him through every vicissitude, and in the evenings still reading Dante's *Inferno*.

Into Battle

The naked earth is warm with spring,
    And with green grass and bursting trees
Leans to the sun's gaze glorying,
    And quivers in the sunny breeze;
And life is colour and warmth and light,
    And a striving evermore for these;
And he is dead who will not fight;
    And who dies fighting has increase.

The fighting men shall from the sun
    Take warmth, and life from the growing earth
Speed with the light-foot winds to run;
    And with the trees to newer birth;
And find, when fighting shall be done,
    Great rest, and fullness after dearth.

All the bright company of Heaven,
    Hold him in their high comradeship,
And Dog-Star and the Sisters Seven,
    Orion's Belt and sworded hip.

The woodland trees that stand together,
    They stand to him each one a friend;
They gently speak in the windy weather;
    They guide to valley and ridge's end.

The kestrel hovering by day,
    And the little owls that call by night,
Bid him be swift and keen as they,
    As keen of ear, as swift of sight.

The blackbird sings to him, 'Brother, brother,
    If this be the last song you shall sing,
Sing well, for ye may not sing another;
    Brother, sing!'

In dreary, doubtful, waiting hours,
    Before the brazen frenzy starts,
The horses show him noble powers;
    O patient eyes, courageous hearts!

And when the burning moment breaks,
    And all things else are out of mind,
And only joy of battle takes
    Him by the throat, and makes him blind.

Through joy and blindness he shall know
    Not caring much to know, that still
Nor lead, nor steel shall reach him, so
    That it be not the Destined will.

The thundering line of battle stands,
    And in the air death moans and sings;
But Day shall clasp him with strong hands,
    And Night shall fold him in soft wings.

Commanding 1 Squadron

The Squadron which Geoffrey Salmond was to command was the famous 1 Squadron, with its origins in the very beginnings of British aviation. As far back as 1878, experiments with balloons had been started by the Royal Engineers at Woolwich Arsenal, where a balloon store was first established. Later, balloons were used for reconnaissance in the South African War. Airships followed at the Balloon Factory at Farnborough, and when the Air Battalion was formed in 1911 one of the companies was named No. 1 (Airships) Company, while the other was No. 2 (Aeroplane) Company. On the formation of the RFC in May 1912, the Airship Company, stationed at Farnborough, became No. 1 Airship and Kite Squadron. 1 Squadron could therefore be said to be the oldest squadron of the Royal Flying Corps and Geoffrey felt delighted and honoured that he had been chosen to command it. The Gamma airship, in which Geoff had flown during manoeuvres in 1912, and the Delta, were perhaps the best known British airships to fly before the war, but on 1 January 1914 the entire control and organization of airships had been transferred to the Navy. The Squadron was then reorganized and became No. 1 Aeroplane Squadron under the command of Captain Longcroft. When he and Captain Salmond were sent out to France, the squadron was temporarily suspended, but was resumed at Brooklands shortly after the departure of the RFC under Captain F.V. Holt.

During the following winter 1 Squadron received about a dozen machines – Blériot monoplanes, Maurice and Henri Farmans, and one Box-kite. Captain Longcroft again took command and the Squadron moved to Netheravon, where training continued, and in November some officers were attached for training as observers. In January 1915 Longcroft, going to France to command 4 Squadron, was succeeded by Major W.G.H. Salmond. By this time, a nucleus had already left to form 12 Squadron. Preparations were immediately made for departure overseas, and Geoffrey found that in only three weeks he had to take the squadron to France.

Peggy soon joined Geoff in lodgings near Netheravon. Only one letter survives, in which he said he had seen Major Fulton who was then Chief Inspector of Aeronautical Material. He said he was with him until a late hour. Geoffrey did, however, write to 'BK', who was convalescing with his wife at a hotel in Sidmouth. On 25 February BK wrote back in light-hearted mood, to his 'dear brother ex-Babboo', congratulating him on his 'mention' and on his 'movement order' to the Squadron. He wrote:

> I saw the General [Sir David Henderson] when I first came back and told him I wanted to leave. He was very nice and offered me a Squadron. The call of my Regiment is too strong, however. You see it is quite different for you, as there are plenty of Gunner officers to go round, allowing for a nice surplus. I was offered the adjutancy of the Welsh Guards with the

bait of considerable seniority etc. [but] I refused. It would have been interesting work in peace-time, but at the moment it would mean being tied to this country for at least three months. Hope to get out with the 1st or 2nd Battalion early next month. You must pay me a visit in my dug-out, and bring Victor [BK's brother, who was to join 1 Squadron] and a select party. I will arrange a battle to amuse you! . . . If I can, I shall run over to see you before you start, just for the day. My wife sends greetings to yours. I believe they have corresponded but haven't yet met. This must be rectified at an early date. The best of luck with your squadron. I am sure it will do really well. Yours ever, BK.

This letter, carefully preserved, was probably the last letter Geoff was to have from his friend.

On 2 March the four BE8s and eight Avros which now composed the Squadron flew to Folkestone. Five days later all twelve machines crossed the Channel and arrived safely at St Omer. Cecil Lewis described the departure of a squadron for France in February 1916, but it could well have been a year earlier. Those left behind knew that some of the pilots might never return. He wrote:

> The machines were lined up in flights in front of the sheds. The February sun glistened on their new white wings. The pilots, muffled up in their leather coats, stamped about in their sheepskin boots, strapping up their haversacks, looking over their machines, polishing their goggles. They collected round the Major for final instructions, consulted their maps, and then were off. Pulling on flying caps and mufflers, they climbed into their cockpits, settled down and strapped themselves in. The mechanics kicked the chocks more firmly against the wheels and sucked in the engines. Contact! The pilots spun their starting magnetos, and one by one the engines sprang into life. Three minutes to warm them up, and then the heavy roar, which rose and fell as pilot after pilot ran up his engine, tested his magnetos and then, satisfied, throttled down again. At last they were all ready, engines ticking over, and a deep thrumming of the planes and wires filled the air. The Major dropped his hand, and a Flight Commander opened his engine up, turned and taxied away down the aerodrome. The others followed him, single file, and one by one they headed to the wind, pushed their throttles open, rose, swaying in ground gusts, and sailed up towards the sheds. We stood on the tarmac and watched them go, and still, after twelve years, my heart swells at the memory of the sight.

1 Squadron landed at St Omer on 7 March. Three days later a tremendous barrage signalled the start of the battle of Neuve Chapelle.

Early in February, Sir Douglas Haig, the Commander of the First Army, had sent for Colonel Trenchard. He told him in confidence of the planned attack in the neighbourhood of Merville and Neuve Chapelle, and asked him what the RFC could do. When Trenchard left he was elated, for Haig had told him that success largely depended on the observation and reconnaissance of the aeroplanes, and had even said that if the weather made flying impossible he would probably postpone the attack. At midnight on 9 March Haig sent for Trenchard. A pilot was sent up at dawn and made a short and satisfactory report. The bombardment started at 7.30 am and the first reconnaissance by 1 Squadron also marked the opening of the battle. The main work fell on the squadrons of Trenchard's 1st Wing, but 1 Squadron was now attached to the newly-formed 3rd Wing, commanded by Colonel Brooke-Popham, and they were given the task of strategic reconnaissance and the bombing of special military objectives.

The beginning of the battle of Neuve Chapelle was the first time that aircraft were used specifically as bombers. Before then some of the more inventive pilots had concocted their own explosive devices, or used ordinary infantry hand grenades, which they often carried in the pocket of their flying jackets, whipping out the pin with their teeth before dropping them by hand over the side of the aircraft. In March 1915, however, orders were given that certain aeroplanes should be used only as bombers and attack strategic transport points behind the German lines. For this reason, on 10 March, at the start of the battle, a BE2C biplane was converted into a bomber by strapping bombs under the wings and fuselage. First to fly it was Captain L.A. Strange of 6 Squadron, and although his maximum speed was little more than 80 mph, he managed to use his makeshift bomb release lever over the station at Courtrai, hitting two railway coaches and thus delaying German transport for three vital days. At the same time as Captain Strange took off, Captain Carmichael of 5 Squadron was briefed to bomb a railway fork just north of Menin. He had had pre-war practice of 'bombing' with bags of flour which the light-hearted pilots of those days had used for the purpose, and he already knew that aiming at a given target was almost impossible. He was to fly the new Martinsyde SE.1, a single-seat scout aircraft, one of the first to arrive in France. Hoping to aim his bombs more accurately, he had a hole cut in the cockpit floor beneath his feet, so that he could look down vertically. It was a very primitive bomb-sight, but he was successful, although, coming down to 300 feet he found himself the centre of a storm of bullets from the German barracks at Menin and only just managed to limp home.

At that time it was vital for all pilots to return to their base to report, as there was no other way for their Commanding Officer to know whether an attack had been carried out. Those first bombing raids were not, however, always so successful. On 11 March Lieutenant Mapplebeck and two other pilots from 4 Squadron took off at 4.45 am from Bailleul to attack the station at Lille at first light. To keep their formation and prevent collision, ordinary hand-torches were strapped to the pilots' backs as primitive navigation lights. They were met at Lille Station by a barrage of gunfire. One aeroplane had already come down with engine failure and both those remaining were shot down. Mapplebeck crash-landed near a wood south of the town. He managed to elude the German search parties and, after hiding till evening, he found sympathizers in Lille who helped him. He was eventually smuggled into Holland and walked back to his unit. He was the first pilot to establish the tradition of escaping from enemy territory, which was to lead to the famous 'Escaping Society' of the Second World War.

On 12 March 1 Squadron, just arrived from England, was ordered to bomb a railway bridge north-east of Douai and a junction at Don. Four BE8s took off, but only two pilots reached the target. One mistook the railway line for the Don Junction and the fourth, Lieutenant O.M. Moullin, was shot down and taken prisoner, the first 1 Squadron pilot to suffer this fate. The battle lasted three days and it was not until after the fighting had lessened that Geoffrey could write to Peggy:

We are probably leaving here soon. I am now staying with the Squadron, as I thought it best to live with them, though I was enjoying being at Wing HQ. I stay with 'B' flight, i.e. with [Victor] Barrington-Kennett, Hewett and the others. It is much the best plan, and you get to know them better.

Captain Ludlow-Hewett (later Air Chief Marshall Sir Edgar Ludlow-Hewett) was to become a great friend and support in the months and years to come.

At the beginning of the battle of Neuve Chapelle Jack, in command of 3 Squadron in Trenchard's Wing, had decided on a daring plan. He wrote:

Our job was to bomb the enemy's Divisional Headquarters, and I had visions of throwing the whole enemy defence into confusion by killing the Commander and his Staff. I flew with Eric Conran, who I knew would put me right on the spot, and if I failed to plant the bombs accurately, it would not be his fault. We started at dawn, and found the house, which had been indicated on a map from higher command, and made sure of it by bombing from 100 feet. It was soon burning fiercely, but it looked such a poor humble little apartment for a German Divisional Headquarters that I gave a large grandiose building a dose as well. Flying back low over the trench-line, we were greeted with an early morning display of Hun spleen. I felt a shock in the stomach, and putting my hand inside my shirt felt a clammy ooze of blood, but on pulling it out there was nothing to see. A bullet had passed through the fuselage brushing my clothes, and imagination had done the rest.

Following this low-level attack Colonel Trenchard wrote to him: 'Dear Salmond, you are splendid, but don't do it again. I can't afford to lose you. It is really a magnificent example you set. You and Conran will not be forgotten.'

During the battle another and far more distressing incident occurred for Jack Salmond. One evening one of his pilots, Captain Cholmondeley, was sitting in his cockpit ready for take-off while bombs were being loaded. One of them exploded, killing him instantly, and the machine burst into flames. Eleven other members of the squadron were killed in the explosion and debris was strewn all over the airfield. Jack Salmond knew the devastating effect this would have on his young pilots and he ordered them to leave everything until morning. During the night he and one of his sergeants, Angel, cleared the airfield and buried the bombs that had not gone off. He wrote, 'Next morning there were no signs left for the pilots to see before they took off on the early morning reconnaissance.' It was an act of typical coolness and bravery. Jack wrote: 'Cholmondeley had been with me at Hendon taking his flying certificate. He had a brilliant brain and was an excellent pilot. His loss to the Squadron was severe, and I mourned him as an intimate friend.'

While the battle raged, Jack wrote that although the plan had in general succeeded, the enemy's guns had smashed telephone lines and other lines of communication to such an extent that commanders soon no longer knew how the battle was faring, or where and how to exploit a success or support a failure. Added to this, the weather was the worst possible for observation, the ground flat and the difficulties of correcting range from ground level were enormous. He wrote:

> From the air, we did what we could. Had the weather been better we could have ranged our artillery on new enemy gun positions and concentrations and on concealed strong points, which had not shown up in previous photographs, and which sprang to life with deadly effect. But the clouds were frequently down to three hundred feet which made it impossible most of the time, and we had consequently to confine ourselves to trying to demarcate the line reached by our infantry and reporting this to the Divisional Headquarters. But Neuve Chapelle was taken and the line brought forward a few miles.

The battle ended after three days through lack of ammunition. The field guns had expended eighty rounds a day and this was far more than could be manufactured at home or replaced.

At the beginning of April Jack was promoted to Brevet Lieutenant Colonel and transferred home to command a Wing at Farnborough. He wrote:

> I said goodbye with deep regret, knowing well that it was the end of a rare experience, which I could never repeat and could never forget. We had

been pioneering all the time, not only in flying under war conditions, but also in gaining recognition from the older Service, which had to be converted from passive scepticism, through a stage of sympathetic interest, to one of active realisation of our indispensability. This had been done, and naturally we considered the success was chiefly owing to the untiring effort and enterprise of 3 Squadron.

Geoffrey, always in close touch with his brother, was bound to miss him. They had discussed and agreed on so many subjects – not only the future of photography and wireless but the whole future of the RFC. Their friendship never wavered, nor their complete devotion to the Royal Flying Corps. Geoffrey felt more and more that his own plan of artillery observation was essential if the enemy guns and concealed strongpoints were to be silenced. He worked untiringly to bring it to the attention of the authorities, at the same time feeling the thrill and enthusiasm of being in command of his own squadron at last. He wrote home in April:

I am enjoying the life most awfully. The Squadron is doing very well. I think, too, that I can see the Wing Commander thinks so – long may it continue. I only hope I am not made a boring CO too soon. I have not dug my toes in, as I threatened, because it is too ripping as it is. There! You never thought, did you darling, that I would write of everything as happily as that, and yet it is absolutely true. I am generally out in the afternoon seeing my various artillery Generals. I feel that at last I can put into play all the various schemes I wish to think out. At last most of those I used to put up are actually in force, but I find there are all sorts of things which I can do as I go along. I have discovered out here a use for a wonderful little aeroplane called a Caudron which everyone laughs at, but which has wonderful qualities. It rises out of very small fields and gets down into very small ones. It is not very fast, but fast enough. The result is that I can use it in all sorts of places where the normal machine could not possibly land without running into something. I am having the pilots trained one by one at another place. One of Jack's old Squadron, Hewett [later Sir Edgar Ludlow–Hewitt], started training. Now he is trained, so he trains another and brings a new man here, as soon as the other can fly alone. He is coming tomorrow. These Caudrons that I am flying are thought so little of that they gave me as many as I asked for, and do not count them on my establishment of twelve machines. But I feel sure [that] in a few weeks all squadrons will be wanting them. I use them on detachments with other troops. They are quite safe – they are not unpopular because they are considered unsafe, but simply because they look so funny. Last night we were attacked by a Zeppelin. I am afraid the Flying Corps cannot really cope with them at night unless we get ample warning, as by the time the machine is high enough they are off. I have explained this to the authorities and they quite agree, so that is all right. The German aeroplane is far from being on the ground and harmless, they are very active just at present. I am organising all sorts of schemes which I can only tell you of later.

At this time the enemy had a good view of the Ypres area from a hill, rising some 60 feet above the surrounding country, south of Klein Zillebeke. This hill, known as Hill 60, Sir John French determined to capture. The surrounding country was reconnoitred from the air beforehand and photographs were taken of gun emplacements and entrenchments. The attack was timed for the evening of 17 April and 1 Squadron was entrusted with the task of keeping all German aircraft away during the day before the attack. Geoffrey wrote to Peggy:

All the week I have been getting up at 4 am and not getting to bed till 12, but we have had rather an exceptional time as there has been a show on. In fact on 16 April our trench line opposite Hill 60 was reinforced, and 1 Squadron, in keeping the air free from hostile aircraft, was given the double object of preventing this reinforcement being discovered and of reassuring our troops. The whole of the Front from Kemmel to Ypres was thus patrolled from 4.30 am until 7.30 pm. In addition, special fighting patrols were sent up to search for enemy aircraft and certain targets were registered. A special flash reconnaissance was made successfully by Captain Ludlow-Hewett. These patrols continued for the next two days.

On the afternoon of the 18th the 5th Division Artillery Headquarters asked for a special effort to locate flashes from 6 pm to dawn, and indicated that great importance was attached to this. Geoff was also told that our troops were going to make a counter-attack (by 11 Corps Headquarters.) As this seemed an exceptional opportunity to locate flashes and so help the artillery, Geoff sent up seven more machines, in addition to the one already on patrol, and the efforts of pilots and observers resulted in the location of thirty-three gun flashes. Because of these constant patrols, the concentration of troops for the counter-attack was not observed by the enemy, so the attack was a complete surprise and in the evening the crest of the hill was brilliantly, if temporarily, retaken. On 21 April the fighting died down.

During this time Geoffrey had been furious with his Wing Commander. This was not Colonel Brooke-Popham because temporarily, at Bailleul in March, 1 Squadron had been put under 2 Wing. On the 25th Geoffrey was writing:

I don't think I like my new Wing Commander. The other day when I was out he telephoned up for me, and when Ludlow-Hewett went to answer he began asking him all sorts of things about our flying, whether they weren't flying too much. Now the amount of time spent in the air by pilots is certainly my show and I watch my pilots to see they are not doing too much. It is really disgraceful to start tampering with what is really the most sacred thing in a Squadron – i.e. its morale – and if you begin to suggest to pilots they are flying too much of course they begin to think of it and that is the beginning of the end. So I am going to tell him straight that I don't like this sort of tampering and, if he argues that he doesn't mean it, I shall tell him that he did. As a matter of fact I have watched that side of it all most carefully, but because I have got a wonderfully capable lot of fellows who do more flying than other Squadrons, he thinks I must be forcing them. Blighter! (My angel, this is just what I feel). Ludlow-Hewett told me all about it directly I came back. He was very sick at being pumped. The Squadron is great fun and are doing jolly good work. The two German machines brought down in Sir John French's despatch were both brought down by my Squadron.

In spite of the success of his aircraft at Hill 60, Geoffrey found that contact between the air and artillery was not always successful. In those early days of wireless, transmissions could be sent to the batteries, but the batteries were unable to transmit to the aircraft. If there was time before take-off, the observer would alert the battery with which he was working to confirm the objective, check co-ordination on the squared map and agree the time. Once in the air the observer, always himself under heavy fire from enemy positions, would let out his trailing aerial and call up the battery in Morse code, waiting for the gunners to put out 'ground strips' in reply. When he received the reply he could then direct the fire by means of the clock code. The clock code had been developed by Lieutenants Lewis and Baron James, and was based on a clock face with numbered concentric rings recording the distance of the impact from the target. Together with the squared map, this system should have enabled the batteries to understand what corrections had to be made, but it all depended upon good communication between ground and air.

Geoffrey, who had been an Artillery Officer before joining the RFC, could well understand the difficulties on the ground, and how hard it was in the midst of battle for the artillery to put out these messages or to listen to advice from the air. During one of the attacks on Hill 60 he had been awakened at dawn by a heavy cannonade to the north-east of Bailleul and he had sent up Captain Ludlow-Hewett to find out what was happening. When Ludlow-Hewett arrived over the lines he found a heavy attack was being launched against the V Corps front. Seeing many targets below him, he sent down message after message to the V Corps artillery, but there was no response; his signals had not been understood. Geoffrey determined to improve matters and evolved a plan for standardizing the procedure all along the line. This method included the observer sending an agreed signal, JJ, meaning 'I see a good target . . . all guns please engage it', followed by an appropriate map reference. Once the battery received the message they were to take immediate action. He brought the plan to Sir David Henderson, and it was immediately considered at a high level. Later, after an important conference in June at Choques, his method was used as a basis for co-operation between the Air Service and the Army. In its amended form in July, the pamphlet formed the basis of co-operation at the Battle of Loos and was later adopted all along the front. Perhaps it was Geoffrey's greatest contribution to the work of the RFC in the field in those early days.

Quite suddenly, without warning, the very worst attack of the war took place on 22 April. A young pilot, Captain L.A. Strange of 6 Squadron, who had earlier carried out the first bombing attack, was flying on reconnaissance when he noticed a thick green and yellow cloud below him. It was poison gas, seeping forward, blown by the wind towards the British trenches. Choking and stumbling, unable to breathe, the soldiers retreated, leaving a four mile gap. As it happened this gap which would have opened the road to Ypres, was not taken advantage of by the Germans, and Australian troops gallantly managed to hold the line, but the whole Army was horrified and stunned.

Geoffrey wrote a letter home which he told Peggy she could send to the newspaper without, of course, mentioning his name. Miraculously, it passed the censor. It ran:

> Our poor soldiers have been having rather a bad time lately. These poisonous gasses are the invention of the devil. They are hideous, dreadful methods. After all, we came into the war under certain rules to which Germany signed and now she proceeds to hit below the belt. That was a low-down thing to do and she deserves everything that may be invented to retaliate. They are brutes, horrible devilish brutes. It is not in the least due to their prowess as soldiers that they have slightly succeeded, it is due to their beastly hellish method of doing underhand things. If we had known they would descend to such depths we would have taken countermeasures, but we trusted to the Hague Convention, and did not even dabble in such horribleness. Anyone could succeed if they chose to go to such depths. I don't think people at home have hardly wakened up to the great danger these gasses mean to the success of the War. The gas creeps along, trickles into every trench and suffocates, if not immediately, it sets up acute bronchitis and people affected die in great pain. And not a single bullet or bayonet has done the work. These are those hulking brutes, simply poisoning, waiting until the hellish cloud they have spewed forth rolls past our trenches. They know that no living being can remain and they simply do nothing after that but walk up. And then the German

communiqué tries to make out they have defeated our men, when they have really done nothing of the sort. It is just the same, only worse, than if they spread cholera. However, we will knock the brutes, but it will be some time before the stupid people of England wake up to the Germans, and it will cost our poor fellows many lives. It is no good arguing that it is war, it is a different method of war to what Germany swore to, and that ends the case. It is, I believe, simply pitiable to see our fellows, poor chaps, who have been affected by the gasses, and have not even had a fighting chance.

The last part of Geoff's letter, however, was crossed out by the censor.

A few days later Geoffrey wrote a more cheerful letter to Peggy. It began:

I have been up since 3.30 am, and now the morning mist has come up and stopped our reconnaissance. We keep awfully early hours in the Squadron but everyone gets used to it. No one feels it really. They go to bed very early. All last night I was being woken up with telephones from a place quite near, saying there was a Zeppelin over that place. The spring has really come and everything is breaking into bloom. The trees are so lovely and these last two days it has been quite hot. The other night I was at a certain hill that was not very far from the fighting . . . There was an awful din going on and places were burning. The men belonging to the H.Q. were playing football! Later on, when I was coming back, I passed a regiment formed up near the road before going into battle. The sun was setting in a red flame and the light was reflected in their faces. Behind me was the awful roar of guns and rifles going on, and I couldn't help feeling what a wonderful sight it was – our splendid men. Then, as I was looking and feeling all these things, suddenly something shot into the sky behind and above their heads, and what do you think it was? – a football! You really cannot get to the bottom of our men.

Again the rest of his letter was censored.

Geoff knew by now that Peggy was expecting another baby. He was so anxious she should not do too much. On 14 May he wrote:

This will probably reach you before your birthday, but I might not be able to write at the time, so in case not, let this be one of your birthday letters – the first one. Dear, do take care of yourself for my sake – I send you my love, darling, I have nothing more to give you out here. I began writing nice things, darling, but the rumble of the transport outside and all the rest of things stopped it, so you will know that although I have not written it I feel so much dearest. The last two days there has been wind and rain making it quite impossible to fly. The clouds are down to 500 feet or so. I have been having great work to do in starting my new system of artillery co-operation with air, on our front. My Corps has adopted the system in toto, so I am actually very pleased. My original report on the subject went into General Headquarters and was favourably commented on, and the latest thing I saw of it was that there is to be a Conference of Armies and the RFC on the subject, calling it 'Major Salmond's Method'. Well, the other day I was sent for by the Chief of Staff of our Army (there are so many Corps, but only two Armies) and put through my feelings on the whole subject. I think he rather tried to down me at first, but was better afterwards. I stuck to my guns on the subject, and although he did not say he agreed with the system, I hope he did, but am not sure. Anyhow I have got my system adopted by my Corps, and that is a great advance. General Furse is the man I principally dealt with. He is the Chief Staff Officer of the Corps I belong to. He is an absolute topper to work with, always ready to push a thing through once he considers a thing is sound. I don't suppose they will offer me a Wing, when there is one going, but if they do I shall be inclined to refuse it. A Wing, in my opinion, is a rotten job. There is nothing like a Squadron.

He went on to report on the day-to-day situation:

I have had a good many casualties lately, three pilots and one observer, but none of them serious. But they have all gone home, which is sad for the Squadron. The observer was hit in both hands and the leg, the pilot in the left hand and leg. The observer told me [that] directly he was hit he turned round to the pilot and held up his hands, showing he had been hit. The pilot showed no sign, but nodded. The observer had no idea the pilot was hit. The pilot turned the machine to come home and stopped the petrol. They were at 1,000 feet at the time, and not very far away from our landing ground. As he came down to the landing ground the pilot tried to turn on the electric socket to get the engine going again, but his left hand was helpless. He couldn't do it. His right hand had to keep control of the elevator. So he had to land in the nearest field. He landed in a field three fields distant from here, jumped a hedge, the machine swung round and landed sort of sideways. The undercarriage went and the machine smashed. Directly I heard of it I went over to them and found the observer lying on his back, wounded but unhurt by the smash. The first he said to me was, 'I have sent up my report, Sir.' Gallant fellow. It had crossed me on my way to them. We got them both away and put into hospital which luckily was quite close. I deciphered his notes, which were covered in oil and a little blood, and within one hour they were being sent over the wires to General H.Q. That is only one instance of how splendidly these fellows do. Wills Bladon was the name of the observer and Richards the name of the pilot. One of my pilots was grazed on the head, a fairly deep cut, and it partially stunned him for a few moments. He wobbled a bit but then pulled himself together and never let the observer know what had happened till he had shut off to come down. Another was hit in the knee. They have all gone home but I hope to have the one who was hit in the head back soon. The German anti-aircraft are improving . . . I think they have a special method. I have sent my views to General Furse, I am sure there is something in it. We have a hospital next door to the landing ground here. It is sickening the way all day long convoys of wounded men are coming in. I do wish people at home would realise what a fight it has got to be if we are to win. Ever and ever and ever your Geoff. PS Thank you for the cigs – cork-tipped are extravagant I think (usually I don't like them very much.)

In another letter he wrote:

I have spent a week in tremendous argument over one part of my system of 'co-operation' which I want but which they will not put up as a regular RFC proposal. In the RFC proposal the main point of my thing is included but not one part which could, I think, make it perfect. It is really great fun having caused such a furore. There is an enormous Conference going to take place soon. I don't know whether I shall be asked to go or not, but I hope I will. The weather is fearfully hot.

Meanwhile, on 10 May, some new machines had arrived. The Squadron now consisted of four Morane Parasols, four Caudrons, three Avros, one Martinsyde and one BE8, and in addition one Morane Scout and one Bristol Scout soon to carry out hostile enemy patrols. After the climax of the Battle of Ypres and the retaking of Hill 60, there was one casualty which Geoffrey found it very hard to bear. On 23 May he wrote to Peggy:

It is a lovely day. I write this before breakfast. All the May is out and it makes me think of you, dearest. One of the saddest things has happened. Barrington- Kennett, the one I was with at the beginning of the war, has been killed. It is so distressing. He was such a real good fellow. I do wish he had never left us . . . It is due to him and him only that the spirit of the men in the RFC is what it is, and everyone is grateful to him for it. I only heard of it yesterday, and told his brother. Poor chap, he went off at once to the part of the country it must have happened in. Poor Mrs Barrington-Kennett – I am so sorry. I wish she could know what we all feel about him. What a stamp his personality, *élan*, and work has put on the Flying Corps, how all his hard work which he put in at Farnborough and out here has done for our country. Our Flying Corps is recognised by all nations as being the best and this is principally due to B.K. Dear Peg, he was such a good fellow.

As soon as he heard the sad news, Maurice Baring came to Geoff's Headquarters at Bailleil and had a long talk with Victor Barrington-Kennett. He wrote:

If ever a man deserved a soldier's death, to die leading his men and the men of his own regiment into battle, it was BK. But of all the bitter losses one had to bear throughout the war, it was, with one exception, this particular loss I felt most, minded most, resented most and found it most difficult to accept.

When BK had left the RFC, Baring had written of him:

BK had been one of the first pilots in the Flying Corps before the War. It is impossible to state too strongly what a loss his departure was to the whole Corps. He had himself laid the foundation of a certain tone; he had always been keen on instilling a certain spirit, and although there was nobody less of a martinet, he had always insisted on the extreme importance of discipline. He had recruited from the Guards a nucleus of excellent Non-Commissioned Officers and had thus established a solid framework of tradition and sound principles, which a new Corps dealing with a new weapon and a weapon such as the aeroplane, and with all the qualities and defects which flying must necessarily entail was, of course, of vital importance. His influence was great.

Later he wrote:

When this particular piece of news came I felt the taste of war turn bitter indeed and, apart from any personal feelings, one rebelled against the waste which had deprived first the Flying Corps and then the Army, of the services of so noble a character. He was the most completely unselfish man I have ever met; a compound of loyalty and generosity and a keen interest in everything life has to offer.

It was on 3 June that Baring went once more to stay at Bailleul with Geoffrey Salmond. He wrote:

At this period there were great discussions going on, as to the organisation of the co-operation of aircraft with artillery by wireless, the system of signalling, etc. and the next day I went to Colonel Trenchard's Headquarters at Choques, where an immensely long Conference took place on the subject.

Meanwhile Geoff was writing to Peggy, in pencil:

I do hope you are feeling well, tell me dearest, you are too unselfish you don't say anything. You are such a trump the way you are working with the wounded. It does make me feel so proud. And you have done it without being fetched. Very soon all women in England will have to work at something, something to bring victory closer. It is splendid out here to feel that England is really waking up, really beginning to feel that she has got to show the world what she can do. My co-operation scheme and its further development has now gone to RFC HQ. My original project . . . has borne fruit and the whole thing has been adopted. Now I am trying to get my plan of cooperation adopted for the whole Front, but it is going to be a tussle as the 1st Wing has put up a scheme. . . . I am, of course, sure mine is the best because it is so simple and I am awfully keen on it.

In another note, he writes of the death of one of his best observers:

I lost one of my best observers the other day – last Tuesday – a fellow called Playfair. He was actually shooting at a German in another aeroplane when one came up behind him and shot him through the heart. He died as I know he would have loved to have died, if it had to be. He was a very true soldier. I will tell you more about these things later.

In his report he recommended Lieutenant L. Playfair for a medal. Geoff had been hoping for five days' leave, but owing to the pressure of work he decided not to go, especially as the Artillery Conference, at which his plan was to be discussed, took place in June. Major General J. P. du Cane, the Artillery Adviser at GHQ, presided, and artillery and flying representatives from the two Armies attended. Geoffrey Salmond's pamphlet was placed before them, and all outstanding instructions were included. In its amended form it was issued in July and formed the basis of co-operation between the Air Service and the Army during the September offensive.

Geoffrey wrote:

The great Artillery Conference took place yesterday, and my scheme was supported by the Army and partially by the others, and has now been referred to the General Staff, so I am really satisfied, although I did not get quite as much as I wanted. Part of it, however, was adopted entirely for the whole Force.

The acceptance of his scheme was to be an enduring satisfaction.

Meanwhile, it became only too clear that, even to hold the line in Belgium, many more aircraft, guns and ammunition were needed. The Germans seemed to bring up reinforcements at will, while our soldiers and airmen fought on in the face of terrible odds. News came through in May of the sinking of the *Lusitania*, and on 31 May there was the first Zeppelin raid on London. The RFC could no longer carry out reconnaissances without opposition from German aircraft and fights in the air became frequent. Geoffrey himself had written a report in May recommending the use of lighter, more manoeuvrable aircraft. Part of the report ran:

> The Germans have done very little in the direction of the develop-ment of the Scout type. Now a Scout type possesses the following advantages:
>> It can be made stable.
>> It can be designed for greater speed than any two-seater type of similar engine power.
>> It is more supple.
>> It can carry a machine gun.
>
> Consequently, as in 1914, by designing a stable Scout capable of going 120 mph it will be possible to attack the Germans in his weakest spot, i.e. in his clumsiness. On the other hand, if we design heavy fighting machines we are faced with the following difficulties, apart from aban-doning our independence of design which gave us our initial supremacy.
>> The difficulty of catching up.
>> The difficulty of manoeuvring, so as to place the Germans at a disadvantage.
>> The inherent lack of suppleness in such a type.

It was almost as if he foresaw the arrival of the German light Fokker aeroplane with its capacity of firing through the propeller, which was to appear later in the summer.

In July Robert Brooke-Popham wrote to Colonel Ashmore, who commanded the Administration Wing in England:

> The German aeroplanes are becoming more active and are making a regular habit of attacking our machines while on reconnaissance, and we are having to fight for our information. We are now having to fight by pairs of machines, as well as individual duels. It will probably be neces-sary to send machines by pairs, or even by flights, on all reconnaissances. The General Officer Commanding, therefore, wants you to practise flying by pairs of machines – simple manoeuvres might also be carried out.

It was not until the beginning of 1916 that the School of Flying at Gosport, under the imaginative Smith Barry, was to fulfil and surpass these recommendations, teaching young pilots to fly daringly and to take swift action, disregarding the old methods of flying for safety alone.

In another memorandum which Colonel Brooke-Popham sent to London, he again wrote that, whereas the Army had grown from four Divisions to thirty since the beginning of the War, the number of RFC Squadrons to supply the Army's needs had only grown from four to eleven. He wrote:

> If the enemy brings his troops over from the Eastern Front, and if he resumes his offensive, he will doubtless make a determined effort to prevent our discovering his movements. Then will commence the real struggle for air supremacy where numbers will be one of the essentials for success.

At the end of July Sir David Henderson saw that a senior officer 'of high esteem' who had had battle experience and also technical knowledge was needed in London. With great unselfishness he decided that he must go himself. He recommended that Colonel Trenchard, commanding the 1st Wing, should succeed him in France, Colonel Brooke-Popham was to succeed Colonel Sykes at Headquarters and Colonel Brancker was to come out to command a Wing. The War was now no longer confined to Europe and the Eastern Front. Turkey had declared war on the Allies in October, 1914, and already her armies were threatening Baghdad and the Suez Canal. Our Army was also fighting in Gallipoli and Colonel Sykes was sent out to command the RFC there.

Meanwhile, Sir David Henderson had appreciated all the work Geoffrey Salmond had done while commanding his squadron and he felt he would have confidence in him in a wider sphere. He had appreciated his now successful plan of air to army co-operation and he had worked with him at Headquarters all through the first testing months of the War. He knew of his vision, his reliability and his loyalty to the Royal Flying Corps. On 14 August Geoffrey was appointed to command 5 Wing at Gosport in preparation for departure to Egypt. He was promoted to Lieutenant Colonel and a thrilling and exciting prospect stretched out in front of him. But the grief, the agony and gallantry of that summer in France, with 1 Squadron, would always be printed on his mind.

3

MIDDLE EAST COMMAND

A Handful of Aeroplanes

Geoffrey was promoted to Temporary Lieutenant Colonel on 18 August 1915. He had already been mentioned in despatches by General French, and he had achieved his ambition of fighting at the Front with 1 Squadron, and of knowing that his plan for artillery to air co-operation had been adopted. Now he was promoted to command a Wing, but not in France as he had always hoped.

5 Wing was stationed at Gosport, in preparation for departure for Egypt, and he had to prepare 14 and 17 Squadrons and all their equipment including BE2c aircraft, for embarkation. These had to travel in crates, to be reassembled on arrival, as it was considered too far to fly to Alexandria.

The move was a godsend for Geoff and Peggy, as they could at last be together for a few weeks. Peggy's third baby was due in October and Geoff made all the arrangements for her arrival, renting a house, 'Brookfields', in Alverstoke, near the sea. Only one letter from this time survives. He wrote: 'The house looks very nice. Never never come via Havant and Fareham. I changed about six times today and gave the porters tips at each change. I have now broken the ice here, and feel I shall like them all. They seem a nice lot of fellows.' Little Joyce, who was three years old, remembers standing at the gate of the Alverstoke house and seeing the tall figure of a soldier walking up the road towards her. She half knew it might be her Daddy but, suddenly shy, she turned to run back into the house, when he swept her up in his arms and said, 'Don't you know me, Joyce?'

It was a very happy time. Geoffrey with his first-hand knowledge of all that the RFC had to face in France, inspired his men, and was able to prepare them for all the danger and hardship of war in the air.

Geoffrey's report in France in July 1915 had recommended 'lighter more serviceable aircraft', showing that he was aware of the new danger, but it was not until 1916, when Geoffrey was in Egypt, that Robert Smith-Barry started his famous school at Gosport, in which pilots were trained to react swiftly, to turn and twist and dive, with all the daring and skill they would need at the Front in France. It was to be a revolutionary change of attitude, recognized by Geoffrey's brother Jack, who, after a flight with Smith-Barry, was so impressed with his new method that he introduced it to training stations throughout the country.

Meanwhile, in the autumn of 1915, while the news from France grew ever more serious and the weather grew colder, when the golden autumn leaves were falling from the beech tree in the garden of the house at Alverstoke, Peggy's new daughter was born on 26 October. They decided to call her Penelope, because while she waited for Geoff's return Peggy felt like the Greek heroine Penelope, who waited patiently for her husband Ulysses' return from the Trojan wars. It was the greatest comfort to her that Geoffrey could be with her at this time, but less than three weeks later all the preparations were completed, the aircraft were packed in crates and the Aircraft Park and the two squadrons were ready to sail for Egypt.

Penelope was so delicate that Peggy was unable to go to London to see Geoff off, and he crossed the ferry to Portsmouth and went up to London alone.

The parting must have been heartbreaking for Peggy, but for Geoffrey the future seemed boundless. Although he had only two squadrons with him, and a handful of aircraft, he set off with every confidence to protect the Suez Canal by air, and perhaps even defend Egypt itself. His departure for Egypt was, indeed, the beginning of great things: the opening out of his career into increasingly complex and fascinating territory where he would eventually win the highest honour. But nothing to come would be so vividly exciting, or more satisfying, than those early years when the RFC was coming into being, and proving its worth so gloriously in France, as he had been sure it would.

Egypt and Action

The arrival of Geoffrey Salmond and the 5th Wing of the Royal Flying Corps in Egypt was not greeted with any great enthusiasm by the Army. It was true that aeroplanes had won their spurs at the Front in France, but in Egypt the Army was still sceptical of their value and Geoffrey soon realised that it was up to him and 17 and 14 Squadrons to show how important aerial photography, reconnaissance and artillery co-operation could be.

In Egypt the situation was growing more and more uncertain day by day. As long ago as 1911 Lord Kitchener, then British Agent and Consul General, had realized the potential threat of a Turkish advance across the Sinai Desert towards the Suez Canal in the event of war, and he had updated the maps of the area between Gaza and Beersheba and the sensitive area of Sinai on the borders of Egypt and Turkey. This survey had been undertaken by Captain Newcombe of the Royal Engineers. A young archaeologist, T. E. Lawrence, was part of the team selected for that survey and he wrote home to his mother: 'We are obviously meant as red herrings, to give an archaeological cover to a political job,' but it was not until October 1914, when the Turkish Fleet had shelled the Black Sea ports, that Britain and Turkey found themselves at war.

A month later, on 4 November, a single flight of aeroplanes under Captain Massey was sent out to Egypt to provide reconnaissance for the Army. The Flight, however, consisted of only three Maurice Farmans, joined by two ancient Henri Farmans acquired from an Italian firm in Cairo, as every available British aeroplane had been needed for the Western Front in France. In spite of all the disadvantages, the Flight did noble work. Sheds and an airfield were created at Ismailia, a town half-way between Port Said and Suez, and in December some reinforcements of engineers and mechanics and one BE2A arrived from Sitapur in India, but they could do little more than act as a reconnaissance unit for the Army. Turkish forces, meanwhile, avoiding the more usual northern route, took advantage of recent rains and advanced across the Sinai Desert from Beersheba towards the Canal. Their advance was reported from the air, but they had even attempted to cross the Canal south of Lake Timsah by pontoons and rafts before British troops drove them back. At length, disheartened by their defeat, the Turks withdrew into the desert, many of their soldiers being transferred to fight at Gallipoli.

During the summer months of 1915, however, the Maurice and Henri Farmans continued their reconnaissance over the wide stretches of the desert on the eastern side of the Canal, often even flying 80 or 90 miles a day. An example of their help to the Army was when they dropped a message to the British cavalry at El Hawarish, giving them the location of the enemy. It was at this juncture, in November 1915, that Geoffrey Salmond arrived at Port Said.

Geoffrey and his Adjutant, Captain Shelmerdine, had intended to arrive at Alexandria well in advance of 14 Squadron, and to arrange everything for their reception, but, after an exhausting train journey across war-torn France, they were delayed at Marseilles, due largely to the activity of German submarines in the Mediterranean, and they arrived only half an hour before the SS *Kaiser-i-Hind* carrying 14 Squadron docked at Alexandria.

Geoffrey was on the quay at Alexandria when the ship steamed into the harbour. As they drew slowly towards the shore, one can imagine the excitement of the men of 14 Squadron on board. Many of them had never been abroad before and the tropical sunrise, the intense blue of the Mediterranean Sea and the busy port must have been a revelation to them. A mass of boats soon surrounded the ship, selling fruit and souvenirs, and small boys dived for coins in the clear water.

War at that moment must have seemed very far away, but soon the squadron disembarked and the tranquillity was broken. Crates containing the aeroplanes had to be landed and billets found for the men in preparation for their move to Heliopolis, a town half way between Cairo and Ismailia, which Geoffrey had chosen as a suitable site for an aerodrome and camp. The crates containing the aircraft had to be opened, the BE2C aeroplanes assembled and everything prepared for action. These aeroplanes, which had been invaluable during the first landings in France, were now already out of date and no match for the German Fokkers and Aviatiks appearing on the Western Front. They were a development of the BE1, the first really stable machine, devised by Burk at the Aircraft Factory at Farnborough in 1913. They had been the standard two-seater biplanes which had accompanied the RFC to France in 1914. The Aircraft Park, meanwhile, took over an old Swiss iron factory at Abassia, between Heliopolis and Cairo.

Very soon, long lines of white tents for the officers and men bordered the airfield, while the Headquarters was in a rather dilapidated empty house in the town. Geoffrey was amazed at the contrast between the grim reality of war in France and the hectic brittle life of Cairo. He wrote to Peggy:

> Just a line with my love. I will write later, but things are in a rush. Everything is CAG MAG [sic] but I'll get it straight by degrees. I am off to Alexandria tonight, again. I came here yesterday to try to get hold of things, but it takes some doing. I do wish I had got everyone out here, and a proper show, but it is all the more interesting, of course, getting it together, and fixing it up. Cairo is like a play at the Gaiety, but I'll write this later . . . Write to me [at] 5 Wing RFC Cairo. I am not there, but I will get it.

It was not easy, when he visualized the cold winter at home and the fighting in France, to describe the sunshine, the palm trees and long lines of camels lurching slowly through the dusty roads of Cairo. Most of all, it was hard to describe the life of the British and foreign residents. He wrote a few days later: 'We went to Gazirah, which is exactly like Ranelagh, people having tea out, all the world in their brightest dresses, far from the idea of war.' He described how the rich Egyptians drove by in their luxurious cars, their wives sitting in the back with their faces half veiled, and the 'yashmaks' of the poorer women with a gold pin over the nose to keep off the 'evil eye' and wrote: 'There are green polo grounds, and lovely gardens made by Kitchener, and a racecourse.' The city was full of officers on leave. Geoffrey met several friends, but determined to only stay in Cairo for a few days.

Almost at once, on 23 November, 'A' Flight of 14 Squadron was sent on to Ismailia to take the place of the original 30 Squadron which had left for Mesopotamia, and which would take part in the disastrous advance of General Townsend towards Kut.

Southern Palestine, 1915-17

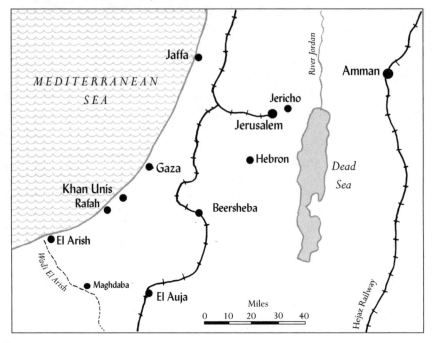

Palestine September, 1918

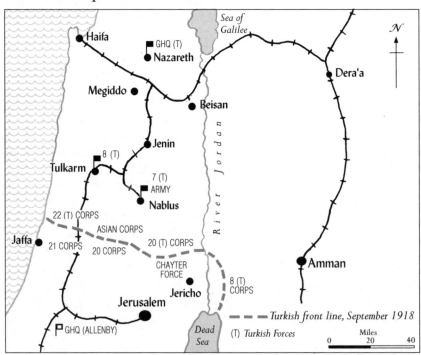

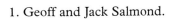
1. Geoff and Jack Salmond.

2. Crossing the Tugela River, South Africa, 1898-9. A photograph taken by Geoffrey Salmond when he was 19.

3. Geoffrey Salmond
   when an officer in
   the Royal
   Artillery, 1908.

4. Peggy, aged 18.

5. A Bristol Boxkite with a 50hp Gnome engine on which Jack took his Certificate and was awarded No. 272.

6. Jack at Hendon in 1912.

7. A Maurice Farman in flight.

8. The Central Flying School, Upavon, 1913. Officers attending the second course. *Back row:* Captain E.G.R. Lithgow, J.H. Lidderdale, RN; Major H.M. Trenchard, DSO; Captain Paine, MVO, RN; ?; Sub-Lt H.A. Lyttleton, RNVR, DSO. *Front Row:* Major D.B. Fulton; Lt A.H. Longmore, RN; Captain J.M. Salmond; Major E.L. Gerrard.

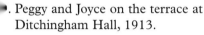

. Peggy and Joyce on the terrace at
   Ditchingham Hall, 1913.

10. Geoffrey Salmond wearing Army uniform
    and RFC Wings.

1. The first reconnaissance flight of the First World War. Captain Joubert de La Ferté flying
   a Bleriot monoplane of No 3 Squadron and above him Lieutenant G.W. Mapplebeck in
   B.E. 26 of No 4 Squadron.   *(From the painting by K.M. McDonough)*

12. Lieutenant Barrington-Kennett, known as 'B-K', in 1914.

13. Geoff *(left)* and Jack Salmond receive a report at St Omer, 1914.

14. Loading an aircraft on to a truck in Egypt.

15. The very first aeroplane to be built in Egypt; made in the Aircraft Factory. Geoffrey Salmond is in the centre, surrounded by his men.

16. T. E. Lawrence in the desert.

17. *(bottom left)* General Allenby.

18. *(below)* Geoffrey Salmond.

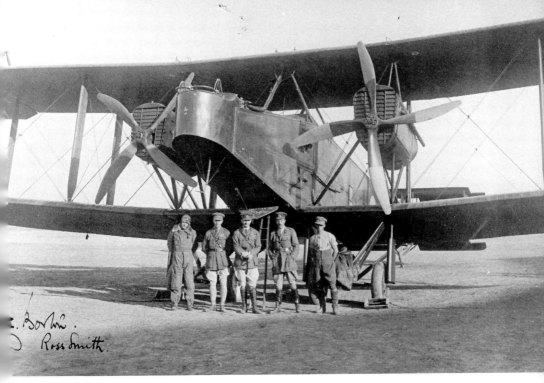

19. The Handley Page 0/400, prior to the record flight to Baghdad and on to India, 1918. The photograph bears the signatures of Brigadier General Borton and of Ross Smith, the pilot.

20. Geoff *(right)* and 'Biffy' Borton during a landing on the flight.

21. Geoff is knighted.
Outside
Buckingham
Palace in 1919
with Joyce and
Anne.

22. Baby John Geoffrey has his first meat from the point of a sword. A family tradition.
General Allenby lent his own sword for the occasion.

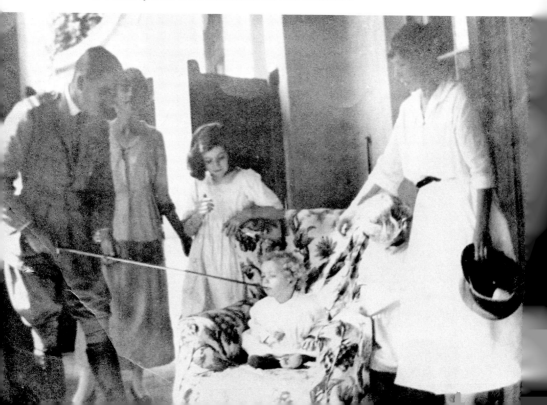

23. The family visit the Pyramids, 1920.

24. Peggy in 1925.

25. Peggy and John in 1925.

26. "Flying the Furrow". An arrow guides aeroplanes flying across the desert.

27. The Cairo Conference, 1920. On the left is T. E. Lawrence; next to him is King Abdullah of Jordan. Geoffrey Salmond is in the centre. Front right is Bill (later Lord) Deedes.

28. Major General Sir William Salmond KCB with his two sons: *(left)* Air Vice Marshal Sir Geoffrey Salmond KCMG, CB, DSO; *(right)* Air Marshal Sir John Salmond, KCB, CMG, CVO, DSO, ADC. Taken after the Levée on 10 March 1925.

29. Geoff is awarded the KCB. He and Peggy outside Buckingham Palace in 1926.

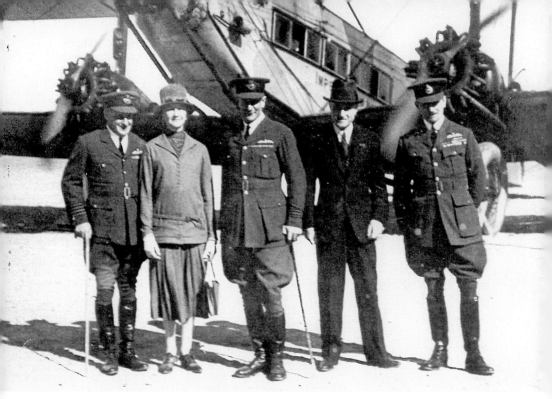

30. Sir Geoffrey Salmond accompanies Sir Samuel and Lady Maud Hoare on the first commercial flight by British Imperial Airways to India, 1926.

31. Re-fuelling the Hercules en route to India.

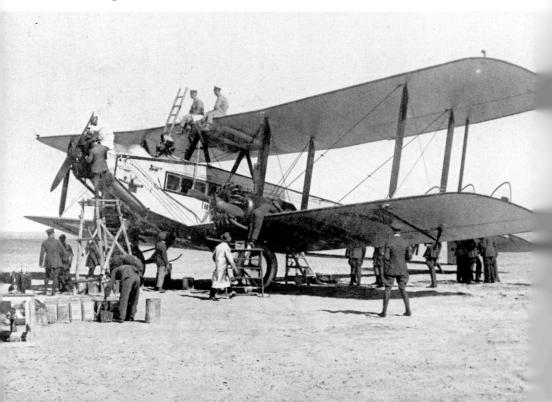

32. The British Legation, Kabul, 1928.

33. A Victoria in flight.

34. A model of the winner of the Schneider trophy – the Supermarine S-6B.

35. Sir Geoffrey
    Salmond in 1930.

At last, on 5 December, Geoffrey was able to write to Peggy:

> My own darling, I am getting things into better order out here, but I don't
> expect to be properly fixed up for another month at least. They have to
> build sheds and all sorts of things. We are in two different places, two
> miles apart, the transport at Abbarich and the other things at Heliopolis.
> We have a house for Wing HQ at the last place, absolutely empty but we
> shall get enough into it to make it comfortable. If I only get enough stuff
> out here, as regards machines etc., I think this will be rather interesting,
> as we have great possibilities in certain eventualities. It is certainly
> different from France in every way. Some of our cars ought to have
> arrived last night so I shall at last be able to get about. Except for an
> occasional car borrowed from the HQ people I have to get about in trams
> and they are so slow. It is quite cold here at nights and cool during the
> day now. The weather is really glorious, it is a stupid thing to wake up in
> the morning and say 'Fine day today' – it is always fine and gorgeous, so
> different from England. I doubt if I shall have time to cable to Baby
> today, but if I don't, I don't forget.

It was Joyce's fourth birthday.

When Geoffrey spoke of 'great possibilities in certain eventualities' he had
already realized the great potential the RFC possessed in support of the Army
in Egypt, for the Turks and their allies had now developed their threat to Egypt
in three quite different directions. There was, first, the ever-present danger to
the Suez Canal for, once more, the Turkish forces were gathering at Beersheba
to prepare for an attack. Secondly, there was unrest in the Sudan, where the
Sultan of Darfur, Ali Dinar, was threatening to attack the neighbouring state
of Kordofan with the help of his slave army. Thirdly, to the west of Cairo, there
was a rising by a wild tribe of Bedouin, the Senussi. They had been infiltrated
by German and Turkish agents during the past year, persuading them to take
part in a Holy War, or Jihad, against all Turkey's enemies and these, of course,
included the British outposts west of Cairo.

In all these areas the only support for the ground forces from the air was
through Geoffrey Salmond and his 5th Wing. With his handful of somewhat
outdated BE2C aircraft he was determined to do his best to inform and protect
the Army. In their plan to surround Cairo, the Turks had persuaded the
Senussi tribe to attack the British outposts east of the city. It was on 26
November, only a few days after the arrival of the 5th Wing at Heliopolis, that
war was declared on the Senussi, and a detachment of 'A' Flight from 14
Squadron was sent out at once to Matruh in support of the Army. The men,
who had so recently disembarked at Alexandria, rose to the occasion. They had
to unpack and reassemble their aeroplanes on arrival, and, because they had
as yet no form of wireless, they flew over the Bedouin and Senussi force

sketching every position by hand, in spite of gunfire, and reported back to Army Headquarters. Their rough maps were of great importance to the Western Frontier Force and on 5 December the Force, supported by the British sloop *Clementine*, attacked and the Senussi were temporarily defeated.

The air reconnaissance, however, continued and in January the main camp of J'afa Pasha, the Senussi leader, was seen from the air. At an oasis many camel lines and tents were observed, and the huge tent of the Grand Senussi himself stood out clearly against the desert sand. Once again, as a result of the RFC report, the tribe was attacked and defeated, although J'afa Pasha himself managed to escape. Even so, Sir John Maxwell, the Commander-in-Chief in Egypt, was determined that his troops should occupy both Sollum and Sidi Barrani. After a further engagement both towns were taken and J'afa Pasha was taken prisoner.

Soon after the battle it was rumoured that the disorganized forces of the enemy had travelled either to the oasis at Sinai or by the southerly route to an oasis at Farafra in Lower Egypt. Lord George Wellesley, a pilot of 14 Squadron, volunteered to fly to Farafra, a six-hour flight, in his BE2C over waterless desert, with no hope of a forced landing, but he managed to return safely and reported the oasis clear.

The courage of the pilots of 14 and 17 Squadrons, when flying over the desert in their outdated aircraft, was to be tragically demonstrated a few months later. It was in May that two aircraft of 17 Squadron were flying across the desert to their base when one aircraft came down with engine failure. The pilot of the second BE2C flew for help, but on returning found that the first aeroplane had disappeared. After a desperate search it was located by the Imperial Camel Corps some miles away, but both the pilot, Lieutenant S.G. Ridley, and his observer had died of thirst and exposure to the intense heat. The observer, 1st Air Mechanic J. Garside, had left a diary showing that they had managed to restart the engine, but after flying some distance, had been forced to land again. Pilots of the RFC invariably had to brave the danger of engine failure every time they flew over the desert, where there was little hope of survival.

On 27 February, soon after the defeat of the Senussi, Geoffrey was writing to Peggy:

> We have just had a victory in the West – the back of the Senussi is broken. The other day the Flying Corps had a real victory. We (the RFC) located about 1000 enemy at a certain place, and the next day the Flying Corps went out and bombed them, with the result that they disappeared altogether. This is a real victory. Love and love, Your Geoff.

Back in Cairo, Geoffrey had written to Peggy:

Everything is going splendidly out here as far as my show is concerned. All the RFC have smartened up, as I wanted them to. You remember what I used to say about the Hounslow Squadron, No. 17? Well, it is getting along and improving daily. Thank goodness, I have got the officers into a state of keenness about signalling, and other things, which is a great thing. I have certain tests which they have to carry out and they are all getting jolly good. I feel that unless I do something I am stuck here until the end of the war. I will still wait a bit before I start agitating – but I can't wait for ever.

Obviously Geoffrey's heart was still with his friends in France but, even so, he could write: 'The Flying Corps protects Egypt on all sides – we are the same as the Silent Fleet at home. It is all wonderfully interesting – only my heart rather longs for France.'

★   ★   ★

It was at this time that Geoff's pilots were able to take the first aerial photographs of the Pyramids, which they presented to the Sultan. He had been lent a horse by an officer who was going home and was able to ride most mornings before breakfast. Often, however, he would get up at 3.30 or 4 am when his pilots were flying at dawn.

The camp at Heliopolis was run on strict lines. Orders were given that NCOs and men walking out would do so correctly dressed, that is, wearing breeches and puttees and webbing belt . . . It was added 'Slacks will on no account be worn.' As the weather grew hotter these rules were necessarily very much modified, but Geoffrey always insisted on a smart appearance. Then it was stated in the regulations, rather desperately, 'Home Service dress or khaki drill may be worn, but not a combination of both.' Many of the instructions reflected the youth of the airmen. Ice cream and strawberries were forbidden to be sold in the camp from 19 January as a precaution against dysentery. Captain Shelmerdine kept a careful eye on the men's health, and every detail of their routine was inspected and reported on daily.

On 26 January there was a visit from the Commander-in-Chief himself, General Maxwell, who Geoffrey described as a 'true Britisher'. He was most impressed and Geoffrey was delighted that the Army was at last beginning to appreciate the help which he could provide. It was at this time, too, that Geoffrey would have visited the Map Room at Giza, on the West Bank of the Nile, two miles from the Army Headquarters at the Savoy Hotel, for it was here that he could see Kitchener's maps of the Sinai Desert, the Suez Canal area and Palestine – all vital to the work of the RFC. In return he would bring aerial maps and information from the reconnaissances his pilots and observers had been carrying out. Here he would have met, for the first time, Lieutenant

T. E. Lawrence, whose slight figure, fair hair and impish smile belied his expert knowledge and who would become his life-long friend.

Sir Ernest Dowson wrote of Lawrence at that time: 'His tremendous keenness about anything to do with the work was remarkable and infectious, with the consequence that his frequent walks round the various offices and workshops had a most stimulating effect on the men.' He also had a quiet sense of humour, and it was once said that he stood behind a pillar in the Savoy Hotel and counted over a hundred Generals passing in and out. This was reflected in a letter from Geoffrey to Peggy on 10 January: 'I was beautifully settled down here and getting everything in order when who should come along but Sir Archibald Murray. There are 107 Generals in Cairo. It was 97 yesterday, but it has now gone up to 107!' Sir Archibald had been sent to Cairo after the disaster of the Dardenelles and in March he was finally to take over from General Maxwell as Commander-in-Chief. Geoffrey ended his letter:

> I hate those Zeppelins coming over Ditchingham. Please make everyone put out all lights at once. You ought to have the big bell rung or some other signal. Anyhow, they have not been near London since the new system was incorporated and for that I take a certain amount of credit. Tell me, darling, more of your doings – I love them . . . Do you remember when I came home from France, and you said, 'I don't know what I am saying – I can't think'? That was lovely. All my love, Your Geoff.

It seemed that Geoffrey, while at Gosport, had been helpful with plans for the defence of London. He certainly recommended one of his best pilots, 2nd Lieutenant John Slessor (later Air Chief Marshal Sir John Slessor, author of *The Central Blue*) from 17 Squadron, to take part in a night patrol against Zeppelins. John Slessor has left an account of his first argument with a Zeppelin, over London at night. There was no black-out in those days, and the lights of the city shone on the huge body of the Zeppelin, which luckily turned away towards the coast. After pursuing it he turned for home, but said that his worst experience was coming down half-blinded by the searchlights which were turned on to help him land. Those were the very early days of any attempt to fly at night.

Geoffrey was right to be anxious about air raids over Norfolk. That winter a bomb was dropped in the drive at Ditchingham Hall. Most of the windows were blown out, and Peggy, the babies and her parents spent the rest of the night in the cellar. It was thought that the lights of a car had been seen by the German pilots, probably flying back to the coast from Norwich.

Iron Horses in the Air

It had been decided in Egypt that the line of defence of the Suez Canal should be pushed back about 11,000 yards (10.6 km), so that the Canal would not be so vulnerable. Geoffrey organized new airfields in the Canal Zone, at Suez and Qantara. 'A' Flight of 17 Squadron was to occupy the Suez airfield, and 'A' Flight of 14 Squadron the Qantara site. Although the Flights and Squadrons were often separated by miles of desert, an interchange of trained officers kept the spirit of the Squadrons together. Geoffrey was to continue with this plan, even when the RFC had become even more widespread in the Middle East. There was always close liaison between the Squadrons, and the latest news from France and all latest developments on the Home front would be passed on to them, while trained officers joined the new Squadrons as they were formed. Geoffrey also moved his Headquarters in February from Heliopolis to Ismailia.

At this time he started a course of lectures for military officers, on Army co-operation and the importance of the Air Arm in warfare. Having been so recently in the Royal Artillery himself he could speak the same language, and it was found that his lectures became immensely popular. He wrote to Peggy:

> Tomorrow we have twelve senior officers coming to be lectured. It lasts two days, and I give a lecture on two of the days – Woe is me! But I expect it will be all right . . . I am having great 'confabs' with the Navy about co-operation, it is all coming out in a few days, and a copy will go to the War Office. I expect that out of it will come a uniform system of signalling from aircraft to both ships and guns of both Services.

According to the official history of the RAF, the lectures to the Army officers 'created a spirit of sympathy and understanding so that liaison between the Royal Flying Corps and the other arms in Egypt and Palestine were always close, cordial and informed.' His correspondence with the Navy also showed a vision of the future. Their co-operation was vital to the success of all operations in Palestine.

Geoffrey also organized an Air Photographic survey on a large scale. This was made in conjunction with the Topographical Section of the Intelligence Branch, so that he was again in touch with Sir Ernest Dowson and Lawrence. Air photography was taken by triangulation and the photographs were transferred to the 1:20,000 squared map. It was a development of Geoffrey's plan in France. Observers were thus able to give pin-point references which would not otherwise have been possible.

Reconnaissance flights were made over Hassana and Nekhl, east of the Canal, and in February the Hassana waterworks were twice bombed. Geoffrey wrote on 21 February to Peggy:

One of my fellows has just been given the Military Cross for destroying a valuable pumping station the enemy had. He came down to 600 feet and dropped an enormous bomb bang into the middle of it, and blew it sky high. I believe the effect of this exploit will be far-reaching. On all sides the Flying Corps out here are doing immense good, but I doubt if they realise it.

The pumping station was at Hassana and aerial photographs had helped in the location of the exact site. An aerial photograph taken at the time showed a direct hit on the Turks' main water tank.

It seemed that at last the Army was appreciating the help that reconnaissance, bombing raids and wireless communication could give them, but in April one disastrous incident showed that the liaison and understanding between the Army and the RFC was still very far from perfect.

At this time the Army was constructing a railway between Qantara and the Qatiya oasis, perhaps one of the greatest contributions which Sir Archibald Murray was to make towards the eventual conquest of Palestine. On 22 April Geoffrey's pilots reported to him that, while flying over the area of Qatiya, they had seen a large army of Turks collecting at the village of Mageibra, only four miles away from the town of Qatiya itself. Geoffrey took the news very seriously and, instead of sending a messenger, he decided to go himself and report the fact that he felt an attack on Qatiya was imminent. In spite of this, and even though another message was dropped by air on the morning of the 25th, the Commander on the spot decided to move all his troops to Mageibra, ignoring Geoffrey Salmond's warning that the town of Qatiya itself was about to be attacked. When the troops arrived at the Turkish camp at Mageibra, they found it quite deserted and, on their return, found, just as Geoffrey had predicted, that Qatiya had been attacked that day and taken. The RFC were up, bombing and pursuing the enemy.

Geoffrey wrote that during the 23rd, 24th and 25th, eight of his aeroplanes flew 4,000 miles in pursuit of the enemy and were in the air for sixty-eight hours:

My fellows have been fighting hard for two days, and have done awfully well . . . I thought it was coming and warned GHQ, and it did come. I can't tell you all about it as it is against the rules, but I asked a good deal of my officers, and they were simply splendid . . . German aeroplanes have appeared and are making things much more lively. My officers have carried out three raids. On one of the first, eight of them attacked a camp at dawn, dropped about seventy bombs from 400 feet and then came down to 200 feet with machine-guns. They did tremendous destruction. Then, on the following day they attacked another camp and after they returned, rested one hour, and then went off and did another. They flew on those three raids 2,400 miles and over. It is a new form of warfare in a way . . . but I am pleased with them all and they are simply splendid. It isn't as if it is safe for them by any means. They got very much peppered. One was hit in the knee and that made him jerk the rudder so badly that the machine began to spin. However, he pulled it out of that – a risky job as he was at 1,000 feet at the time, and then dropped four more bombs – he was so angry with them for hitting him. He had 50 miles to go to get home and lost a lot of blood, and as his left leg was useless he had to hold the left rudder control with his hand, but he did it all right, and landed safely. Grant Dalton was attacked by a German machine, and the first he knew about it was the wood splintering by his feet. He looked up and there was a German quite close. The German was faster than he was, and cleared off. But they did well, didn't they?

In spite of these gallant attacks by the RFC, the lack of co-operation with the Army at Qatiya was a disastrous example of the lack of confidence in RFC reports which still existed among some sections of the Army. Such misunderstandings were, however, becoming increasingly rare.

A few days after the bombing of Hassana water works, Geoffrey was writing to Peggy:

My course of senior officers has swollen to one of 16 officers now and the last day I had a Corps General and a Brigadier General listening to my lecture. Rather terrific! However it went off all right. It is good practice for me. . . . I hear from Father that Jack is coming home, and is to be a Brigadier General. Father is awfully pleased, and of course Mother will be too, and so am I. Really these things are astounding but everything is possible with this war while it lasts. I have more or less got to the bottom of what is happening at home, and in France, which made all these new Wings so necessary – but I don't quite understand why Trenchard came home and General Henderson has gone out, nor do I quite understand what has happened to Brancker. Webb-Bowen, Ashmore and Higgins have Brigades in France, apparently. This attack on Verdun looks rather bad, but I expect they will be stopped all right – the Germans die hard, don't they?

Geoffrey felt it was due to General Trenchard that more aeroplanes were sent out to Egypt in April 1916, but, even in August, RFC aeroplanes never totalled more than seventeen in any engagement. Even early in 1917 the strength of the 5 Wing was only twenty BE2Cs and 2Es, two Bristol Scouts and five Martinsydes, all of them out of date compared to the German Rumplers and Fokkers.

In April the arrival of an Australian unit, 67 Squadron of the Australian

Flying Corps, was a tonic to the RFC in Egypt. Although they arrived without aeroplanes, Geoffrey wrote that they were sent to 17 Squadron for training and later they were to form 60 Australian Squadron, RFC. It was a member of this very famous Squadron, McNamara, who was to win the first VC for the RFC the following spring.

Also at this time, letters were found on a captured Austrian prisoner stating that the Germans were sending Fokker single-seater fighter and Rumpler aircraft out to Egypt in support of the Turks, and it was these aeroplanes which had attacked the RFC at Qatiya. Unlike the British Government, Germany sent some of her best fighting aeroplanes to the Middle East, which contrasted with the out of date aeroplanes allotted to the Royal Flying Corps at home. The British Government seemed unaware of the crisis in Egypt. But the spirit of the men was high and, as always, the standards set by the early pioneers of flight and BK had not been forgotten.

During the spring and summer of 1916 in France, the need for more pilots and observers was growing desperate. German Fokkers, Aviatiks and Rumplers were taking a heavy toll of our aircraft, in spite of the new FE.2b and Geoffrey de Havilland's DH.2, which were our answer to the Fokker. For some time General Trenchard had been pressing Sir David Henderson for more trained pilots, as the average of only ten pilots a week was scarcely enough to replace the heavy casualties. In March John Salmond had been sent home from France to improve the situation and he at once took command of the Fifth Brigade, which was to become the Training Brigade and, in 1917, the Training Division. He at once laid down minimum standards for pilot training and, in order to speed up delivery of aeroplanes to the training squadrons, he commandeered every theatrical scenery truck in the country. Using these he had the machines earmarked for training sent direct to the squadrons, where they were tested and inspected. In this way the supply of machines in England was doubled. Before his arrival, new machines had had to be dismantled and sent in crates to Farnborough for inspection and then repacked before they could be delivered to the squadrons.

Later in the year, too, after hearing of the success of Robert Smith-Barry's training school at Gosport, Jack visited him and was taken up by Smith-Barry and shown his revolutionary method of training. Jack was so impressed that he ordered the same method to be adopted in every RFC training school in Britain.

Meanwhile, in Egypt, Geoffrey too was very conscious of the need for more trained pilots and aircrew. As he watched his BE2Cs taking off from Heliopolis and Ismailia in cloudless skies day after day, he realized that the long days of sunshine were ideal for flying training. So often in England a pilot's training was dependent on the weather. Mist, rain and cloud only too frequently grounded the aircraft and in 1916 it was vital that the pilots should have as much training as possible. Geoffrey perceived that conditions in Egypt were ideal. He wrote to Sir David Henderson, suggesting that the good weather and climate in Egypt would be ideal for a training ground for officers and men of the Royal Flying Corps, not only for Egypt but for France too. To his delight, he was supported by General Trenchard. Very soon the Government was persuaded to agree and it was decided that no less than three Reserve Squadrons were to be trained at Abu Quir between June and September. It was the start of one of the most ambitious programmes of the war in Egypt.

While these events were taking place yet another demand was being made on the Royal Flying Corps. In March, while a flight of 17 Squadron was operating against the Turks in the Sinai Peninsula, a message was received from none other than Sir Reginald Wingate, the Governor General of the Sudan. He asked for aeroplanes to be sent out to Darfur, far south of Khartoum, to help him, as Ali Dinar, the Sultan of Darfur, was threatening to attack the neighbouring province of Kordofan. Ali Dinar had been among those whom Kitchener had defeated at Omdurman in 1898, but he had been allowed to stay and govern his province, as long as he remained loyal to the Crown. Ever since that time he had hated the British and, hearing of the revolt of the Senussi in the North, had taken the opportunity to send an insulting message to Sir Reginald Wingate, while massing his forces on the border. Sir Reginald replied that he would be in Ali Dinar's capital before Ali Dinar could arrive in his. Sir Reginald knew the wild tribes that Ali Dinar had collected round him, and he felt that the mere sight of an aeroplane appearing from the skies would terrify them. It was for this reason that he made his request to Geoffrey Salmond.

Immediately 'C' Flight prepared to leave Suez, with four BE2Cs and their 90 hp Raleigh Factory engines in crates. They had to be dismantled, cased and then taken by rail. Oil and petrol had to be transported as well. Lieutenant Groves was put in charge of the overall operation. By May the heat in the desert had become intense, often reaching 120 degrees Fahrenheit. The cases containing the petrol had to be protected from the sun by a double layer of grass matting. The first stage of the journey was 800 miles (1280 km) from Suez by boat to Port Sudan. From there the aeroplanes in their crates could only reach Rahad by way of Atbara and Khartoum, another hundred miles (160 km) by train. At Rahad the two first BE2Cs were assembled in some old locomotive sheds, for it was too hot to construct them outside, while all the spares, stores and equipment were carried a further 350 miles (560 km) by loudly-protesting camels. The country was flat sandy desert, covered by low scrub and tebeldi trees. All water for the party was transported by the only motors available.

At last the two aeroplanes were ready and, after flying to Jebel El Hilla, prepared for their first reconnaissance. Captain Ballantyne, in charge of the flight, had sheets of white calico spread on the ground to help guide his aircraft back to base, but these soon disappeared! Eventually, the two aeroplanes flew the last 350 miles successfully to Jebel El Hilla, where an extra tank was rigged up on the aircraft so that the engine could be topped up with oil every two hours during flight, thus preventing evaporation of the fuel.

On arrival at Jebel El Hilla, everything was prepared for the first reconnaissance. Leaflets were dropped on the tribes, written in their own language, asking them to evacuate all women, children and old people from their villages before the bombing raids began. It was an effort to protect the innocent population and was a method which was to be used throughout the Middle East during the war. It was also used later on the North-West Frontier of India, where it was hoped to cause the maximum disruption while saving as many lives as possible. Often the fear of a raid would be all that was necessary to end a tribal rising. One cannot doubt that Geoffrey Salmond was the author of this plan. Just as Sir Reginald had guessed, the sight of the two aeroplanes was enough to terrify the motley soldiers of Ali Dinar's camp, although he boasted that 'he did not care what the Sirdar's iron horses which flew in the air could do'.

After a short battle on 22 May, the Dervishes were driven back, but the next day they were terrified to see a single aeroplane flying once more towards their camp. It was piloted by 2nd Lieutenant John Slessor, who, although seriously wounded in the thigh by a stray bullet, managed to drop several 20lb (9 kg) bombs on the camp. Two of the Sultan's servants and his own camel, which he was about to mount, were killed. The remnants of the army fled in terror into the desert, fearful of this new form of warfare from the skies. Ali Dinar himself survived a few months longer, but the revolt was over and 17 Squadron was recalled once more to Heliopolis. Although the wound in John Slessor's leg healed successfully, it left him lame to the end of his life.

As Geoffrey had predicted, the role of the Royal Flying Corps in Egypt had become far more varied and of far more importance than anyone could have guessed.

4

BUILDING AN AIR FORCE

In May, 1916, the heat had become so intense that both armies had almost ceased to function, but Geoffrey knew that he could not allow the Royal Flying Corps to relax, for German aircraft now numbered fourteen Rumpler two-seater aeroplanes, powered by Mercedes engines, and supported by Fokker single-seater fighters. He felt certain that a crisis would arise soon. Meanwhile, he wrote: 'They say the heat is unprecedented. It is extraordinary . . . A hot blast strikes up from the sand all round, and makes it hotter than ever.' In spite of this, the R.F.C. continued their reconnaissance over the enemy lines.

Quite suddenly, the Germans bombed Port Said. Confident in their superior machines, they had not taken into account the intensive training in bombing, artillery spotting and reconnaissance which the RFC had undergone in the previous six months. Nor had they appreciated the high morale of the pilots and observers. At once, on 18 May, a retaliatory raid was made on El Arish. Six aircraft set off before 06.00hrs to bomb the German base and to fight any enemy aircraft in the neighbourhood. Photographs of El Arish were taken, bombs dropped and a reconnaissance made. Three days later German pilots again bombed Port Said and again four BE.2Cs retaliated by attacking five enemy camps around El Arish.

Geoffrey wrote to Peggy: 'The heat is terrific, I am writing this in my shirt sleeves. There is a towel round my neck. In spite of this I am going to walk up to the aerodrome this afternoon to see my fellows who are going on a show.' He saw that some form of warning system was essential. A new airfield was hastily laid out at Port Said. Half a Flight of 14 Squadron was to man it, and they were to be in touch by telephone and wireless with the garrison at Romani, so as to warn of any approaching attack.

Perhaps the most distressing of the German raids took place a fortnight later, on 1 June. A single Rumpler, flying at 8,000 feet, dropped eight bombs on the camp of the 1st Light Horse Brigade of the Anzac Mounted Division. One of the officers and seven men were killed, while twenty-one were wounded. Thirty-six horses were killed and the others all stampeded. Yet another attack was made in the next few days on Qantara and the British garrison at Romani was attacked with machine-gun fire. Geoffrey Salmond determined on a reply.

While these stirring events were taking place in Egypt, news from home grew even darker. The agony of Verdun was followed in July by the Battle of the Somme, in which thousands of lives were sacrificed for the sake of a few miles, as Sir Douglas Haig determined to follow up the offensive. In England the casualty lists grew longer, and in May a personal grief overwhelmed the family. Jack's beautiful young wife, Joy, had been expecting her first baby in May and Geoff had written saying how much he longed to hear news of her. Sadly, Joy only survived a few hours after the birth of her baby on 8 May in London. Jack was heartbroken. The baby was a little girl and Jack called her Helen Amy Joy Lumsden, after her mother. Geoffrey wrote at once, offering to care for the baby in his own family. He wrote to Peggy: 'I have written to Jack telling him he is always to look on our home as his, for his mite.' But Jack decided to bring up his little daughter himself, rented a flat in London and hired a Nanny, though, always afterwards, little Joy was to feel much more than a cousin to Geoffrey's family and was more like a sister to Joyce, Anne and Penelope.

In Egypt Geoffrey now was planning a reprisal on a much larger scale. With the help of the Navy he decided to approach El Arish from the sea. Eleven BE.2Cs took part, two of them flying with observers, the others flying solo so that more bombs could be carried. They took off from Qantara and approached El Arish from the sea at 600 feet. There was stiff opposition from anti-aircraft fire and one British aircraft came down in the sea, but the pilot was rescued by motorboat. Captain Tipton, one of the pilots, reached the German airfield, but was shot down, crashing outside the airfield, but was able to set fire to his machine before being taken prisoner by the Turks. Perhaps the most exciting adventure was that of Captain H. A. van Ryneveld. A bullet had passed through the sump of his machine and he was forced down on the beach. Just then Captain Grant-Dalton's aircraft was passing overhead. The observer, Lieutenant D. K. Paris, saw van Ryneveld on the shore and Grant-Dalton immediately glided down and landed beside him. In a moment he had scrambled into the observer's cockpit with Paris and the BE.2C carried all three men safely back, 90 miles (144 km) to Qantara. One German aircraft was destroyed in the raid, one was damaged and two hangars were set on fire, while bombs were dropped on a Turkish camp.

Geoffrey wrote:

My own darling, I am proud of my fellows, the attack on El Arish was wonderful. I wonder if you have heard of it. Unfortunately I lost one of my best officers, but I think he is all right, as his machine landed in a good place and was seen to burn, all of which shows he set it on fire and was all right. I do so hope so. He was such a good chap. It was undoubtedly the first aerial attack from the sea that has ever been made. I was lucky to have the sea to help me. Darling one, I am in a great hurry and unable to tell you about it all, but everyone is very pleased out here. Grant-Dalton has been given the DSO, Paris a Military Cross and McLaren who blew up the German machine, a Military Cross. His was a wonderful feat. We have photography of the burnt machine on the ground! . . . Groves has just come back [from the Sudan] and really our fellows did wonderfully. It is extraordinary how much they helped in the actual defeat of the enemy. I am proud of my Wing – a really wonderful lot of officers. I started all these fellows off for El Arish, I stayed there overnight. It was a perfect day. The Navy helped me – they were most gallant in rescuing one of my fellows. Darling, no time at all, so hot. Your Geoff.

At last, it seemed as if everyone had recognized the gallantry of the RFC. Already Geoffrey had heard that he himself had been praised by Sir David Henderson, and he wrote: 'It was nice of him to say these things about me, I hope I deserve them.' Now congratulations were coming from all sides and he was writing:

My own darling, I was so glad to get your letters when I came back from Suez yesterday. I had just that afternoon heard that I had a Brevet. The CGS telephoned his congratulations to me at Suez, and it was brought to me in a railway carriage. The very first thing I thought was of you, darling. Then I got your letter when I came back. I am being rushed just at present, so this will be a very short letter. The great Trenchard wrote a letter to congratulate me. He said, 'Many congratulations on your Brevet Lieutenant-Colonel. You thoroughly deserve it. You are making Egypt one of the chief, bright spots of the Flying Corps. Your reports are always intensely interesting and we all read them.' So I have received something like a smack on the back. I am so glad old Jack has a brevet too. Three of my fellows get the Victory Crown, van Ryneveld, Wellesley and Morse, and one the DSO – Ross. But all this is nothing to the joy it will give me to be with you again to have you to kiss and look at, darling. I have just had a letter from the CGS about the show we carried out at El Arish the other day. He says ' . . . [but this was censored].' No, I simply can't go on writing this sort of thing, although I know you would love to hear, but I can't do it. I will reserve it for your ear alone.

Quite suddenly, on 1 July, Geoffrey heard that he had been promoted to Brigadier General. All detachments in Egypt, Mesopotamia and East Africa and later in Salonika were to be under his command and were to form the Middle East Brigade. It was a tremendous encouragement to feel that all his work in the last six months had been appreciated and that now he was to be trusted with so great a Command. Lieutenant Colonel P. R. C. Groves, who had organized the campaign in the Sudan, was to be Chief Staff Officer and Joubert de la Ferté was to be in charge of the 5th Wing. This was now to include 14 and 17 Squadrons, also 1 (Australian) Squadron of 28 officers and 195 men which, in September, was to be retitled 67 Squadron. When the creation of the Middle East Brigade was announced, there was an official announcement:

> Brigadier Lieutenant Colonel W.G.H. Salmond RA was mentioned in a Despatch from General Sir A. J. Murray KCB GCMG CVO DSO for gallant and distinguished service in the field.

Perhaps the most exciting development for Geoffrey was permission to form the 20th Reserve Wing. It was all he had hoped for and was to include 21, 11 and 23 Reserve Squadrons and was to include an aircraft park and aircraft depot. 30 Squadron was still to serve in Mesopotamia and 26 (South African) Squadron in East Africa.

Between June and September the three Reserve Squadrons were to arrive at Aboukir in Egypt. They were to train pilots for the Middle East Brigade and were also to form a general training establishment for the RFC as a whole. The aircraft park which had originally accompanied the 5th Wing to Egypt now had to supply technical equipment and stores to all the RFC squadrons in the Middle East. The author of the Official History of the RFC wrote later:

> A sense of unity undoubtedly permeated the Brigade, caused partly by moving personnel to suitable positions so that one could find, in any squadron, officers and men who had seen service on the ground or in the air in all theatres of the Middle East. So many squadrons were representative of the whole Brigade.

Training establishments, depots and repair centres were expanding all the time now and local labour was also used to help in their construction.

On 17 July Geoffrey wrote to Peggy:

> My own darling, your letter saying you were proud of me was ever so sweet, it is all I ever want, darling. I believe I am really off to Mesopotamia on the 1st or thereabouts. I could not go before although the War Office cabled because I had so many things in process of formation out here. I have been making things. I feel like Wallingford in the play, 'Get rich quick, Wallingford.' The school I have made at Aboukir and the Aircraft Depot is a regular city, all to my design. I have only to say, and it is done. Whereas in May there was nothing there but a blank space, it now has buildings, office quarters, workshops, power stations, enormous sheds,

electric light plant, railway sidings, men's barracks, bomb stores, petrol stores all mostly erected. Roads all over the place, just where I want them, altogether now when I go to see it, it is wonderful. I shall never get the chance again. I have just been seeing one of my squadrons off. The Australian Squadron is trained and is now doing its work. On 23 April they arrived with just 200 men with no stores, training, aeroplanes or transport. They have been all trained out here – and are jolly good. Oh dear, how I wish I were in France in that wonderful offensive [the beginning of the Battle of the Somme] . . . I am proud of my country. You were quite right about the 'raids' idea. I did write to General Robertson about that, but probably someone else did at the same time. However, I told no one except Groves about it so don't tell. But I love to think that what I did will help the show on, for I do believe these raids have a great deal to do with our successes. They blood the troops and take away their fear of war and also alarm the Germans as well as confuse them as to when or where the real offensive is coming. All this I wrote, and I see by *The Times* that the Germans were confused.

At this time also he wrote to his sister Gwen, saying he did not feel he could possibly come home. 'I don't see how I can, for a long time. What with travelling to Salonika, East Africa and Mesopotamia etc. carrying on the School and fighting out here I don't see my way clear at all. I left England about November 9th and I haven't seen Peggy since.' To Peggy, knowing he could not go home, he wrote: 'It is so hopeless-.'

The next few months were very full ones for Geoffrey. Not only was his vision of a training ground for the RFC in Egypt becoming a reality so swiftly, but his enormously extended command meant that from July to November 1916 he was to travel to Mesopotamia, East Africa, Salonika and even to India, inspecting, organizing and extending the areas in which the Royal Flying Corps could operate.

Lack of the latest machines was compensated for by the enthusiasm and devotion of pilots and observers, supported as always by the technicians and engineers at the Aircraft Park. For Geoffrey possessed that effortless quality of leadership which inspired all those who worked for him. Always friendly, outwardly unruffled and able to see the funny side of things, he was tireless in visiting every squadron under his command. According to the Official History:

The shape of the Air Service in the Middle East during the war was moulded chiefly by Major General W. G. H. Salmond. He had experience, vision, sane judgment and great charm of manner, a combination of qualities which enabled him to get things done with the minimum of fuss. It was due to him that the scattered detachments of the Royal Flying

Corps east of Malta enjoyed unity of command from the beginning. The command, extending from the Balkans to India, and embracing operations, training, repair and construction, as well as the creation of new squadrons, was a remarkable one.

On 27 July 1916 Geoffrey wrote to Peggy from Ismailia:

My own darling . . . I am off to Alexandria tonight again by the night train, and then back here tomorrow evening. I am off to Mesopotamia in about four days, or less. The C–in–C cabled home, and they cabled I had to go as soon as possible. Evidently there is something we mean to put right. I don't like going when so much is in the making here, but there it is. I am very fit but very hot. The C–in–C said very nice things to me the day before yesterday, this for your private ear. Also I am leaving here, although I know things are going to be a little exciting which disgusts me. But the sooner I get all this Mesopotamia business done, the better. Then there is the question of Africa. When am I to go there? It would perhaps be better to do everything at once.

Mesopotamia had become a very vexed question ever since the tragic fall of Kut in April 1916. Although in March a deputation had gone out to Kut, consisting of Aubrey Herbert, Colonel Beach, Head of Military Intelligence in Mesopotamia and T. E. Lawrence, they had only succeeded in persuading the Turks to free 1,000 ill or disabled prisoners, and the remainder of the garrison had been forced to surrender. 30 Squadron had done everything possible to support the Army. Early in March they had organized an airlift of food into the besieged town. General Townsend had said that 5,000 lbs of supplies were needed for everyone to have only the minimum of food every day. Four BE.2Cs, two Naval Farmans and two Short seaplanes had dropped 19,000 parcels of food between 15 and 29 of March in 140 flights. The Squadron had flown tirelessly and at great personal sacrifice, but all to no avail. Kut had fallen on 29 April. By June Sir Percy Lake, soon to hand over his command to Major General K. S. Maude, had to report that the enemy had been able to establish what was very nearly a mastery of the air. The Naval squadrons were withdrawn and, owing to the fearful climate and exhaustion, all but two RFC pilots had been admitted to hospital. The aircraft were also in need of repair, as fierce sun had warped the wooden airframes. Moreover, fever had played havoc with the pilots and the ground staff.

It was for these reasons that the Commander-in-Chief had ordered Geoffrey to go to Mesopotamia. He worked rapidly. By August, 30 Squadron had thirteen serviceable BE.2Cs in the air, with seven more under repair and a further seven arriving at Basra. Immediate help was given to Major General Maude, and considerable damage was done to the enemy airfield at Shumran.

Soon Lieutenant Colonel J. E. Tennant was to be put in command of the RFC in Mesopotamia; there could have been no better choice.

Meanwhile, in Egypt things had become 'a little exciting', as Geoff had predicted in his earlier letter to Peggy. Heavy gatherings of Turkish troops were seen from the air at Birel Mazar, 42 miles east of Romani, which had now become of very great importance to the enemy, for the railway, built under orders of Sir Archibald Murray, had reached the town and could prevent their plan of using Romani as a base for attacking the Suez Canal once more. On 3rd August the Turkish army attacked and the battle of Romani was joined. Although only seventeen British aircraft took part in the battle, vital information was continuously passed to the troops. One aircraft was lost and one officer killed, but the determination and spirit of the RFC could not have been higher, although German aircraft were backing up the Turkish attack, and for the first time in the Middle East pilots experienced air-to-air combat. The bravery of the aircrew was shown in the courage of Lieutenant E. W. Edwards and his observer, 2nd Lieutenant J. Brown. Returning from a reconnaissance flight, their BE.2C was attacked by a German Rumpler, which soon showed its ability to out-manoeuvre the ancient BE.2C. Edwards was hit by seven bullets, two of which broke his jaw and one broke his shoulder. In spite of his injuries he managed to evade the German machine and force-landed at the Headquarters of General Chaytor, who commanded the ground forces. His first thought was for his observer, Lieutenant Brown, who was unable to move as he had been shot through the chest. Bravely, Brown refused to be moved from the aircraft until he had dictated his report from his cockpit. He heard it read back before he consented to be moved. He then fainted and died two hours later.

Owing to the courage of aircrew such as these, the RFC managed to support the Army. The battle of Romani was won and eventually, before the end of the year, the threat to the Suez Canal was temporarily removed.

Problems in Sinai and in Mesopotamia were not the only ones which Geoffrey had to face in his widely scattered Command. He had also to face difficulties in Macedonia and in the far-flung continent of India. In July, soon after his appointment, the Greek Government had appealed to Britain for help in their fight against the Bulgarians, and immediately Geoffrey's Chief of Staff, Colonel Groves, so recently returned from his successful expedition in the Sudan, was sent to Macedonia to arrange for the arrival of 17 Squadron. This was to be under the command of Major E. M. Fuller, and was to be stationed at Mikra Bay. Its place in the Sinai Campaign was taken by the Australian squadron. On arrival the Squadron members found that their work was to be mainly reconnaissance, patrolling the desolate hills and valleys between the two rivers, Vardar and Struma. Their aircraft were no match for the German Fokkers, as they were BE.2Cs and BE.12s, but they were supported from the sea by the *Ark Royal* and seaplanes stationed on the islands of Imros and Thasos.

Later in the year, in September, 47 Squadron and 17 Balloon Section were to join them at Salonika, thus forming the 16th Wing. It was then that Geoffrey Salmond flew himself to Salonika. One of his most brilliant pilots there was Captain Murless-Green of 17 Squadron, who had already succeeded in shooting down three German aircraft. This was a particularly skilful action as in Macedonia his BE.2C was no match for the German machines. Later he fought the famous German aviator von Eschwege and managed to shoot down three further German aeroplanes.

There was still a spirit of chivalry in those early aerial contests over Macedonia. Notes would be dropped from British aircraft giving the number of casualties to the enemy and almost friendly greetings would sometimes be exchanged. Lieutenant von Eschwege, after arriving at Drama, the German Headquarters, soon became the most admired of the German pilots, as he combined chivalry with courage. When a British pilot, Lieutenant Owen, burnt his aeroplane, after being forced down in a battle with him, the Bulgarians brought him to trial, but von Eschwege fiercely defended him. He fought many duels and brought down at least twenty British aircraft, flying Fokkers and, later on, an Albatross. In the end, he lost his life as a result of a *ruse de guerre* on 21 November 1917. The basket of a captive balloon belonging to 17 Section, which had operated since the autumn of 1916, was filled with 500 lbs. of explosives, and a dummy observer made of straw. Von Eschwege dived on it, but his aircraft was blown up and he himself killed. When his body was recognized as the great von Eschwege the RFC were deeply upset that he had not died in a fair fight but as the result of a ruse and he was given a funeral with full military honours.

While on other Fronts during 1916-17 specialization became the rule, in Macedonia the pilots felt a sense of greater freedom. They were called upon to fly fighters, bombers or reconnaissance aircraft as the occasion arose, and this encouraged them to greater initiative and independence.

Fighting the Turks with Allenby

It was during the late summer that Geoffrey visited India, travelling by sea to Bombay and then by the Kalka Railway up to the mountains of Simla, where the Viceroy and the Commander-in-Chief were spending the summer months and where he could discuss the future of the Royal Flying Corps in India.

It is interesting to note that the British & Colonial Aeroplane Company of Bristol had sent three Bristol biplanes to India as early as 1911, to demonstrate their military value. They took part in the Army manoeuvres and a young Captain, William Sefton Brancker, went up with his pilot, Henri Juilleot, and brought back a detailed report of the opposing forces' movements in an hour and a half. The then Chief of Staff, Lieutenant General Sir Douglas Haig, had been suitably impressed.

On his return from Calcutta Sefton Brancker joined the RFC. He was promoted to Head of Military Training and in that capacity, and in other appointments, was closely associated with the Salmond brothers until his untimely death in the *R101* disaster in 1930.

After Geoffrey's return to Egypt he was able to write to Peggy once more about the progress of the Training Brigade, which was so very close to his heart. He wrote:

> I have just been down seeing my city that I have made by the sea. It is wonderful, and grows even larger. It is a hive of activity and that pleases me more than I can say. All the same, this Brigade of mine takes some looking after, there are all sorts of pitfalls you have to be looking out for . . . I took the General who is the Director of Works out with me this morning and in an unguarded moment he said, 'I have never been up in an aeroplane.' So I said, 'All right, now is the time!' and before he knew what had happened I had him strapped in with the best pilot I had, and off he went. He came down frightfully pleased, and now his sympathies with all my projects are absolutely certain, not that they were not so before, but now they will be stronger than ever. . . . have given one month's allowance to an officer who has just lost his brother, and whose mother is in a bad financial way. This fellow told me all about it as he wanted to get home to try and arrange something, and he told me he had to support the whole of his family and he is married as well. So I made him take my allowance as a loan, in case when he gets home he should find he was really hard driven, and I gave it in memory of his brother. It makes no difference to me as when I got back from India I had three cheques for £18 apiece in allowances waiting for me, and one of them made no difference, while it might make such an enormous difference to him.

This was only one small instance of Geoffrey's thoughtfulness for his men; he was always willing to listen to them and, if possible, to find some solution. He told Peggy not to tell anyone.

In November, while Sir Archibald Murray was making preparations for yet another attack on El Arish, an RFC pilot, flying over the town early in the morning, brought back the news that it had been completely evacuated by the Turkish Army. The town, which was surrounded, was easily occupied and in a few days the first supplies were being brought in to El Arish by sea. Having secured the position, Sir Archibald conceived the more ambitious plan of pushing yet further into Palestine, supported by the Royal Flying Corps. At this time Geoffrey would fly whenever possible to inspect his squadrons, and on New Year's Day he wrote to Peggy from Cairo:

My own darling, a happy New Year to you all at Ditchingham and a kiss to Penanjo [his private name for his daughters] with the accent on the Anne! I have just returned from El Arish, where I have been seeing my fellows and doing certain things. I flew from Ismailia, I flew myself to the aerodrome, about eighty miles, and then went on with Joubert. I came back yesterday, by air. There was a strong headwind. I was surprised I wasn't tired . . . I tried singing in the machine, but came to the conclusion that my voice hadn't much chance against the roar of the engines. I enjoyed it very much. I had no passenger to think about. My servant went by rail. I carried my washing things and hairbrush in my despatch case, in the front seat. It was a wonderful sight seeing all this astonishing country down below me, the sea on one side and the desert on the other. I passed over all the battlefields of Katia and Romani and then went down the defence line on the Suez Canal.

It had been Geoffrey's second Christmas without Peggy. On Christmas night he had some officers to dinner, including Colonel Groves.

The first daylight raid had taken place on London. Geoff wrote to Peggy, trying to cheer her up: 'Poor old Jack being bombed in Basil Street. Rather good it stopping in the milk cans. That does sound like home. Newcombe is here, on a sort of mysterious job which I can't talk about. He dined with me last night . . .'

Colonel S. F. Newcombe was one of a dedicated band of British soldiers under the direct orders of Sir Reginald Wingate. A brilliant and daring demolition expert of the Royal Engineers, he was an equally genuine but less known hero than Lawrence was to become.

Almost certainly Newcombe's 'mysterious job' was connected with the Arab rising, in which Lawrence was to play so pivotal a role. It was known that Sherif Hussein, the hereditary ruler of the Arabs, had returned to the Holy City of Mecca in June from his enforced stay under the Turks in Constantinople, bringing his four sons with him. It was rumoured in Cairo that he might possibly lead the Arabs in a revolt against the hated Turks, but only the Diplomatic Service knew the real facts.

Quite unobtrusively, the young archaeologist Lawrence had asked for a fortnight's leave in October, so that he could accompany Sir Ronald Storrs on a diplomatic mission to meet Abdullah, the second son of Sherif Hussein. In June Lawrence had transferred from the Map Section to the Arab Bureau in Cairo. A brilliant linguist, he was able to edit *The Arab Bulletin* and where he was working with such congenial men as Aubrey Herbert, Philip Graves and even, for a time, with Gertrude Bell, the archaeologist and traveller whom he had met in his excavating days at Carchemish. Sir Ronald Storrs was delighted to have him. Members of the Arab Bureau could not have foreseen that Lawrence's 'fortnight's leave' was to extend to several years.

Once at Medina, Lawrence persuaded Abdullah to allow him to meet his brother, Feisal, who was then at Hamra, and Abdullah kindly lent him one of his favourite camels. As soon as Lawrence met Feisal he felt the magnetism and power that lay behind the tall, dignified young prince and felt too that he, above all, could lead his Arabs to victory. Because of his convictions and his own enormous enthusiasm, confidence and energy, Lawrence was able to convince first Sir Reginald Wingate in Khartoum and secondly the Army in Cairo that an Arab revolt was a real possibility. Lawrence soon became regarded as an authority by the Army in Cairo, and was appointed as Military Adviser to Feisal. Sir Archibald Murray and his staff were only too pleased to feel that the rising need not be entirely their responsibility, and were willing to supply Lawrence with money and artillery. And so the amazing story of the revolt in the desert began.

Even at this stage Geoffrey was involved. In late September six aircraft of 14 Squadron had been sent to Rabegh, a port on the Red Sea, under Captain Freeman, and an attempt had been made to cut the railway line to Medina which was held by the Turks. In January the Flight was transferred to El Wejh after Lawrence and Feisal had taken it. The six aircraft were quite a generous assignment, as the whole strength of the 5th Wing in Egypt at that time was only twenty BE.2Cs, two Bristol Scouts and nine Martinsydes.

Meanwhile, the whole of southern Palestine was being systematically mapped by air photography. Wireless co-operation with artillery was being perfected and the zone call system was introduced in conjunction with 'Contact Patrol'. Geoffrey was determined that the latest developments on the Western Front in France should be communicated to him in Egypt as soon as possible, so that they could be sent out to all the squadrons under his command. At the end of December the RFC had discovered 2,000 Turks with mountain artillery entrenched at El Hagruntein, several miles north of El Arish. The pilots photographed and plotted their positions from the air and, on 8 January, additional troops were seen arriving. General Chetwode, who commanded the Desert Column, decided to lead a raid against them himself and moved out of El Arish. As neither the railway nor the water pipe line was yet completed, it was not possible for the Column to capture Rafa, but it was hoped to raid it from the air. As the troops advanced, the RFC flew over the town at seven am. Five wireless receiving stations were in use, transported on sand sleighs, the operator riding on horseback. Two aircraft stayed up all day, observing the enemy. The result was that the garrison of 1,655 Turks was captured.

Beersheba airfield was also bombed in January but in February attacks by bombing were discontinued as German retaliation terrified the workers on the railway. Reconnaissance, however, was continued and in March the Turks were seen to evacuate their defences and retire to Gaza.

Meanwhile, during January and February 1917 the German submarine menace in the Mediterranean was becoming more and more dangerous to shipping. Many letters were lost when ships were torpedoed, but a letter arrived from Peggy dated 5 January saying how upset she was that Geoff's name had not appeared in the New Year's Honours list when he had done so well. However, in a few days he was to write:

> I have a surprise for you. The C-in-C sent for me the other day and gave me the DSO. In fact, I am really awfully pleased and it is rather nice having been given it by the C-in-C out here. He really only gave me the ribbon, and made a little speech which I can't repeat. A French officer and one other were given it at the same time. The CGS and French Military Attaché were present and the Military Secretary.

The Citation, published on 3 March, read:

> Citation for conspicuous ability and devotion to duty when personally directing the work of the Royal Flying Corps during the action. The striking success was largely due to his magnificent personal example.

At this time Geoffrey was also delighted to receive a letter from Major Ludlow-Hewitt, who, after working so closely with Geoff in 1 Squadron in France, had been promoted and at the beginning of November had taken command of 1 Squadron himself. He wrote:

> I have had a ripping letter from Ludlow-Hewitt who is in France. He tells me that my artillery co-operation theories have all come into their own at last, and that to use his own words 'the strapping son of my parent ideas is universally adopted, patronised and applauded from the sea to the Somme'. He says 'Do you remember the struggles we had – the birds we launched – the sermons we preached – the campaigns we inaugurated? And now it has all come true. After you left I carried on the work as a good apostle and led the infant to the front in 1915. From then he had a hard life, until about July, 1916, when after enlisting, month by month, many distinguished supporters, he leapt into sudden fame and his efforts were crowned with success.' Isn't that nice? Ah! I wish I was out there. I am sure I could do things. I flew down to Qantara to see a squadron that was leaving us. I was in a new type of machine which I had never flown before and was rather apprehensive as to what sort of landing I would make as the whole squadron were out to see me, but it came off all right. I do enjoy these trips so much.

Sadly, at the beginning of February, he had a really bad attack of lumbago. He wrote from the Hotel Cesino at Alexandria:

I am alone here. I have had to come down here about a new scheme which really is growing into a very big affair, I think, but which I had better not write about. The worst of it is that I flew a machine down to Ismailia yesterday and got very cold and halfway there I realised I had got lumbago again. It just started in the air. Now I know where I get lumbago as it is always after flying and comes from not wrapping up my legs so that they keep warm. They were very cold yesterday. My first go of lumbago was at Brooklands, the next at Netheravon, always after flying and in each case my legs were half frozen. It is my own fault, because I can draw warm things from stores and will do it always in future. Luckily this attack is not overpowering.

However, it *was* overpowering. He had insisted on going to Alexandria for two days and afterwards the pain became worse. His next letters were from hospital, where he spent two weeks. He said the lumbago had developed into the worst attack he had ever had.

Letters were pouring in congratulating him on his DSO, and he wrote:

Dearest, honestly, I don' t deserve it and it makes me feel horrible. I have never done anything magnificent or heroic as the announcement implies, I wish I had. I make the plans generally, and have my fellows carry them out. But they do it and they want no example from me. They are all so absolutely splendid. The action I suppose they refer to is Rafa but I wasn't there. I am sorry I cannot describe to you something really wonderful. There seems to be a general conspiracy to ascribe all the splendid work my fellows do to me, why I don't know, and it is most appalling to read praise like this when it is wholly undeserved. I don't know what to do. The only real laugh I have had about it is your letter when you say, 'Now write and tell me all about it as I shall think someone else did it.' You hit the nail right on the head and it really makes me laugh. It is the only thing that appears to make me happy about the whole business. I shall write to Brancker and General Henderson and to Jack and tell them the truth, it is too stupid. Of course Mother and Father are wonderfully pleased and both write to know when and where it happened as everyone is asking them, and, pathetic to relate, I can' t.

He was in great pain, but wrote:

Darling, do not worry about me. I get furious at times with feeling so well and yet being a crock, but it cannot be helped. . . . My fellows have been doing wonderful things lately. Here are some of them. One came down while attacking a railway and was rescued under fire by another machine which already had a passenger. The following day another had to come down and was rescued by another machine whose pilot was already shot in the leg and it was done under hot fire.

Geoffrey was here describing the courageous action of Lieutenant McNamara, who was awarded the VC for his action. Lieutenants McNamara and Ellis had been ordered to bomb a train with 4.5-inch howitzer shells. Unfortunately, the last shell exploded prematurely and McNamara was wounded in the right leg. He wisely decided the best course was to return to base before he fainted but as he turned he saw that a BE.2C piloted by Captain Rutherford had force-landed and the pilot was igniting a distress smoke signal. With no thought for his own safety, McNamara landed beside him, although he could see Turkish cavalry approaching. Rutherford climbed onto the engine cowl of the Martinsyde single-seater, but the aircraft swung to one side and crashed. The Turkish cavalry dismounted and opened fire. Ignoring them, McNamara set his aircraft on fire before dashing to the stranded machine which had originally crashed. Just as the two airmen reached the machine McNamara's burning aircraft exploded. This so shocked the Turks that they hesitated. McNamara, weak from his wound, flung himself into the cockpit while Rutherford swung the propeller. Miraculously, the engine fired and they took off unevenly, the Turks now almost near enough to touch the wings . . . It was not until he was in the air and flying the 70 miles back to base that MacNamara realized how faint he was from loss of blood. Several times he almost lost consciousness but at last managed to reach his base and even to achieve a good landing. He was recommended by Geoffrey for his extreme bravery in rescuing his friend and escaping from the Turks. On 17 June he was awarded the Victoria Cross – the first Australian airman to receive this highest award.

Geoffrey's letter continued:

> Another fellow's machine was hit and he had to come down in the sea. He swam ashore but was fired on from the land. He then swam some four miles, made five attempts to land and eventually escaped. Another fellow's Very signalling light was hit by a bullet and the machine caught fire in the air. Although over enemy country he stuck to it and landed the machine eventually in our lines, with his back rather burnt. Having put out the fire, he flew back to his aerodrome. He then had a little leave to recover, went back and yesterday brought a German machine crashing to the ground. They are a wonderful lot. The only thing I do to help them is to make much of them when they do these things, and tell other people about them. I feel anxious about the food question at home. I do hope things are all right. I cannot say anything about leave – yet.

The pilot who swam four miles along the coast to escape capture was Lieutenant Seward, who had been compelled to land near Ashkelon. He discarded his clothes as he swam and eventually found himself behind British lines and was able to return to his base.

By March Sir Archibald Murray felt that he could advance on Gaza. The railway and pipeline were almost completed and he felt his supply line was thus assured. Unfortunately he did not take into account the superiority of the enemy aircraft over our own for, in spite of Geoffrey's repeated requests for more sophisticated aircraft, they had not been supplied. In consequence the British troop movements were observed by the Halberstadts and Fokkers of the German Air force which could easily outfly and outmanoeuvre the BE.2Cs and Martinsydes, however gallantly they might fight. When Sir Archibald advanced the Turks were ready for him and, although the Desert Column reached the gardens outside Gaza, the attack, without the help of surprise, was a failure.

The desperate need for more modern and sophisticated aircraft is shown in a cable sent by Geoffrey Salmond dated 3 April 1917 to 'Adastral London'. It was only one of many, but showed how urgent the matter was. It ran:

Martinsyde machines overheated during first spell of hot weather. Besides engine seizing one occasion 3 pilots overcome by fumes and heat. In addition enemy has 2 Halberstadts, information states they are expecting more, making hostile total 20. These Halberstadts attacked our machines at intervals in Gaza operations, doing serious damage in each case, wounding 2 pilots, killing 1 observer and seriously damaging 6 machines, bringing down 2. German policy is to give some of their best machines to all their detachments. As numbers of aircraft cannot alone compete with superior types, request this policy should be adopted by us. Urgently request you to send out six of the best types.

This request was followed by a letter to the Director of Organization, Air Board House, The Strand:

Reference my cable 3/4/17 I write to confirm and explain. In every theatre in the Middle East, except East Africa, the Germans possess a few of their very latest types, which reinforce their machines of more ancient pattern. This policy of theirs is extremely sound, as it makes possible for them to greatly reduce the advantages we derive from our numerical superiority. Incidentally, it inflicts a heavy strain on our pilots and machines as besides necessitating constant escorts it enables them by their mobility to attack machines which are, in every case, inferior to them in speed and climb. Apart from this it enables the enemy with a single machine to carry out reconnaissances over our lines with impunity, as they do it from a great height and in perfect safety as no machine we possess can tackle them. This state of affairs now exists in Mesopotamia, Palestine and

Salonika. I press, therefore, for the adoption by us of a similar policy. If each of these theatres possessed one flight of up-to-date machines, no complaints could be made. They would clear the air, prevent hostile reconnaissances and enable all ordinary aerial work to be carried out by our slower reconnaissance machines. I suggest therefore that one of the existing flights in each theatre should be regarded at the War Office as a flight possessing machines of the very latest types. Thus, as a new type of fighter or Scout was evolved and approved for France, twelve of them (or a proportion of twelve) should be immediately allotted to the Middle East Brigade as a matter of normal procedure. Only by adopting such a policy can the full value of the efforts of Royal Flying Corps pilots be obtained for, gallant as they are, they cannot compete with a mechanical superiority which compared to the small amount of German effort involved, confers on him such advantages. It is recognised that first claim goes to France but it is thought by only asking for 1 Flight for each theatre this claim is satisfied. Geoffrey Salmond. Brigadier General. Cairo 1/5/17.Commanding Middle East Brigade, Royal Flying' Corps.'

In spite of letters and cables it was not, unfortunately, until General Allenby arrived that any appreciable difference was made in the supply of aircraft.

Despite his lack of success at Gaza, the Cabinet ordered Sir Archibald Murray to press on, defeat the Turks and enter Jerusalem. Once again he decided to attack Gaza as he felt this was the only course open to him. The advance began on 17 April and was, at first, successful. Next day the bombardment opened by sea and by land, but on the 19th the main assault failed, as the position was once again too strongly defended. The RFC was up continuously and on the next day they discovered on reconnaissance some two thousand Turkish infantry with eight hundred cavalry in a wadi, about to launch an attack on the British right flank. Four aeroplanes dropped forty-eight 20 lb bombs on the Turks and they fled in confusion. Once again the RFC had done all they could in support of the Army.

It was at this point that affairs at home profoundly influenced the Middle East, for when Lloyd George succeeded Asquith as Prime Minister in December 1916 he decided that the only alternative to the long and desperate battle in the Western Front was, as he said 'to strike the enemy where he is weakest'. And it was obvious that by knocking Turkey out of the war the Central Powers could be exposed to invasion from the rear, while the main German armies were held fighting in France. This was his strategy, and thus the failure to take Gaza after two attempts infuriated him and he demanded more resolute leadership. Sir Archibald's great contribution, the construction of the railway and pipeline across the waterless desert, was not fully appreciated, although it was a real contribution to the eventual victory.

At this time Jan Christian Smuts was in London attending the Imperial

Conference. He had recently been in command of the campaign in East Africa, where he had cleared the colony of German forces and had been received in London in some triumph. The Prime Minister now invited him to take over command of the Egyptian Expeditionary Force. Smuts considered the proposal carefully but, after consultation with General Robertson, the CIGS, who considered the whole plan a waste of manpower and wanted all forces to be concentrated in France, he decided to refuse. He felt that Egypt was only a 'sideshow'. Later he wrote: 'Sir William said to me, quite frankly, that if I were to accept the offer under the impression that something first class could be done in Palestine I would be making a great mistake.' He added, 'Lloyd George often afterwards told me I had made a great mistake, and it is a question whether he was right.'

As General Smuts had refused, Lloyd George then pressed General Robertson for a suitable successor to Sir Archibald Murray and Robertson suggested Sir Edmund Allenby, who had been in command of the cavalry at the outset of war and who had then been promoted to be in charge of the 3rd Army. He had been knighted in 1915. There was no one more forceful nor more determined than 'The Bull', as he was called. Enormously strong and tall, he had the reputation of never giving in under any circumstances. Both Lord Kitchener and Sir John French had admired him and it seemed that he was the right man for Palestine. The War Cabinet confirmed the appointment on 5 June and a telegram was sent the same day ordering Sir Edmund Allenby to return to London at once.

Jerusalem Before Christmas

At first Allenby was devastated. However, on arrival in London he was inspired by the Prime Minister's obvious enthusiasm. He learnt that he was to have great freedom of action, and was told by Lloyd George that he was to ask for all the reinforcements and supplies that he might need. Lloyd George also told him that he expected 'Jerusalem before Christmas.'

On 28 June Sir Edmund Allenby took over command in Cairo.

★   ★   ★

While these events were taking place at home, Lawrence, riding his white camel and dressed in the clothing of an Arab prince, which had been given to him by Feisal, was leading a wild army of Arabs on camels across the desert towards El Wejh, a port on the Red Sea. Already his enthusiasm had inspired Feisal and his brothers to rise against the hated Turks. As he advanced with Feisal, more and more tribes joined his banner. El Wejh was taken, with the help of a bombardment by the Royal Navy. The elusive Newcombe had also appeared

107

out of the desert and taken part. Almost immediately, Lawrence was sweeping northwards at the head of an ever-growing army of wild followers and enthusiastic tribes.

Then Lawrence conceived his boldest plan. While lying ill with fever, he remembered the military tactics of the great soldiers of the past whose lives he had studied at Oxford and he decided to follow their example. The port of Aqaba, some 300 miles north of El Wejh was one of the Turks' most strongly held garrisons. Almost impregnable from the sea, it was flanked on the shore side by inaccessible mountains protecting it from invasion. Lawrence, however, saw that it could be the base for an invasion of Syria. On 18 June he set out with 800 Bedouin of the Toweiha tribe, two hundred Sinerats and ninety Kawashiben. Auda, the magnificent fighter and leader of the Abu and Taya section of the Howarti tribe rode beside him, as did Nasir, Feisal's right-hand man, who was nominally in command of the expedition. Lawrence decided to lead a 'flying column' not directly to Aqaba but 1,000 miles into the interior, hoping to upset and mystify the enemy. He realized that the Arab tribes, mounted on their camels, were a law unto themselves, quite unsuited to conventional warfare. Brilliant at surprise attacks and swift raids, they were individualists who could disappear into the desert without trace. Lawrence had trained himself to be as hardy and independent as they were. They made a wide circle from oasis to oasis, eventually approaching Aqaba from the East.

The Turkish army camped just outside Aqaba at Au el Lissal were taken completely by surprise. Auda galloped into their camp at sunset, followed by five hundred wild Bedouin on camels. The Turks scattered, and the battle was won. Aqaba had fallen. Even so, the situation was almost desperate. The huge army of Arabs was almost starving and there were now seven hundred prisoners to feed. Lawrence saw the situation and, exhausted though he was, he rode on towards the Suez Canal with only two men, covering 168 miles in two days. He then crossed by boat to Suez and there, worn out, he was able to have a hot bath, six iced drinks and a comfortable bed, something of which he could only have dreamed during the long months in the desert.

★　　★　　★

On 2 June 1917, before the momentous arrival of General Allenby in Cairo, Geoffrey, having visiting Salonika in May, was given six weeks leave in England. He had served continuously in Egypt since November 1915 and one can imagine the delight of Peggy and the family when he at last returned home. Colonel Board was to be in charge of the Middle East Brigade while Geoff was away. Unfortunately there had been some difference of opinion between him and Colonel Groves while Geoffrey was in Salonika, but Geoff did his best to pour oil on troubled waters before he left.

Part of Geoffrey's holiday was to be at the Spa at Harrogate, where it was hoped that he could have treatment for his lumbago, which had still not been overcome. However, he would first have gone to Ditchingham to see Peggy and the children. He had not seen Penelope since she was three weeks old. During the first weeks of his leave he would also have gone to London to the Second Air Board, an organization which had taken a tremendous amount of heartache and negotiation to form. As early as February 1916 the Joint Air Committee had been formed under Lord Derby in an attempt to draw the Admiralty and the War Office closer together on Air Policy. It had failed, as it had no executive power. The First Air Board was then formed under Lord Curzon in May 1916, and he, in the words of the official history 'explored all possibilities, especially the formation of an Air Ministry and a separate Air Service.' But the First Sea Lord, Lord Balfour, had totally rejected the suggestion, and when the Asquith Government fell in December the First Air Board had been dissolved.

Lloyd George, however, inaugurated the Second Air Board on 3 January. He appointed Lord Cowdray as its first President and in June it was still very active. This success was largely due to the creation of a Fifth Sea Lord, to have powers similar to Sir David Henderson, and to the fact that the design of aircraft now rested with the Ministry of Munitions. Cowdray saw a separate Air Force as inevitable and that it could be achieved, although he still felt it was not possible in time of war. During this time Geoffrey would certainly have seen Sir David Henderson and told him of the problems created by the lack of fighters and modern aircraft in Egypt, about which he felt so strongly.

The last part of his holiday was spent at Harrogate with Peggy. It was decided that Joyce, now aged five, and Anne aged three, could join them. Jack also managed to get some leave and was with them all at the Crown Hotel. To the children it seemed as if sunshine had broken out in their lives. Their mother was laughing and happy and their father was full of fun. The hotel had a lovely garden with red geraniums growing in pots on the terrace, the sun shone and the children fed baby ducks on a tiny pond. In the midst of the dark days of war, it was unforgettable.

While at Harrogate, early in July, the first result of Allenby's arrival in Egypt was felt. A cable which arrived at the hotel for Geoff ran: 'Dear General, Herewith a copy of a telegram we have today sent to Egypt regarding the formation of a new Fighting Squadron there which I thought you might like to see':

To G.O.C. Middle East Brigade, Egypt. 10/7/17. It has been decided to raise a fighter Squadron in Egypt, the officers, pilots and personnel to be found locally so far as possible. Squadron equipment and transport will be sent from England. No further allotment of aeroplanes will be made at present beyond those already allocated at the beginning of this month, nor will any definite type of machine be laid down at present, but for the next two or three months it is assumed that its equipment will consist partly of Bristol Fighters, Bristol Monoplanes and Vickers Bullets. If assistance is absolutely necessary in personnel, please cable particulars of minimum requirements. The Squadron will be designated No. 111.

To Geoff this telegram would have seemed an answer to his most fervent prayers. He could not have asked for more.

The holiday in England passed all too quickly. At the time, the summer of 1917, elderly ladies, in a mistaken effort to support the war, went up to any young man who was not in uniform and tried to shame him into joining the army. Jack, Geoff and Peggy were in the train after their holiday, travelling back to London, Geoff in civilian clothes and Jack wearing his greatcoat. Two old ladies were travelling in the same carriage. They looked at each other and one bent forward to tap Geoffrey on the knee. 'You should be up there!' she said, pointing to an aircraft flying by. Jack joined in at once, putting his hand over his medals. 'Yes, you should be up there!' he remarked accusingly. Geoff of course joined in: 'Why should I?' Peggy laughed until the tears streamed down her cheeks! Feeling very uncomfortable, the two ladies moved into another carriage.

A similar incident happened to General Trenchard some months later. At that time there was a 'drive' for mothers to have more babies. He was sitting on a bench in Green Park, deeply meditating on the future of the RAF. At that time those in reserved occupations wore a badge. An old lady approached him. 'Sir,' she said, 'where is your badge?' 'Madam,' replied Trenchard in a tired voice, 'where is your baby?'

★   ★   ★

The months following Geoffrey's return to Egypt were perhaps the most exciting and the most rewarding of his whole command in the Middle East, for it was announced by the War Office that yet another Squadron, 113, was also to be raised, this time entirely in Egypt at Ismailia. The War Office also offered to send out two Kite Balloon Squadrons. The 21st Balloon Company arrived in August and was attached to the 5th Wing. 'C' Flight of 14 Squadron also returned from the Hejaz and rejoined the Squadron at Deir el Balh with the whole of 5th Wing.

In September Geoffrey wrote a long report suggesting that, as the Middle East Brigade had by then extended to include the two new squadrons and many more aeroplanes including Bristol Fighters, Vickers Bullets, RE.8s, Bristol monoplanes and BE.l2As besides the Balloon Company and Aircraft Parks, that it would be advisable to create a new Palestine Brigade, which would be entirely operational. This was approved in principle and Brigadier General

A.E.Borton DSO, who had succeeded Joubert de la Ferté in February, became second-in-command to Geoffrey during General Allenby's forthcoming advance, while Geoffrey Salmond himself was still in charge of the whole Middle East Brigade, including the 20th Reserve Squadron, in which no less than a thousand pilots had been trained since October 1916. In his report he also said he was responsible for the early establishment of an aircraft factory in which it was hoped aeroplanes could actually be constructed. He included details of the establishments in Salonika, Mesopotamia, East Africa and India, all within his commission.

He had the aircraft he so desperately needed, and he was determined that with them he would support General Allenby to the hilt in his great advance into Palestine. The Bristol Fighters which he was to send were far more sophisticated than the BE.2Cs and were quite able to take on the Halberstadts and Fokkers which flew against them. The Bristol Fighter was a two-seater biplane designed in 1916, and had only come into service in 1917. Its pilot was seated in a cockpit immediately behind the wings, while a Vickers machine gun fired by synchronizing gear through the airscrew. An observer sat behind and had one or two Lewis guns mounted on a Scarff ring. The engine was a 250 h.p. Rolls-Royce. Geoffrey was delighted and his pilots at last felt that they could face the enemy on equal terms.

As soon as General Allenby arrived, he had transformed the attitude of the whole staff in Cairo. Lawrence wrote: 'Allenby's coming has remade the English. His breadth of personality swept away the mists of private or depart-mental jealousies behind which Murray and his men had worked.' A senior Intelligence Officer, Colonel Richard Meinertzhagen, who was almost as unusual an officer as Lawrence himself, also wrote:

> Was introduced to Allenby, to whom I talked on Intelligence matters for a short while. My word, he is a different man to Murray. His face is strong and almost boyish. His manner brusque, almost to rudeness, but I prefer it to the oil and butter of the society soldier. Allenby breathes success, and the greatest pessimist cannot fail to have confidence in him.

On Allenby's first day in his office in Cairo a pile of papers was brought in for him to read. He swept them all onto the floor, saying they should be the work of a junior staff officer. When he had only been in Cairo a week, he crossed the Canal to inspect his troops and, soon afterwards, moved his headquarters from the luxury of Cairo to the hardship of life in the desert, to be with his men.

The force before the 'Gaza Line' now lay over 200 miles from Cairo. The temperature often rose to 110°F, there was little shade and the supply of water was still a nightmare. Allenby wrote: 'The men are burnt as black as Arabs. One sees them sitting in the blazing sun, often with practically nothing on but a helmet, and apparently enjoying it.' He drove round to inspect them, usually in an old Ford truck, although soon he was to drive in an ancient Rolls Royce. An Australian history described him at this time: 'Troops who caught only a fleeting glimpse of him felt that here at last was a man with the natural qualities of a great driving Commander. At last they had a Commander who would live among them and lead them.'

When Geoffrey returned to Cairo he had felt an immediate rapport with Allenby. Both men had left for France in August, 1914, both had fought in the retreat from Mons, the 'race for the sea' and the first battles of Ypres and Neuve Chapelle. They had seen the horror of war and, like General Allenby, Geoffrey never spared himself in training and inspiring the men under his command. In France Allenby had already realized the tremendous potential of the aeroplane and also, as a cavalry man, he valued their success in reconnaissance as much as their achievements in aerial warfare. It was he who had immediately ordered the Bristol Fighters to be sent out to Egypt. Now he had two alternatives before him — he could either advance on Gaza once more, by the expected route, where his troops could be supported from the sea but where the German Commander, von Kressenstein, would almost certainly be waiting for him, or he could advance by the inland route to Beersheba. Allenby asked for two more Divisions, more aircraft and tanks. It was said that his final plan was not entirely his own invention but, according to Lawrence, might be attributed to Guy Dawnay, for General Allenby had surrounded himself with a brilliant Staff. Colonel Bols, with whom he had fought in France, succeeded Lyndon Bell, and Guy Dawnay and General Shea were also at his side. His force was divided into three Corps: the XX under Sir Philip Chetwode, the XI under Lieutenant General Bulfin and the Desert Column Mounted Corps, a brigade of which was always mounted on camels. Allenby chose his main attack, not at Gaza, but at Beersheba.

Meanwhile he decided to confuse the enemy. All preparations were made around Gaza as if for the main attack; tents were put up, armoured cars drove around, only retiring silently to their camps at sunset, and, above all, the RFC was up continuously, keeping all the enemy aircraft on the ground so that not one enemy reconnaissance could be made. Two aircraft flew over the enemy airfields in relays. Rumours were also put out that Cyprus was to be a base for the invasion of Gaza.

But perhaps the most brilliant feint was by Richard Meinertzhagen. His first suggestion was to drop cigarettes every night, with propaganda leaflets, by air over the enemy camps and the night before the battle to dope the cigarettes, but Allenby refused to agree to this. His next plan was brilliantly conceived and carried out by himself personally. As an officer ostensibly on reconnaissance, he rode out on one of his swiftest horses in front of the Turkish outposts to provoke a chase. He galloped away and when they shot at him he swerved, dropped a haversack containing papers, and galloped swiftly on. The papers had been carefully contrived to suggest that there would be an important attack on Gaza in the next few days. They were packed with innocent-looking sandwiches and letters and stained with a little blood, as if Richard had been wounded. Later he wrote: 'I saw one of them stop and pick up the haversack and rifle, so I now went like the wind for home and soon gave them the slip, well satisfied with what I had done and that my deception had been successful. If only they act on the contents of the notebook, we shall do great things.' The Turks were completely taken in and their main troops were removed from Beersheba.

Meanwhile, Allenby had made meticulous preparations. As water was always the most desperate need in the desert he arranged for 30,000 camels to transport water to his troops in Beersheba. It was still vital that the wells in the town should be captured, and this he was determined should be his first priority, but he could take no chances, so roads were built. The RFC continued reconnaissances and maps were completed of the whole area. Allenby was everywhere with his men, and the letters BL were signalled as he left one Corps for another, rather affectionately meaning 'Bull Loose'! At the time of the battle the RFC had no less than fifty-three wireless stations, fully equipped and manned, and many observation flights were made. As the aircraft, laden with wireless equipment, could still only rise to 5,000 feet, they were constantly protected by DH Scouts, Vickers Bullets and Bristol monoplanes. Bristol fighters, which only arrived in October, were held in reserve until the night before the battle.

At this crucial moment, while preparations were being made for the great battle and advance on Jerusalem, Geoffrey was suddenly ordered home. It was a terrible blow. He wrote to Peggy on 18 October 1917:

My dearest, I have been ordered home. I am so very glad for your sake, but miserable for mine. I was so revelling in all my work out here, and here I am at HQ in the Field commanding the RFC as well as running all the training in Egypt and the other RFC elsewhere. Brancker is coming out to supplant me of my birthright and I am disgruntled. But he won't be here for a little time so I am still free. I am not leaving until I have handed over everything. But my heart is bound up with this baby of mine; I have seen it grow and grow till it was at last nearly walking and then I should have been really satisfied after I had shown it to the world as a fully fledged child. But Bang! orders for home, personal even to the C-in-C, and I have to return to do other work. Of course it is all muddled up with Jack having DG IIA and Brancker's position becoming impossible. On the other side I recognise that Brancker fully deserves a spell of active service, so from his point of view it is all justified. Well, there it is. Now, darling one, for the best side. I expect I shall be in London although I have not the faintest idea what it is I am going to do. We will have a house or flat – you must choose – I prefer a flat. You must decide whether it is to be in London or Roehampton or where. A house, if at Roehampton. I suppose I am going to be in London, though I don't know. You must find out from Jack. We will enjoy it, darling, and I do so look forward to all this part of it. I am extraordinarily fit now, I went for a long flight today and saw all the Turks' trenches and got potted at by them from their trenches. I didn't realise, however, they were firing or I would have fired back. Thesiger is very disconsolate at this news that has fallen like a bolt from the blue and everyone is so ripping about it. But alas. Mind you get a really nice house or flat. We will enjoy it so. All the children with us, how ripping it will be. I don't expect I shall leave here for at least three weeks, but it might possibly be earlier. I will let you know. There are so many changes going on at home that I do not know what I am intended for. We brought down another Hun the other day, I saw him fall. Horrible sight anyhow, especially as I was not certain whether it was one of my own. I was with the C-in-C, and he was very pleased.

But, as Brancker did not arrive for three weeks Geoff was in charge of his RFC during the great battle. The night before, 30 October, the troops were moved up to Beersheba and the RFC were up on defensive patrols from dawn to dusk, to prevent even one German aeroplane from slipping through the defences. That very day, however, one German aircraft *did* manage to avoid the RFC. On its return it was shot down, the pilot was captured and papers and maps were found on him showing that if he had returned safely the position of the troops would have been given away. Allenby congratulated Geoffrey and the disaster of the 1st Battle of Gaza was avoided. Eighteen months earlier the siege of Kut might have been avoided if the aircraft flown by Major Reilly had not come down behind enemy lines.

Geoffrey again wrote to Peggy on the same day:

My darling one, I am writing this on the eve of a battle. The letter will not go until after it has begun so no secret is out. I have been at it all day and for many days and feel happy about most timings. We brought down a Hun today, making the third. Isn't that good? We captured the pilot. Brancker is expected to land about the 1 November and will take this all from me! Crunch!! But it means I ought to see you before long and that is a great joy. The C-in-C sent his congratulations over the Hun brought down. I like him so much. He is a real man and that is everything. I do not know whether Brancker will come up here post haste or whether he will mess about in the Delta. I hope the latter. I wonder also whether he comes out as a Major General; I rather think he does, but am not sure. I can see him enjoying this, it is so ripping. And such a good lot of fellows to work with. But under its present organisation it is hard work.

On 31 October the attack on Beersheba began. It was a complete surprise. Fifteen reconnaissance sorties were made and five out of six hostile batteries seen from the air were silenced. All hostile aircraft were driven off, while most of the German air force was still grounded. The 4th Brigade of Australian Light Horse charged on the town and captured the wells intact just as they were about to be destroyed. By evening Beersheba was in our hands.

Next day, 1 November, the day Brancker was to arrive at Port Said, 14 Squadron supported an assault on Umbrella Hill. In a Naval bombardment 48 hours later the *City of Oxford*, the *Empress* and the *Raven II* took part. The German Commander, von Kressenstein, had no idea from where the next blow might fall. Meinertzhagen wrote later:

> The enemy's resistance was feeble and he was taken completely by surprise. A captured document shows the enemy believed our camouflage, and the dummy notebook was a great success, for the enemy had all his reserves in the wrong place . . . So far so good, and we enter on this Seventh Crusade, once and for all to evict the Turk from the sacred places of Christianity.

X Corps followed the capture of Beersheba with a tremendous push beyond the town. The 10th, 60th and 74th Divisions attacked all along the Turkish front and the entire left wing of the enemy line was in retreat. Von Kressenstein wrote: 'Many formations began to retreat without orders and broke into flight.' One hundred and twenty-six targets had been hit as a result of reconnaissance by the RFC, and retreating columns were bombed.

It was on 5 November, just as the battle was almost won and General Allenby was advancing on Jerusalem, that Geoffrey was relieved. Two letters from Allenby, written in his own hand from his Headquarters as he moved towards Jerusalem, survive. He wrote on 10 November:

> GHQ Egyptian Expeditionary Force: My dear Salmond, I hear that you are still in Cairo, stopped by the congestion on the Italian railways. I take the opportunity to write and thank you for the splendid work of organisation and training you carried out while you were here. Its results are shown in the mastery of the air which our flying men have attained. Their exploits have been wonderful – nothing stops them – in fighting or reconnaissance. We have won a great victory; and I wish you were with us, to take part in the success you have done so much to ensure. It must be galling to you to have missed it. I wish you the best of good fortune, and am yours gratefully and sincerely . . .

This was the best letter Geoffrey could have wished for, and he answered at once. Another letter followed, in which Allenby thanked Geoffrey for his 'kind congratulations'. Geoffrey treasured these letters. Agonizing though it was to leave Egypt, he had to return home.

A First Class Row

It seemed to the Royal Flying Corps in Palestine, and to the Egyptian Expeditionary Force itself, that the recall of Geoffrey Salmond at the height of the battle for Jerusalem showed that the War Office in London was unaware of the part the RFC was playing in the battle. In fact, it was the situation at home which had been responsible for his recall and on his arrival in London he was to find himself in the midst of a crisis. He was to find that the whole structure of the RFC was being remodelled, and that his brother Jack was to be the new Director General of Military Aeronautics in place of Sir David Henderson.

A daylight raid on 7 July in which Gothas had bombed the centre of London, killing fifty-seven people, had led to a great outcry and had sparked off a series of momentous decisions by the Government, not the least being the appeal to General Smuts on 11 July to examine the air organization generally and the direction of Air Operations. After only one week General Smuts produced his Report, which was later to become famous. In it he recommended that an Air Ministry should be formed as soon as possible, and plans worked out for the creation of a third fighting Service into which the Royal Flying Corps and the Royal Naval Air Service would be absorbed. He wrote prophetically:

> And the day may not be far off when aerial operations with their devas-
> tation of enemy lands and destruction of industrial and populous centres
> on a vast scale may become the principal operations of war, to which the
> older forms of military and naval operations may become secondary and
> subordinate.

The idea of a third fighting Service was not new, as it had been suggested by Lord Derby in 1916, and General Henderson had himself urged it in a memorandum. But to Smuts must go the credit for his vision and for its far-reaching consequences. The Report was to lead to a new attitude to the Royal Flying Corps and a reshuffle of personnel. Sir David Henderson, whose wise counsels had helped General Smuts, was to run the Air Organization Committee to work out details of the new Service and was to be succeeded as Director General of Military Aeronautics (with a seat on the Army Council) by Major General John Salmond. This appointment was to take place in October.

At this time Jack was only thirty-six years old. His appointment had been hailed enthusiastically by the Press. The *Sunday Pictorial* wrote:

If any man can make Britain supreme in the air, that man is Major General John Maitland Salmond, the new Air Chief. . . . All who have come into contact with him have recognised in him 'the man of the future' in the development of air organisation. His appointment is a triumph of youth coupled with practical and imaginative ability. General Salmond is, above all, a great organiser and that is the quality which is needed most in the direction of our Air Service. Here is the man who, in little over a year, has multiplied the monthly output of pilots for the British Air Service [sic] by ten. Since he became responsible for the complete flying training of the RFC he has greatly improved the standard of efficiency. The new Air Chief is one of the finest pilots in the Air Service. He has flown and does fly now, day and night, every conceivable type of machine.

Jack was to take over his new appointment in October. In the same month Sefton Brancker, who had worked so devotedly in London for the RFC, was to be transferred to Egypt. He was astounded at the news, and wrote to General Trenchard in France: 'They have got me all right at last! I am to go to Egypt. Jack Salmond is to take Henderson's place on the Army Council, Henderson is to go to the Air Ministry permanently . . . Everybody's sins have eventually fallen on my head.'

So it was the situation in London that had led to Geoffrey's sudden recall from Egypt in the midst of Allenby's advance on Jerusalem. He had to leave the pilots whom he had inspired and trained, and the Middle East Brigade which he had created and which he had been so proud to command.

Just before leaving on 10 October Geoff had written in his report on the newly formed Palestine Brigade:

On handing over the command of the Royal Flying Corps, Middle East, I have to report as follows on the work recently accomplished in Egypt and Palestine. On my arrival at General Headquarters on September 10th it was decided to form the Royal Flying Corps in Palestine into a Brigade with an Army and Corps Wing organisation. On September 10th 1917, the Royal Flying Corps in Palestine consisted of two complete squadrons and one incomplete. By 20th October there were four service Squadrons, one emergency bombing Squadron, one Artillery Wing, Army Wing and Brigade Headquarters. Special efforts were made to expedite 'Contact Patrols' and at the same time our artillery cooperation was reorganised in accordance with the latest developments in France, modified to suit special conditions in this country.

Geoffrey went on to report that machine-gun mountings had been fitted to the aircraft, as well as bomb racks. Photography was also organized so that photographs of enemy trench systems, which were taken in the morning, could be despatched by air to the Army within five hours of the machine's landing. He then described how, in addition to the normal duties of reconnaissance and air co-operation, the RFC had to ensure that the enemy had no definite information as to the movement of troops from the Gaza area to the east. By patrolling the area and by sending up Bristol fighters, the enemy were kept ignorant of the real state of affairs.

At the end of October he wrote:

> Our patrols were concentrated over Khalasa and Asluj. One hostile machine was engaged on the 30th in this area, and brought down between our lines, the observer and pilot being wounded and captured whilst trying to escape. The observer and pilot quite possibly had obtained information of the final concentration at Asluj, but, owing to their being brought down, this news did not reach the enemy . . . I think it may be claimed that the measures taken for the denial of information to the enemy of the concentration eastward were successful.

He went on to say that the total number of aircraft on this front on 30 October was thirty-three. He then especially recommended Lieutenant Colonel Borton, commanding the 5th Wing, and his other officers, also his Staff, Lieutenant Colonel. P. R. C. Graves, Colonel Fraser and Captain Anne. His report ended: 'On November 17 1915, before the arrival of the 5th Wing in this country, the only Flying Corps unit in Egypt consisted of one Flight stationed at Ismailia. The Middle East organisation is now as shown on the attached plan.'

Just before Geoffrey's return, Peggy received an express letter at Ditchingham Hall, written by Jack from his office in the Strand. In it he wrote:

> Please excuse my writing. I am so dreadfully busy I must send you a type-written letter. I am so sorry I did not get your letter until yesterday or, of course, I would have made a point of seeing you. All I can tell you is this. When, on the upheaval that occurred, I was put into this job, Brancker was ordered to the Middle East Brigade. At the same time Geoff was ordered home. I believe he has started and when he does come, he will go to York and, as soon as possible after that, to France if he wants to. I am afraid he will be awfully disappointed, as everybody knows that Egypt was his show, not anybody else's. All this was done without my knowing a word about it; naturally it was before I came here. Yours ever, Jack.'

When Geoffrey arrived in England, however, he refused to go to York. Later in his life, Geoffrey always rather enjoyed what he called, light-heartedly, a 'first class row'. This was because he was always defending the Air Force against attack from whatever quarter, political or military. But now, although he had plunged into the middle of a 'first class row', he could not enjoy it, as it only concerned his own future. His whole heart and mind was with the Middle East Brigade and the pilots of whom he felt so proud. From his hotel in South Audley Street, he presented his report on the Palestine Brigade to the Air Board. He wrote to Peggy: 'I am still furious at four am every morning.'

While in London Geoff heard of Allenby's fantastic march towards Jerusalem. Although his army was exhausted after marching for forty miles, Allenby determined to press on, regardless of fatigue and the shortage of water for the horses. On 10 November Jaffa, the sea port of Jerusalem, fell, captured by the left wing of his Army. Leaving one mounted and one infantry Division on that flank, Allenby assembled the rest of his forces in the foothills of Judaea to advance on Jerusalem. He refused to fight in the Holy City itself and consequently had to make a long detour in the hills, but at length the 75th Division took Nebi Samwil, a commanding height overlooking the city. Pouring rain, however, made slippery mountain roads impassable for his cavalry, who had to retire, but Allenby himself, determined to be with his men, ordered his headquarters to move forward and himself dwelt under canvas.

At length the 60th Division broke the Turkish defences west of the city and at dawn on 5 December the city fell. Colonel Newcombe, after a gallant battle fighting until his ammunition was exhausted, had eventually been taken prisoner. 'El Aurens', as Lawrence was now called by the Arabs, had made a brave but unsuccessful attempt to blow up the Yarmuk River bridge. He was actually in Allenby's tent, explaining the failure, when a Staff Officer entered to inform Allenby that Jerusalem had been evacuated. Allenby immediately asked Lawrence to join him for the triumphal entry into the city. And so, on 8 December, Allenby entered Jerusalem on foot, by the Jaffa Gate, and Lawrence, in a hastily borrowed uniform, walked with other Staff Officers behind him.

It was always a private agony to Geoff that he had not been with them on that day. General Allenby wrote later:

> We entered on foot by the Jaffa Gate, and from the steps of the Citadel, hard by, issued a proclamation in many languages to the assembled multitude. Great enthusiasm – real or feigned – was shown. Then I received the notables and heads of all the Churches, of which there are many, including Abyssinian. After this, we reformed our procession and returned to our horses, which we had left outside the walls.

In the Proclamation Allenby had declared that, as the city was the home of 'three of the greatest religions of mankind', he would protect all the Holy Places, of whatever faith.

News of the taking of Jerusalem was received in London with wild delight. It was announced by Bonar Law in the House of Commons and for the first time for three years the great bell of Westminster Abbey was rung. The bells of every Church in Rome rang for an hour and there was a special service at Notre Dame in Paris. Congratulations poured in to Allenby himself. General French wrote to him: 'I regard the capture of Jerusalem and Bethlehem as the finest feat of the War.' During all the agony of the Western Front, the taking of Jerusalem fired the imagination of the world.

Meanwhile, in the midst of his own victory, Allenby had not forgotten the RFC and the Middle East Brigade. In spite of rain and bad weather in the battle, 113 Squadron, by dragging their aeroplanes up a hill and putting down tarpaulins under the wheels, had managed to take off safely and had made continuous reconnaissances. 14 Squadron had also managed to drop a hundred 20lb bombs on enemy installations. Now, in December, after the victory, General Allenby recommended to the War Office that the RFC command in the Middle East should be reorganized, in view of the great expansion of the Service. He recommended that RFC Headquarters should be raised to the status of a Division, under a Major General, while the training group in Egypt and the Palestine Brigade should be decentralized as separate commands, each under a Brigadier General. These recommendations were approved. Brigadier General A.E. Borton took command of the Palestine Brigade on 14 December and Brigadier General P. L. Herbert of the training camp. By General Allenby's special request, Brigadier General Geoffrey Salmond was asked to return to take over command (as Major General) of the Royal Flying Corps Middle East. Major General Brancker was to be free to return home to become, on 3 January, Controller General of Equipment in the newly appointed Air Council, of which Trenchard, as Chief of Staff, was to be a member.

Whilst in Egypt Brancker had been loyalty itself. He understood only too well the high regard in which Geoffrey Salmond was held. He himself had worked with Geoffrey so closely in the early war years and he understood the whole situation. However, he had no passionate feelings about the Middle East and was delighted to return to London and become part of the Air Council. Geoffrey, who was now in a small flat with Peggy and the children in London, was overcome when he heard the news. On Christmas Eve he was to sail. Only vague memories of that anxious time, so different from the happiness of Harrogate, remain with the children. Black curtains over the windows in the evening because of the air raids – and a cross nurse grumbling that there was no jam or cake on Christmas Day!

Peggy's father wrote one of his rare letters on 27 December:

My dearest Pegoty, I don't like to think of you alone in your flat, and I think the sooner you come down here the better . . . A lot of snow on the ground, and everything looking very wintry. We had the wounded here yesterday – about 26, and everything went off all right. Hare soup, roast beef, plum pudding without plums. Your loving father, W. Carr.

They all went back to Ditchingham, but nothing mattered to Peggy. She knew that Geoff had his dearest wish. He was on his way back to Egypt.

Return to Egypt: Shipwreck

Of course no one really expected it. As the troopship neared Alexandria on 31 December 1917 the hopes of many on board were running high. There was a group of nurses and VADs, excited at going abroad, officers and soldiers going out to join the Egyptian Expeditionary Force, and Geoffrey, who had travelled across Europe and joined the ship at Taranto in Italy, thrilled to be going back to Egypt. Only three miles from Alexandria disaster suddenly struck. The ship was mined. For many there was no time to leave the deck and everyone was swept into the sea. Geoffrey, a strong swimmer, did his best to save other exhausted people in the water.

He wrote later the same day, from Alexandria, hoping to reassure Peggy:

> My own dear darling, this will be a short letter, just to wish you a Happy New Year, and may this time next year mean the end of the War, a Victorious Peace, and myself at home with you. Today has been a terrible day in some ways – we were mined coming into harbour and the ship sank in about four minutes. Wooldridge is safe, and so am I. Our Gieves waist-coats held us up splendidly. But, darling, my heart grieves so much for the men and women who were drowned, it is so pitiable. Oh dear, I am so miserable. I was never once unhappy about myself, except perhaps for one tiny moment, and this makes me feel tormented with the idea that had I thought more, I might have done more. It all happened so quickly that one had hardly time to realise the tragedy of it all. We were about three miles from land. We struck the mine at 10.30 am I will tell you more in my next letter. My darling, I thank God that I am alive. I wish, I wish I felt quite happy that I could have done no more to help the ones who were drowned. Your ever loving Geoff.'

He actually had rescued several men from drowning but, as always, he wished he could have done yet more.

Three days later, on 4 January, anxious that Peggy had had a gap in her letters since he left on Christmas Eve, he wrote a long letter, for a letter he had written in Rome was still in his breast pocket at the time of the shipwreck. It was soaking but he dried it and sent it on, and it is still in the family. He sent Peggy a cable to say he was all right, and then wrote:

> We were all on deck at 10.30 in the morning and the pilot had just come on board when bang! At once there was commotion, everyone rushing to

their places. I went off to help to get rafts overboard but found these particular ones were in an impossible place, so had to give it up. So then I went on the bridge to see what Glover who was OC Troops was doing. I was no use there, and so went down thinking I might get my despatch case before she sank, but the cabin door was locked. When I came out the ship was obviously going to sink any moment so I stepped over the rail and jumped into the water. She sank in four minutes. I went overboard about one minute before she sank. Curiously enough I had filled [inflated] my Gieves waistcoat [a life jacket] half full that morning, and was carrying it about in my hand at the time of the explosion. Once in the water I felt quite all right. I had my Burberry without the lining, and field boots on. I floated wonderfully well and the water was not cold. I felt so much all right that I could not imagine that people were drowning. Poor things, they were, but I never saw or realised what had happened when the ship went down. Some people could never have come up from below, others must have been caught by the explosion, others would not leave the ship and others were so frightened of the water that they literally drowned themselves in fright. I had no idea that people could be so hopeless over water. But I realise now that lots of them, poor chaps, only read lurid accounts of disasters at sea, they have never been in the water except in a bath and they don't, or can't, believe in lifebelts, with the result that either they go down in the ship because they can't trust themselves to the sea, or they do go in and are so frightened that if they swallow any water they are done for. Well, after swimming for about eight minutes I came up to a man, a RNR officer, who kept saying 'I am done, I am done'. He was floating quite well, and was really all right but he imagined things. I caught onto a plank and gave it him and eventually pushed him to a destroyer.

A Japanese destroyer had come to the rescue, and the sailors were letting down ropes to save the men in the water. Geoff went on:

I was feeling so absolutely all right that I refused to be taken on board and swam about to help fellows who might be done. I did this for some time until I got hold of one poor chap who was in a bad way. He got his legs round me and wouldn't let go. Luckily it was at the destroyer's side so there was no real danger although it was not at all comfortable. I got a looped rope round his shoulders and he was pulled up. After this, and because an overturned boat floated up and kept pressing me against the side, I decided to be pulled in . . . I shouted to the sailors in Japanese, much to their surprise, and made them make a loop at the end of the rope as I could not keep a grip on a plain rope. It was only when I was pulled on board that I realised that there would be loss of life, because a man came alongside who was hauled in, but though we worked on him with artificial respiration for quite two hours he never came round.

Geoffrey told the sailors to put loops at the end of all the ropes, as they let them down. His year in Japan as an interpreter had proved invaluable in the crisis. He went on:

The mine went off at 10.30 am and we did not get into port until 3.30 pm. It was extraordinary how the time simply flew. You can imagine I was pretty cold. I had my thermogene wool on my back and the salt water made it quite hot, and it felt like a furnace, so that probably helped things. The saddest part was we lost seven or eight Sisters. I believe some of them, thinking they were so close to land, had left off their life belts. They were all detailed for boats and the usual horrible things happened. Only one boat really got away. The rest were overturned. Looking back on it, I feel bad about the Sisters because although I only saw one boat overturn whilst it was being let down, I ought to have thought it might contain Sisters. But the truth is that so many people were already in the water and so much was happening so quickly – she sank in four minutes – that it did not strike me at all as anything very dreadful. I don't suppose I could have helped much, but I might have prevented other boats being let down in the wrong way, or overloading, which, I understand, was the chief cause of their turning over. There were 37 Sisters and VAD on board. One Sister was simply splendid in the way she worked. A number of men (about 190) were drowned. (I can't imagine how, unless they were imprisoned by the explosion). On shore we were given a fresh suit of Tommy's clothing, and I was a fine sight in Tommy's coat, trousers and rope shoes. All my clothes were dried in 24 hours and look quite all right. But everything I had was lost, including my photograph of you, darling, you must at once send me some out. Write to the Harrogate man and send out some of those. I must have them. All the rest of my kit I can get out here. I am gradually collecting it, and can carry on quite well now. Only one or two officers were drowned, all the rest including Glover, Caddell and the old man Mackenzie were saved. Also General Burney. I am living here at present; I am undecided when to leave. I suppose I was twenty minutes in the water, but it was so warm that I did not feel it. It was waiting about afterwards that made me cold. Your present, dearest, of the Gieves waistcoat and Woodridge's was what chiefly saved us. Thank you darling one, so much. I am sending you by this mail my letters written from Rome . . . I had them in my breast pocket, also one for mother, and they have dried all right . . . I do not yet know whether I am a Major General. I have never received anything official. Dalmeny is coming down from the front tomorrow, and I shall hear then. I met Lady Allenby after Church today and she seemed very nice. Dearest darling, all my love and my kisses. Ever your ever loving Geoff.'

A few days later Geoffrey's briefcase, containing important documents from the War Office for the Expeditionary Force in Egypt, was washed up on a beach near Alexandria. After the papers had been dried they were handed to General Allenby.

Geoff's next letter to Peggy was quite cheerful. He wrote:

You are a dear to be packing up parcels for prisoners, dull as it is, it must give them tremendous joy to get them. General Bols came down from the front and I took him over all the schools and workshops here yesterday. He was very impressed, and so he should be! I did the same for the C-in-C a few weeks ago. I dined with them one night and we went to a show afterwards. This Cairo life is like London, I wish I wasn't doing it.

He said he would much rather be in France and went on:

I am still hard at work; there is so much to do. I am so sorry you got anxious, it was the first cable going awry. I do hope you have got some of my letters by now. I hear of some that have arrived home, from the shipwrecked ones, that are censored out of all recognition, so that may account for a lot. I am so glad you got my cable before you heard about it. I felt anxious about that but I knew Jack would know I was all right.

During December Lloyd George had been so delighted with the capture of Jerusalem that he had pressed Allenby to advance further towards Damascus without delay, but General Allenby had demurred. His men needed to recover and to rest and he needed to reorganize his army before attempting a further advance. He cabled to General Robertson that, if an advance on Aleppo was required, he would need sixteen infantry divisions. General Robertson, of course, felt that this was impossible and Lieutenant Colonel A.P. Wavell, who at that time was liaison officer on General Allenby's staff, was sent home to mediate between London, the Supreme War Council at Versailles and Cairo. Fortunately General Wilson, one of the leading figures at the Council, recommended that Allenby should have all the support he needed, subject to the security of the Western Front and his suggestion was adopted on 8 January. Nevertheless, a mission was sent out to Egypt under General Smuts to report back to the War Office and to consider how best the Council's directive should be carried out. It was Geoffrey's first meeting with the great general.

Meanwhile, Allenby was most co-operative and helpful. When Smuts returned, he took to London suggestions which were almost identical to Allenby's own plans, the main difference being that owing to the crisis on the Western Front, reinforcements consisting of three Divisions and one Cavalry Brigade should be drawn from Mesopotamia, supported by one Indian Cavalry Division from France. After these reinforcements were trained, he recommended that Allenby should attack across the River Jordan, after which there would be an advance up the coast, isolating Damascus. Railways for supplying the Army must be reconstructed, while the Hejaz railway should be destroyed, thus isolating the Turkish Medina force. The result of General Smuts' report was that soon the three Divisions from Mesopotamia were returned to Egypt to take part in the advance and one Indian Cavalry division arrived from France.

Allenby had moved his Headquarters yet further from Cairo, to a point between Jerusalem and Jaffa. He also arranged with a reluctant Lawrence that Feisal's Arabs should now become officially a part of his Army and directly responsible to himself, rather than being a wild collection of tribes who were a law unto themselves and only spiritually obedient to their venerable ruler, Hussein, in Mecca. They were to be called 'The Arab Army of the North'. Lawrence accepted Allenby's judgment, although he knew that the Arabs were far happier sweeping down on the enemy, blowing up trains and disappearing into the desert in a cloud of dust than being drilled into any conventional pattern.

⋆   ⋆   ⋆

While General Smuts had been making his report in Egypt, things had been moving very fast at home. Lord Rothermere had been chosen by the Prime Minister to become the first Secretary of State for the newly-formed Air Council, which had replaced the Second Air Board. After consulting General Haig, Trenchard had agreed to become the Chief of the Air Staff. Jack Salmond was to take Trenchard's place as Commander of the Royal Flying Corps in France. He was delighted at the prospect of once more being in the field 'to command a force which he had helped to create and which he had trained'.

The Air Council met first in January at the Hotel Cecil in the Strand, which had been chosen after much deliberation, the Victoria & Albert Museum or County Hall also having been suggested. It was here that the first plans for the new Service, combining the Royal Flying Corps with the Royal Naval Air Service, were to be thrashed out. Sir David Henderson's previous work proved invaluable, but even so there was not a happy atmosphere and tensions and difficulties inevitably arose.

In only three months General Trenchard resigned, unable to agree to a system in which he felt he was not given enough scope for his own plans for the RAF. Always intensely loyal to General Haig, who was so gallantly resisting the enemy in France, he could no longer bear the confines of the Hotel Cecil and its atmosphere of intrigue. It was said that he retired to a seat in Green Park. Major General Frederick Sykes, Geoffrey's old chief in France, was recalled from the Supreme Council at Versailles and appointed to succeed Trenchard as Chief of the Air Staff. Thus it was that to Sykes fell the honour of being the first Chief of the Air Staff when the Royal Air Force was formed on 1 April 1918.

With all the events that had happened in Egypt and Palestine since the arrival of General Allenby, and with things in such a state of flux in London, it is easy to overlook the steady progress that had been made in Mesopotamia since Geoff had been ordered out there in August 1916. His mission had been to command the Air and he had put Lieutenant Colonel Tennant in command of the RFC in that theatre.

By March 1917 General Maude had captured Baghdad in an operation in which the Army had been well supported by the revitalized RFC wing under Tennant. Shortly after the fall of Baghdad Geoffrey had once more visited the area and had put in hand a series of lectures on air co-operation for the Army, as he had in Egypt on his arrival in 1915. He also established an Aircraft Park just outside the city.

Maude had decided to advance on three fronts, along the Euphrates, the Tigris and the Diyala rivers, supported by the RFC. Colonel Tennant, still in command of the Wing, had carried messages to Russian Cossacks operating in Persia, and a flight of 30 Squadron had even flown over the mountains to Teheran. The arrival of 63 Squadron of R.E.8s from Northumberland was intended to reinforce the RFC, but became, at first, a disaster. They arrived in August at Basra, and the intense heat took a terrible toll of the Squadron; of thirty officers only six remained active and seventy men were in hospital in September. Temporary hangars of matting protected the aeroplanes from the sun, but the wooden frames of several machines buckled in the heat.

At length a Major Bradley, from Egypt, took over 63 Squadron, which flew to Samarra, the R.E.8s being at last supplemented by Spads, Bristol Scouts and Martinsyde Scouts. In December they carried out a successful attack on a convoy while bombing enemy fields. Eventually the Turks retired to Tikrit.

Meanwhile the arrival of 72 Squadron in March 1918 enabled the offensive to be resumed on the Euphrates front. Ramadi and Hit were occupied, with the RFC in support. An enveloping movement by the Cavalry Brigade with horses, armoured cars and Ford vans was assisted by air reconnaissance, resulting in the capture of 4,000 Turks. Further advances along the Aleppo road resulted in the capture of the Turkish Army Commander himself, complete with his Staff. It was at this time that Lieutenant Colonel Tennant and Major Hobart of the 8th Infantry Brigade were shot down. Both men survived the crash and managed to burn their aircraft before being captured.

After a gruelling interrogation they were mounted on camels and, without rest, sent as prisoners along the Aleppo road, guarded by twelve fierce Tartars on foot. At once Major General Brooking sent a signal to Brigadier General Cassells on the spot – 'Get Tennant back'. Cassells immediately set off for Ana, only to find that the prisoners had left at 04.00 the previous day. Captain Tod of the Cavalry Brigade was then ordered to give chase with eight armoured cars along the Aleppo road. At length he caught sight of them some 32 miles beyond Ana and machine-gunned the escort. The two officers, amazed at their good luck, sprang from their camels, dashed to the armoured cars and fought their way back to Ana and Khan Baghdadi.

This was, perhaps, the first concept of co-operation between the air and armoured cars in Geoffrey's command, which would lead to the control of vast tracts of desert and which was to be one of the methods used so successfully by Jack Salmond in his operations in post-war Iraq.

It was on 7 March, soon after General Smuts had returned to England, that Geoffrey was able to visit Jerusalem. He found it a most moving experience and wrote to Peggy:

> I have returned from the most wonderful Inspection. I have been to Jerusalem and Jaffa and all sorts of other places. Tuesday, a week ago, I left by the 6.15 pm train from Cairo and went direct to GHQ, which must be nameless as regarding locality. Well, having arrived and spent an afternoon going into things, I saw the C-in-C and Bols [the Chief of Staff] in the evening and then spent the whole of the next day (Saturday) discussing our affairs and slept the night in the same place. In the afternoon Borton, MacEwen and I went for a walk. The country is like Salisbury Plain and full of flowers, anemones red and blue, cyclamen, black iris (wonderful these) and all sorts of flowers. I got up at 6 am every morning and went for a ride on my old horse, which is still there. The whole of Southern Palestine is full of German colonies with wine presses and orange and lemon groves – wonderfully developed – they remind me of Boer settlements . . . On the Sunday morning we went off inspecting and passed through the Biblical country of Jerusalem. Up to a point about ten miles west of Jerusalem there is rolling undulating country and this continues down to the sea, but at that point and eastwards as far as the valley of the Jordan the country is mountainous and it was a revelation to me what our troops had accomplished after getting to Jaffa when they swung eastwards and fought the Turks through the mountains to Jerusalem . . . I had always imagined Jerusalem in a plain. It is nothing of the sort, it is situated high on the side of a mountain and is surrounded by mountains. Passing through the outskirts I stopped at one house occupied by a Gunner General, the same old boy with the helmet who was at the station at Charing Cross when I was leaving this time, and who

was wrecked with me on the *Osmenie* and nearly got done in – well, he is stationed in Jerusalem now. I stopped for a pow-wow about co-operation and then went on to Rafi Allah which is not far from Samuel's tomb, where we had a balloon. I went up in this and saw Jerusalem, Jericho, Dead Sea, etc. A wonderful view. I had never been in a balloon before and was terrified at the prospect. I must say it is a nerve-shocking introduction as they make you get in with all sorts of braces, which is the harness you wear and is attached to the parachute, and they give you a dagger to use in case you have to parachute, to cut the rope of the parachute just when you are landing. Otherwise you may get dragged. By the time I got into the balloon basket after all these preparations I was almost speechless, my legs shook but I don't think anyone could see them. My voice sounded extremely small when I spoke to the Balloon officer with me! It is a curious sensation being cooped up like that, just quiet, 2,000 feet or more above the earth. Gradually I got used to it, my voice grew louder, my legs got stronger and I began like a baby to 'take notice.' If I had remained much longer I should have probably begun criticising the equipment in the balloon and end up by making the balloon officer sorry he had taken me up!

It should be noted that parachutes, though allowed for those in balloons in the First World War, were not introduced into the RAF generally till 1927.

Geoffrey was only up for about a quarter of an hour and then went on to Jerusalem with MacEwen. He said there was a wonderful view from the Mount of Olives over Jerusalem and the surrounding hills. He continued:

The Monday morning we spent with a Turkish Catholic guide going round Jerusalem. I could not spare longer than half a day. But such a morning – so, so wonderful. I saw the places where Solomon's temple used to be, and where Christ overthrew the money-lenders' tables. I saw the Beautiful Gate where Christ entered riding on the donkey. I picked some grass plants growing between the flagged stones to send to you because I thought it so wonderful that actually here He had trod . . . I saw the place where Pilate judged Christ and where He took His Cross and struggled up the hill, where He could go no further, where Simon took the Cross and where He was crucified. Peggy darling, it was so enthralling to think that here the Man we have all chosen as our model, our God, had lived and endured the supreme tragedy while knowing He was doing it all for us. People talk of miracles and question the miracles in the Bible in their arrogance, but the greatest miracle of all to me is that within the comparatively small compass of Jerusalem lived this Man, the example of whose life has spread and spread until it embraces millions of people. Nothing brings it so home to one as Jerusalem with its historical places and every race in the world walking about it like any other town.

Geoffrey bought a little gold cross for Peggy and a pearl one for little Joyce. He flew over the 'wonderful Judean Hills', saw Bethlehem below and landed to inspect a squadron, leaving for Jaffa in the evening. A dried flower, an anemone, picked by Geoff in Jerusalem, has still survived among Peggy's letters after seventy years. It was an experience Geoffrey was never to forget and he wrote his heart out to Peggy in the midst of all the anxiety and tragedy of war.

At this time Geoffrey was presented with the Order of the Nile by the Egyptian Government - a great honour. He wrote begging for photos of the children. He knew some photographs had been recovered but wrote: 'Until they turned up from the shipwreck from the bottom of the sea I had nothing but memories, and they are difficult to see!'

Mastery of the Air

On 20 January 1918 Jack Salmond arrived in France to take up his new command. Almost at once he began making preparations to combat a German advance, which he felt sure would soon take place. In February he briefed his Wings, preparing them for an enemy breakthrough between the 3rd Army and General Gough's 5th Army, between the Sensée River and St Quentin. He also moved his own headquarters to St André-en-Bois, close to General Haig's headquarters at Montreuil, to improve communications.

It seemed astonishing to those at home that the Front which had been held for so long in France, throughout the winter, should be breached in only a few hours, but on 20 March, after a short bombardment and gas attack, the Germans, augmented by thousands of troops from the Russian front, pressed forward towards Amiens, hoping to drive the British back to the sea. Although the British were forced to retreat on the Amiens front, they held Arras in the north, and Ludendorff decided to concentrate his troops on that position rather than follow up his initial advantage. It cost him dear, for the British and French had time to reorganise their defence. General Foch was made supreme commander on 26 March and the tide began to turn.

From the outset the RFC fought with the utmost courage, attacking enemy aircraft and bombing their supply routes. Brigadier General Philip Game, Chief Staff officer to General Salmond, wrote at this time:

'The Germans have concentrated a lot of squadrons against us, but our men make short work of them. Salmond is splendid at these times, and keeps absolutely cool and unfussed, and decides everything at once, which is such a relief.'

Trenchard also wrote congratulating him, saying, 'You are splendid.'

On 25 March Jack sent this order to the 9th Wing:

> These squadrons will bomb and shoot up everything they can see on the enemy's side of the line. Very low flying essential. All risks to be taken. Urgent.

The Squadrons obeyed him heroically. Sopwith Camels, Bristol Fighters, DH4s, SE5s and RE8s flew day and night and Sopwith Dolphins also took part. On the 26th pilots reported that German forces were advancing towards Montdidier. Had that position been taken it would have severed the British lateral railway and exposed the Channel ports. Jack again ordered all available squadrons to concentrate on low bombing and machine-gun attacks in the area. The *Official History* recorded:

> The fighting pilots during the March retreat knew how dire was the position of the armies for which they worked, and they knew, also, theirs was the opportunity and power to take effective action to stem the German advance. They flew down, time and again, day after day, to within a few feet of the ground and performed many gallant deeds that will go for ever unrecorded. Apart from the casualties they inflicted and the undoubted effects which the attacks had on the morale of the German troops, the delaying action of the attacks was important.

A German officer wrote: 'Several [British pilots] flew so low that the wheels of their aircraft touched the ground, attacking us with their machine guns.' Airfields were bombed, although the pilots had often to fly through not only bullets but snow and hail. 102 Squadron was in action for seven hours and dropped 502 bombs. Many of the pilots became well-known heroes. McCudden had shot down 57 machines and was awarded the VC. On 21 April, the famous German ace, Baron von Richthofen, was shot down after a fight with Captain Roy Brown and his squadron of Camels.

On 30 March His Majesty the King himself visited the field of battle and invested Jack with the insignia of a Commander of the Royal Victorian Order. The Air Ministry also telegraphed congratulations to which Jack replied:

> Very many thanks for Air Council's congratulations, which are much appreciated by all concerned. All ranks have their tails well up, and the superiority of the British over every German has never been more marked.

From then on, Jack was always known in the Royal Air Force as 'Tails Up Salmond'. It was one of the most heartening messages in the dark days of the war.

When the news of the German advance in France reached Egypt, many troops were sent back to Europe as reinforcements. Within a few weeks two complete Divisions, the 52nd and 74th, had been returned. In addition twenty-four British battalions, nine yeomanry regiments, five and a half heavy batteries and five machine-gun companies were also sent to the Western Front, about 60,000 front-line troops altogether. The two Divisions were replaced by those from Mesopotamia, but the twenty-four battalions had to be replaced by unseasoned and often ill-equipped Indian troops. Meanwhile Australian Flying Corps units were flown to Egypt to combat the renewed German strength in the air, and fast motor launches were brought up to operate on the Dead Sea. Their flagship, *Miranda*, had once been well-known on the Riviera, where she had won prizes for her owner, the Duke of Westminster.

★   ★   ★

Throughout the summer of 1918, while it was far too hot and humid for the Army to take any decisive action, the troops were trained and reorganized.

Meanwhile Geoffrey Salmond, whose Wings were now well equipped with Bristol fighters, RE8s and Vickers Bullets, was determined that he should have control of the skies before the great offensive in the Autumn. He had fighters now which could face the German Fokkers and Halberstadts and was determined to keep the enemy's aircraft out of action during the advance. That he was successful is shown in a despatch written by Allenby himself in October:

> Brilliant work has been done by the Royal Flying Corps, not only in the actual operation but in the preceding months. The process of wearing down the enemy's strength in the air had been continuous throughout the summer. Our ascendancy in the air became so marked towards the end of August that only a few of the enemy's aeroplanes were able to fly, with the result that my troops were immune from air attack during the operation, and the whole strength of the Air Force could be concentrated on the enemy in his retreat. Besides taking an active part in the fighting, the Air Force provided me with full and accurate information as to the enemy's movements.

Geoffrey could not have asked for a more generous acknowledgement.

He had by no means forgotten his 'City by the Sea'. He was determined to increase and perfect his Training Wing, his School for Aeronautics and his Cadet Wing. He was also especially proud of the Eastern Aircraft Factory, which he had himself created. It was in the summer of 1918 that the very first aircraft, an RE.8, was produced there. The RE.8 was a successor to the BE.2

two-seater observation aircraft which had been designed by Geoffrey de Havilland at Farnborough in 1912. A photograph of this first aircraft shows it surrounded by mechanics, riggers and fitters, and of course, standing proudly with them was Geoffrey Salmond.

The Palestine Brigade now consisted of the 5th Wing (14, 112 and 142 Squadrons) and the 40th Wing (111, 114 and 145 Squadrons) plus a Balloon company, an Aircraft Park, an aircraft depot and an engine repair depot. By September 1918 the number of new squadrons had increased to seven.

One of the most significant events of the summer was the arrival in Egypt of the great Handley-Page O/400 twin-engined bomber, successor to the 0/100, which had first flown in 1915. The O/400 was now to be flown out from England, a tremendous adventure in those days, by Brigadier General Borton and Colonel MacEwen on the very first non-stop flight to Egypt. Geoffrey planned to meet them when they arrived and decided to meet them in the air. From Aboukir he wrote to Peggy:

> August 8 1918. I came down here by air yesterday afternoon to meet Borton and MacEwen, on hearing Borton was arriving at Aboukir. I called up Heliopolis, had lunch, went back to the office, motored to Heliopolis and the machine that was to take me up arrived as I drove up and we left at 3.45 pm. I stayed up quite a long time (I was being flown) in the hope of meeting them in the air. But in the end our petrol was running short so we had to come down. However, we had no sooner landed than they loomed up in the distance. I can't say more than this, because of the censor. I am going up with them to Cairo this afternoon by air. Last night I dined with them here, and tonight we mean to have a great Air Force gathering.

On the way to Cairo, Geoff took the controls and piloted the huge Handley-Page himself. This aeroplane was the only machine of its class in Egypt and according to Lawrence, the 'apple of his eye'.

The success of Geoffrey's offensive against the German Air Force was vividly described in a lecture he gave later in the year. He said:

> In August 1918 the Palestine Brigade had attained mastery in the air. By this I mean that although occasionally German machines did fly, if they once saw our machines approaching they never fought, but went to ground, the personnel ran off, whilst our machines flew round and round and set them on fire. This position was not attained without hard fighting, but by August over ninety hostile machines had been destroyed. I want to make the point clear in order to explain how it came about that we were permitted to use the Royal Air Force to such great advantage in the campaign that was shortly to open up.

The battle, which was to start on 19 September, was to prove one of the great battles of history. It was not only to contain the last major cavalry advance but it was the first absolute proof, in Egypt, of the power of the RAF in modern warfare.

It was said that General Allenby himself had conceived the plan after a morning's ride. He strode into the office of his Operations Staff and announced it in outline. It was to be the Gaza-Beersheba movement in reverse. Allenby and Smuts had already decided to attack the Turkish right along the coast, and Allenby now decided that, after an infantry assault, the Cavalry Corps would ride through the breach across the Plain of Sharon and then turn eastward across the range of hills, some forty miles behind the enemy line, cut the Turkish lines of communication and, after forcing a capitulation, move on to Damascus. Geoffrey wrote describing the plan:

> The General's scheme was based on surprise. The 21st Corps, on the coastal sector, was to force the enemy's left, wheel half right and force him to the foothills. The remainder of the Army, i.e. the 20th Corps and Chaytor's force, were to hold the enemy. As soon as the 21st Corps had opened up a way, the cavalry were to stream up the coast, protected by two torpedo destroyers, and reach Affule, a nodal point on any possible line of retreat. Then, stretching out still further, they were to reach Beisan, a further point on the Jordan. At the same time the 21st Corps with a further advance by the 20th Corps were to press the attack and force the enemy to retreat, when they would finally be met by the Cavalry who would block their lines of withdrawal. General Allenby's scheme, therefore, envisaged the complete encirclement of the enemy, imprisoning him between the Army in the south, the coast on the west, the cavalry to the north and the Jordan to the east.
>
> No special instructions were given to the Air Force beyond asking for their general assistance. Immediately this general plan was received, the senior Air officers were called into conference and the enormous opportunities of realising to the full the possibilities of the air arm, to achieve results we had dreamed of, were realised. To start with, our command of the air enabled us to practically guarantee the concealment from the enemy of General Allenby's plans; it enabled us to suggest plans for still further misleading the enemy, it made it possible to destroy his communications centres and lastly it enabled us to contemplate the destruction of his retreating forces. We had the means, we had the power, with any ordinary luck, of greatly adding to the success of the operation.

Geoffrey suggested, from his knowledge of air reconnaissance of the area, that the sector on the right should be made to appear as normal as possible. Dummy horses replaced the Australian Mounted Division when it moved to the coast, camps were left pitched and horses dragged brushwood behind them to make dust and give the appearance of army activity. The area was left almost un-patrolled, to allow the German aeroplanes to observe this, while on the left a perpetual patrol was mounted. Between 12.30 and 14.30, when horses were allowed to water, the patrol was strengthened. Captured German maps after the battle showed that this ruse was successful. In addition, in order to give the enemy no hint of Allenby's plan, no air activity or bombing took place until the very day of the battle, starting at 01:00. Geoffrey wrote that he was pressed to carry out bombing raids before this date but decided against it. He continued: 'Meanwhile Allenby made great use of the Arabs under Feisal and Colonel Lawrence. They were a sort of flying column on the extreme desert right.'

In September Colonel Lawrence entered Amman secretly and made arrangements for £4,000 worth of forage to be collected in various villages in the neighbourhood by 20 September. This information was immediately trans-ferred to the Turks. On the 15th, 16th and 17th, Arabs under Lawrence attacked the Pavaan Junction. Geoffrey wrote:

> This junction is strategically very important, for here join the railways from the south of the Hedjaz, via Amman, the railway running east and west to Haifa and the railway to Damascus. The Royal Air Force co-oper-ated to such effect that captured documents stated that all signals, telegraph and telephone communications were destroyed.

After this attack several German aircraft were transferred to this area and a reserve battalion was hurried up to Haifa, thus depriving the German High Command of a reserve to block the British cavalry when they advanced.

At last all preparations were complete. On the night of 18/19 September at 01.00 hours the Handley-Page, piloted by Ross Smith, took off with sixteen 112lb bombs and scored direct hits on the Turkish Headquarters and central telephone exchange at El Afula, thereby denying the whole of the Turkish Seventh and Eighth armies in the Plain of Sharon any knowledge of Allenby's movements during the next two vital days. Ross Smith returned that evening and again early next day and bombed the railway and airfield at Jenin.

Early on 19 September General Allenby stood outside his headquarters with his watch in his hand. At precisely 04.30 hours his great voice boomed 'Zero'. Immediately the sound of the barrage was to be heard. The attack had begun. After a short opening bombardment, the cavalry began to stream forward along the coast road. Geoffrey was determined that on the day of the battle no German machines would leave the ground. This was achieved by placing two SE5s with two bombs each, all day long, over the enemy's airfield at Jenin. Describing this he wrote:

These machines were relieved every two hours, and before leaving came down and machine-gunned the hangars. On the slightest sign of movement during these patrols, bombs were dropped. This threat, thanks to the low state of the German morale, was entirely successful and no machines left the ground.

It had been a magnificent piece of organization. Perhaps the most anxious time had been the very early morning of the 19th. It had been vital that no inkling of the enormous mass of cavalry – three Divisions – waiting to burst through on the coastal road should be conveyed to Turkish Headquarters. Their discovery would have been disastrous to the whole plan, but the air patrols had been entirely successful and the cavalry advance achieved complete surprise.

It was now seen that the German VIII and VII Armies could only retreat along certain roads, which had all been photographed prior to the operation by the RAF and were watched throughout by Bristol Fighters with long-range wireless. Once the enemy columns were located, a message came through to RAF Headquarters and bombing reserves sallied forth. In addition to these special precautions, the usual reconnaissances were carried out.

Two of Geoffrey's own inventions were used. The first, a special message-picking-up apparatus, which was used by Wing Commander Primrose, in liaison with the cavalry, proved especially effective. Secondly, the air-delivered smoke-screen was used on three occasions, but the cavalry there moved so swiftly that it was no longer found useful.

Geoffrey flew with General Borton to Affule aerodrome on 19 September, soon after the arrival of the cavalry. Afterwards he wrote to Peggy:

> I followed the Cavalry Division out to Beisan, in fact, we hid them for a short time. It was grand. Before leaving, I brought a message back by air from the Cavalry Corps Commander to General Allenby and dropped a message on an Infantry Corps telling them all about the Cavalry and where they were. So I actually did some RAF work and I think it was probably the last time that a Major General did actual co-operations. The next day I stayed in, and during the afternoon commanded the Brigade during Borton's absence.

Nine thousand horsemen had thundered through the breach, the majority armed with swords or lances, and in ten minutes the van of the column was behind the Turkish lines and leading the way up the coast.

Allenby wrote to his wife on the 20th:

> My Cavalry are now in rear of the Turkish Army and their lines of retreat are cut. One of my Cavalry Divisions surrounded Liman von Sanders'

Headquarters at Nazareth at 3 am today, but Liman had made a bolt at 7 pm yesterday.

Geoffrey wrote:

> The Turks had long been known to have contemplated a retreat . . . and a comparatively orderly retreat was possible, given the normal condition of a heavy British attack, but they had not reckoned on the effect of attack from the air.

The Turks, attacked from the south by XX and XXI Corps, now found themselves surrounded. During the evening of the 19th and 20th the Eighth and Seventh Turkish Armies tried vainly to escape. Warned by the Bristol Fighters, General Borton, under the command of Geoffrey Salmond, sent up DH.9s, SE.5As and Bristol Fighters to bomb the retreating columns. The result was wild confusion. Geoffrey described it:

> Without real instructions from Headquarters, with telephones and signalling carts blocked on the road, with all the evidence of destruction from the air before them, and pressed by a persistent enemy in the rear, it is not to be wondered at that cohesion was lost and the retreat became a rout.

He said that many Turks, in their flight, would spring on their horses with two in the saddle and gallop to safety. The Turkish Eighth Army had collapsed and 500 Australian Light Horse rode into Jenin on 19 September and received the surrender of 5,000 Turks. The remainder of 7th Army retreated along the valley of the Nablus-Beisan road, attempting to reach and cross the River Jordan before XX Corps under General Chetwode could head them off.

It would, in fact, have been almost impossible for the Cavalry to reach them in time, even though they had marched all through the night. As it was, the aircraft were ordered to fly over the retreating column every three minutes, dropping bombs and strafing the transport. In one hour the whole column was in ruins: over 100 guns, 55 motor wagons and 900 horse transports were utterly destroyed. Many Turks were killed, others fled into the hills, never to reform. The whole of the Seventh Army was defeated and scattered. Lawrence wrote afterwards:

> The climax of the air attack, and the holocaust of the miserable Turks, fell in the valley by which Esdraelon drained to the Jordan by Beisan. The modern motor road, the only way of escape for the Turkish divisions, was scalloped between cliff and precipice in a murderous defile. For five hours our aeroplanes replaced one another in series above the doomed column:

nine tons of small bombs or grenades and fifty thousand rounds of SAA were rained upon them. When the smoke had cleared it was seen that the organisation of the enemy had melted away. They were a dispersed horde of trembling individuals, hiding for their lives in every fold of the vast hills. Nor did their commanders ever rally again. When our cavalry entered the silent valley next day they could count ninety guns, fifty lorries, and nearly a thousand carts abandoned with all their belongings. The RAF lost four killed. The Turks lost a corps.

The attack had been intended to last for five hours but in fact it was all over in 60 minutes.

Geoffrey, in a letter to Peggy just afterwards, wrote to say he had determined to walk out to see the destruction of the column:

No picture of retreat that you have ever seen can equal this column, over six miles long, packed with dead horses, dead mules, dead oxen, dead Turks, motor lorries overturned, lorries that had eventually caught fire, guns, over 80 of them – all abandoned. All control of personnel went by the board, and the result was the most complete demoralisation. This is the true secret of the extraordinarily rapid victory. We walked for 16 miles that day, and at the end I was pretty done up – so were the others, but I kept ahead of them.

During the battle Lawrence flew back to Allenby's Headquarters on the 20th to explain that all his prospects with Feisal's army were being wrecked for lack of air support. All available aircraft had been used in the main attack. Lawrence described the scene:

From Ramleh the Air Force gave me a car up to Headquarters and there I found the great man unmoved, except for the light in his eye as Bols bustled in every fifteen minutes with news of some wider success. . . . . I explained our prospects, and how everything was being wrecked by air-impotence. He pressed a bell and in a few minutes Salmond and Borton were conferring with us. Their machines had taken an in-dispensable part in Allenby's scheme. The perfection of this man who could use infantry and cavalry, artillery and Air Force, Navy and armoured cars, deceptions and irregulars, each in its best fashion and had fulfilled it. There were no more Turks in the sky – except on our side, as I hurriedly interpolated. So much the better, said Salmond; they would send two Bristol fighters over to Umtaiye to sit with us while we needed them. Had we spares? Petrol? Not a drop! How was it to be got there? Only by air? An air-contained fighting unit? Unheard of! However, Salmond and Borton were men avid of novelty. They worked out loads for DH.9 and Handley-Page, while Allenby sat by, listening and smiling, sure it would be done. The co-operation of the air with his unfolding scheme had been so ready and elastic, the liaison so complete and informed and quick. It was the RAF which had converted the Turkish retreat into rout, which had abolished their telephone and tele-graph connections, had blocked their lorry columns, scattered their infantry units. The Air chiefs turned on me and asked if our landing-grounds were good enough for a Handley-Page with full load. I had seen the big machine once in its shed, but unhesitatingly said 'Yes' though they had better send an expert over with me in the Bristols tomorrow and make sure. He might be back by noon, and the Handley come at three o'clock. Salmond got up: 'That's all right, Sir, we'll do the necessary.' I went out and breakfasted.

Lawrence continued:

Clayton and Deedes and Dawnay were friendliness itself, and also the Air Force staff; while the good cheer and conscious strength of the Commander-in-Chief was a bath of comfort to a weary person after long strained days . . . Before dawn, on the Australian aerodrome, stood two Bristols and a DH.9. In one was Ross Smith, my old pilot, who had been picked out to fly the new Handley-Page, the single machine of its class in Egypt, the apple of Salmond's eye. His lending it to fly over the enemy line on so low an errand as baggage carrying, was a measure of the good-will toward us.

Ross Smith anxiously paced the airfield at Lawrence's base, at Umtaiye, and said that the ground was OK for the Handley-Page. Meanwhile Lawrence wrote:

The three shining aeroplanes had much restored the Arabs, who lauded the British, and their own bravery and endurance, while I told them the scarce credible epic of Allenby's success – Nablus taken, Afuleh taken, Beisan and Semakh and Haifa. My hearers' minds drew after me like flames. A shiver of self-assertion and confidence ran across the camp. Meanwhile, it was breakfast time, with a smell of sausage in the air. We sat round, very ready: but the watcher on the broken tower yelled 'Aeroplane up', seeing one coming over from Deraa. Our Australians, scrambling wildly to their yet-hot machines, started them in a moment. Ross Smith, with his observer, leaped into one, and climbed like a cat up the sky. There were one enemy two-seater and three scouts. Ross Smith fastened on the big one, and, after five minutes of sharp machine-gun rattle, the German dived suddenly towards the railway line. An 'Ah!'

came from the Arabs about us. Five minutes later Ross Smith was back, and jumped gaily out of his machine, swearing that the Arab front was the place.

The sausages were still hot when yet another aeroplane was sighted. Again Ross Smith and Peters jumped into their machines, but the aircraft fled, only to be reached further afield. Ross Smith, longing to stay with the Arabs, had to leave to fetch the Handley-Page, and bring petrol, food and spares. He was to alight at Um-el-Surab. Lawrence and Feisal drove in their Vauxhall to meet him and the Handley-Page.

Lawrence wrote:

> Twenty miles short of Um el Surab we perceived a single Bedawi, running southward all in a flutter, his grey hair and grey beard flying in the wind, and his shirt (tucked up in his belly cord) puffing out behind him. He altered course to pass near us, and, raising his bony arms, yelled 'The biggest aeroplane in the world', before he flapped on into the south, to spread his great news among the tents. At Um-el-Surab the Handley stood majestic on the grass, with Bristols like tiny fledglings beneath its spread of wings. Round it admired the Arabs, saying, 'Indeed and at last they have sent us THE aeroplane, of which these things were foals'. Before night rumour of Feisal's resource went over Jebel Druse and the hollow of Hauran, telling people that the balance was weighted on our side.

While Lawrence was being supported by the Handley-Page, congratulations were pouring in for Geoffrey Salmond. Before he left the advanced Headquarters he went to see General Allenby, the Commander-in-Chief, who thanked him for what he had done. Geoffrey described the interview to Peggy:

> I told him Borton was to be thanked and he said no, it is all organisation etc. which is true, but Borton's handling was magnificent. Since then I have had cables of congratulations from Sykes, as Chief of Air Staff, and from the Air Council. Of course, we are so far away that the magnificent part the RAF played in the victory cannot easily be known. We forced them to abandon over 120 guns alone, leaving them on the roads, until we came to collect them.

It was a splendid victory, and the way was now open for General Allenby to advance on Damascus. Later *The Times* wrote: 'The part played by the Royal Flying Corps in the final advance in Palestine was particularly well conceived and brilliantly executed.' Geoffrey was also called 'The man who destroyed an

Army'. But he himself never liked to talk about it afterwards. He had realized the terrible potential of the aeroplane and the awful possibilities of bombardment from the air.

Victory

General Borton had accompanied the giant Handley-Page himself when it was flown by Ross Smith to meet Lawrence. Ever since his flight from England to Egypt in July, the first flight ever to have been made between the two countries, he had found it hard to part with the great machine and already both he and Geoffrey Salmond felt it capable of ever further flights which had never been attempted before. But they realized this was for the future, when the war was over.

After his return to Headquarters, he and Geoffrey decided to take a few hours off, away from the fighting. They flew in a small aircraft to the Sea of Galilee, hoping perhaps to rest by the lake for a few hours. In fact, the cavalry had been fighting there that day and, after talking with them, they realized they could not stay any longer as it was becoming late, which would mean landing in the dark. It was still an adventure to fly at night in those days, and the return flight proved to be a more rewarding experience than they could have imagined. In their small aircraft they flew above the clouds and found that the sunset was shedding a soft golden light over the banks of cloud below. Geoffrey wrote afterwards to Peggy:

> The sun was setting in the west and a great sea of cloud came up, shutting us off from the land below, like an enormous sea of cotton wool. The reflection of the sun in this was truly magnificent. There we were, right above the sea with only the setting sun and stars beside ourselves, perched between the sky and the clouds. We weren't in the clouds but above them, so our view was just unimpaired. It became darker and darker and nothing could be seen below except the occasional flicker of a campfire that looked up through a narrow opening of the cloud. On and on, darker and darker, till a glance at my watch told me we should be near our destination. But cloud, cloud, cloud – nothing to be seen. Minutes passed, still we went on, when suddenly flickers could be seen, the cloud was breaking. Staring at these, no aerodrome lights could be seen, but after a time they suddenly appeared. Then, brrr-rr – the engine throttled down, down, down – till Borton made a perfect landing on the aerodrome we started from.

Later, of course, a flight above the clouds at night was not a new experience but in their small aircraft, with its open cockpit, lack of instruments and fragile wings, it was a new and thrilling adventure, especially as General Borton was piloting it himself. The aircraft was not only an instrument of death and destruction – once again it had been, for a few hours, a miraculous machine which could conquer the air. Both 'Biffy' Borton and Geoffrey Salmond felt the magic returning, and it was then that they decided on more adventurous flights together. They were now to plan further record-breaking flights in the huge Handley-Page, perhaps to Baghdad or India, or even south to the Cape. The possibilities seemed endless.

Meanwhile Lawrence, supported by his Bristol fighters, pressed on towards Deraa and Damascus, while Allenby's forces, particularly the ANZAC Cavalry, were sweeping forward in pursuit of the retreating Turks.

Mounted on their swift camels, the Arabs were first to reach Damascus and poured into the city to a tumultuous welcome. Sadly, the bitter political strife which then broke out, particularly over the future of Syria, put Lawrence in an impossible position, torn between his loyalty to both Allenby and the Arabs.

The main difficulty was the Sykes-Picot Agreement, which had given Syria to the French. Lawrence declared that he did not know of it and had always felt that Feisal would be ruler of Syria including the Lebanon, but excluding Palestine. Feisal himself came to the meeting and Allenby described him: 'He was mounted on a big Arab [horse] with a large escort of Arabs, all mounted. He is a fine, slim, sharp-featured man of about 35. Lawrence was there too, and interpreted. I had a long and satisfactory talk with Feisal. He will take over the administration of Damascus, or rather will put in a Military Administration. His flag now flies.' But Feisal refused to work with the French. He was only responsible to Allenby directly, and Allenby persuaded him to wait until a conference could be arranged to decide on his claims. With these political tensions around him, and torn between his conflicting loyalties to Allenby and the Arabs, Lawrence no longer felt he could stay in Damascus, and immediately asked for leave, which was granted. He left at once for the long journey to London. As he drove away cries of 'Aurens! Aurens!' followed him. After he left, Allenby cabled to the War Office, asking that Lawrence should be granted an interview, not only with the Foreign Office to explain the Arab claims, but also with His Majesty the King.

★   ★   ★

Meanwhile, in France, the attack on 27 May had been almost the last great effort on the enemy's part. It was originally meant as only a diversion, as Ludendorff was still hoping to attack the British front at Hazebrouk. But so successful was the initial advance that the German High Command had been tempted into throwing in more reserves and so had maintained the attack too long. Strangely enough, the fighting was over the same ground as the British retreat in 1914. Fère-en-Tardenois and Soissons were reached on 29 May and by the following day the German 'flood' had swept on to the Marne. But here, as they had intended in 1914, they turned towards Paris. Petain ordered up fresh reserves and the advance was checked.

In June, General Ludendorff moved his reserves up to capture Reims, hoping that after securing the railway he could divert some of his forces to take part in his proposed attack in Flanders. This attack, however, was never to materialize as the Allies, strengthened and encouraged by the arrival of Americans, were able to plan a brilliant counter-attack. Just as the Marne had been the turning point in the retreat from Mons in 1914, so now, four years later, the second battle of the Marne was destined to be the point at which the first German retreat began. The tide of the German advance was checked on 18 July, and three days later the German collapse started, under pressure from the Allies. At the same time the Americans, under General Pershing, had counter-attacked at Château Thierry. The tactical success of the German Army had proved a strategic reverse.

In all these battles, the RAF under John Salmond had never ceased to fly over enemy lines, keeping their aircraft low to the ground wherever possible. They had also fought large formations of German aircraft in the air. Sometimes as many as 50 or 100 aircraft would fly to the attack together, and the battle would develop, almost as though there were two armies fighting in the sky.

At this time, Philip Game wrote to his wife:

> Salmond is a good soldier and I have an enormous admiration for him. He is a real commander, exempt from petty faults. We had a man staying with us last night who is on leave from Egypt and says that Geoff Salmond has done perfectly splendidly there. They really are a fine pair, the Salmonds, aren't they?

As the Germans fell slowly back to the security of the Hindenburg Line, the Allies, determined to keep up the pressure and maintain the initiative, began to prepare for a massive offensive in early August. Just as Geoff was doing for Allenby in Palestine, so was Jack winning complete air superiority across the 14-mile front of General Rawlinson's Fourth Army, enabling the Staff to make their extensive preparations in absolute secrecy. Thanks to a brilliant deception plan and the unfailing efforts of the Royal Air Force, when the blow fell on 8 August absolute surprise was achieved.

More than 450 tanks and every available aircraft, working in close co-operation with a huge artillery fire plan, supported Rawlinson's infantry in the most intense assault of the war. The Germans were devastated and the Hindenburg Line, which had for so long seemed impenetrable, was shattered. Ludendorff would later describe 8 August 1918 as 'the Black Day of the German Army'.

But the war was by no means over. Throughout the ensuing period known as 'The Hundred Days', which saw some of the bloodiest fighting of the year, Jack's pilots got little rest as they harassed the retreating Germans and fought to keep the skies clear over the advancing BEF. Meanwhile Trenchard's Independent Air Force, which had an in-depth bombing role, was concentrating on the German bases and several major cities, with a commensurate impact on the enemy's morale. Co-operation between the ground and the air forces was particularly effective.

Ludendorff's dream of a Flanders Victory had vanished and the Kaiser was lamenting: 'We are at the end of our resources'. It was clear that the only way forward was to negotiate as advantageous a peace as was possible in the circumstances.

Late in October Geoffrey had written to Peggy:

> Isn't the war going wonderfully? It is like a miracle. Bang bang go the props upon which Germany has rested for so long. She is collapsing all round. I only hope President Wilson does not listen to their last piece of window-dressing on the part of Max of Baden – I don't think he will.

★   ★   ★

It was now November, 1918. Far away, in the quiet of the Norfolk countryside, Peggy was still nursing wounded soldiers at her aunt's hospital and William Carr was still drilling his Volunteers in the park at Ditchingham. Food was becoming scarce and there was a rumour of an epidemic of influenza. Joyce and Anne, on 11 November, were at their great grandfather's house, having their lessons. They were never to forget that morning. The library door opened and the old butler stood there holding a huge Union Jack in his hands. Tears were pouring down his cheeks. 'The War is over, sir,' he said. 'Shall I hang this on the gatepost?' Little Anne felt the blood rushing to her face: if the war was over her father would be home. Of course, he was not, but on their walk through the country lanes back to Ditchingham Hall, they saw flags, Union Jacks and Stars and Stripes, hanging from all the cottage windows. Early next day Peggy wrote to Geoff:

> My dear darling old thing, peace was declared yesterday and I write this at 6.45 am before going to the hospital. Isn't it glorious and splendid and wonderful and seems far too good to be true? I feel so wonderfully glad and happy I don't know what to do. I can imagine you, too, back in Cairo again now I suppose, with all the plans of invasion through the 'back door' blown to the winds. (I imagine that was what you went to Salonika to arrange!) The hospital will be off its head with excitement this morning. Think, there is no barrage in France today, and the armies are resting and no more bomb raids tonight. I wonder what Jack is doing? (Wednesday)

I had no time to finish this yesterday . . . of course I am hoping every minute of the day to get a wire saying you are coming on leave. If I didn't think you were quite certain to come I would come out and I hope you will take me back with you. I do wish I had been in London on Monday. Doro says it was too thrilling for words. Everyone went quite mad and rushed about shouting, swarming on to the taxis and buses, dancing, and even kissing the policemen! (This last I can't quite believe of Englishmen but she says she saw it!) I expect you were very happy in Cairo. We down here were very quiet, with church bells ringing and guns and fireworks, but nothing wildly exciting! Don't you think the terms are more than you ever hoped for? I must say they astonish me. It must be simply too awful for the Germans. The downfall of the Kaiser, War Lord, is quite tragic and almost incomprehensible – he seemed to have such absolute and overwhelming power, even a year ago, didn't he?

Peggy ended her letter by warning Geoff of the influenza which was spreading like wildfire. She said their own doctor at the hospital had died of it, and begged him to be careful. She wrote that she would go out to Egypt herself . . . 'but it would be so lovely to have you back first.' And so, with the Arab flag flying in Damascus, the Armistice signed in France, bells ringing out across Europe and policemen being kissed in London, the long and tragic four years of the Great War were at last over.

5

THE FIRST FLIGHT FROM EGYPT TO INDIA

Whether it was their flight together after Allenby's great battle which had inspired Geoffrey Salmond and Brigadier-General Borton, or whether it was Geoffrey's vision of the capacity of the aeroplane to reach far wider horizons, or just the plain fact that the huge Handley-Page O/400 was lying temptingly idle on the airfield at Aboukir, whatever the reasons, Geoffrey and his friend decided on a daring long-distance flight together, which was to go down into history and even find a place in the Guinness Book of Records.

They decided, only a few days after the Armistice was declared, to fly together in the O/400 to Baghdad, a journey which normally would have taken three weeks by car and train. The journey by air would take them across 500 miles (805 km) of unmapped and waterless desert, where there were no roads or signs to guide them, only the occasional tracks of camel caravans which wandered slowly between Amman and Baghdad. Then, if all went well, they hoped to fly on to the furthest reaches of Geoffrey's command — India itself. It would be the first flight ever to have been made direct to Baghdad and on to Karachi. Geoffrey played it down in his letter home to Peggy, written on 28 November:

> I am off to Baghdad in a few hours. I do hope, dear, that you are coming out. We shall have such fun together. It will be lovely. I hope to be back in a week. I am going to Baghdad to (a) inaugurate the journey, (b) discuss post-war policy there and (c) inspect my squadrons. I am going with Borton and Ross Smith.

Both he and General Borton had complete confidence in the O/400 and also in the pilot who chose to accompany them, none other than Captain Ross Smith, the brilliant young Australian aviator who Lawrence had described as 'climbing like a cat up the sky' only a few weeks earlier in pursuit of the German Fokker aircraft.

Plans were swiftly made, perhaps all the more so as there was no knowing in the euphoric climate at home whether the great aircraft might be recalled or, with 'demobilization' on everybody's lips, whether the vital partnership of Geoffrey Salmond, Borton and Ross Smith might be broken by orders from home.

And so it was that, only seventeen days after the war was over, the three set out, the two Generals who had supported Sir Edmund Allenby all through his advance and the pilot whom they had both admired so much in the final rout of the Turks. Two mechanics accompanied them and they took a ten-day supply of water and food, which was essential if they were forced to land in the desert between. The stakes were high: there was the danger of being lost and perhaps never found in the vast desert and also the danger of falling into the hands of unfriendly tribes. The distance between Cairo and Damascus, which was comparatively well known to them, was 385 miles (620 km.), while the distance over the desert between Damascus and Baghdad was 523 miles (842 km.).

Perhaps the best description of the flight was given by Geoffrey himself in a lecture a few years later. By that time a regular route had been established from Cairo, but his words bring back his own feelings during that first adventurous flight. He said:

> You leave the aerodrome at Heliopolis at 5 am and rising rapidly you see the Delta unfolding itself before your eyes. The Pyramids, looking like tiny hillocks, lie just over the tail of the machine. Stretching away to the northwest and northeast, and from the apex of a triangle, lies the desert fringe of the Delta. To the west, dimly, you can see the blue haze of the Mediterranean, whilst to the east the Bitter Lakes on the Suez Canal can be distinctly seen. Striking north-east, you skirt the north-eastern edge of the desert and pass the sector Ismailia Qantara at 6 am, crossing the Suez Canal at the same time. At 7 am you are traversing the great battlefield of Gaza and at 8 am you see the churches and mosques of Jerusalem. At 8:10 am you are over the Jordan.

On that first flight, they stayed at Damascus for the night and set off the next morning for Baghdad. Geoffrey wrote:

> The country beneath you becomes absolutely waterless and at first it is marked by great stretches of black lava for 60 miles – but at 11 am, leaving the lava behind you, you are sailing steadily over the desert. No living habitations can be seen for miles and the majestic solitude of the desert surrounds and penetrates every fibre of your being. At 7 pm, however, a shimmer is seen to the east, and gradually this forms itself into the Euphrates which is crossed at Ramadi, the first inhabited place to be seen

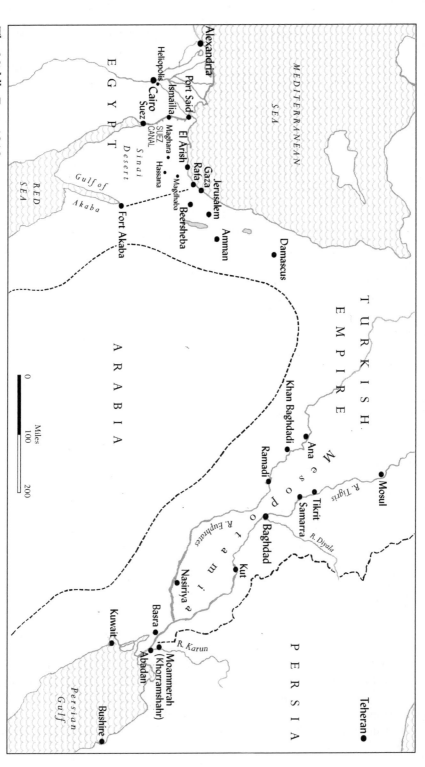

The Middle East, 1918

MEDITERRANEAN SEA

EGYPT

Alexandria
Heliopolis
Port Said
Cairo
Ismailia
Suez
SUEZ CANAL
Maghara
El Arish
Hassana
Gaza
Rafa
Magdhaba
Bersheba
Jerusalem
Amman
Damascus
Sinai Desert
Gulf of Akaba
Fort Akaba
RED SEA

ARABIA

Miles
0
100
200

TURKISH EMPIRE

Mosul
Khan Baghdadi
Ana
Ramadi
Tikrit
Samarra
R. Tigris
R. Diyala
Baghdad
M e s o p o t a m i a
R. Euphrates
Kut
Nasiriya
Basra
Kuwait
Moammerah (Khorramshahr)
Abadan
R. Karun
PERSIA
Teheran
Bushire
Persian Gulf

since leaving Amman. Steering due west, you are over Mesopotamia and from this area the country appears desolate and waste except on the banks of the river, and even these banks do not appear to be richly cultivated. In about half an hour's time, the domes of Baghdad appear, and at 3 pm you are landing.

Although the times must differ, from this later description one feels that in every line Geoffrey was remembering his own first flight to Baghdad.

On Geoffrey's arrival, Mr. Scott Liddell, the representative with the Expeditionary Force in Mesopotamia, cabled as follows:

Baghdad. December 1st 1918. General W. G. H. Salmond, commanding the Air Force in the Middle East, arrived at Baghdad this afternoon, having flown from Cairo. They left Damascus this morning at 7.40, arriving at Baghdad in 6 hours 50 minutes. Today's distance of 510 miles was a non-stop flight. After flying north-east along the Jebel Esh Sharki Range to Palmyra the machine was steered due east till the Euphrates was reached and followed the stream to Ramadi, thence across to Baghdad. The flight was made in a Rolls Royce-engined Handley-Page over a waterless desert. . . . General Salmond on arrival told me that the weather was perfect and the conditions ideal. The importance of the flight lies in the fact that it marks a direct route to India and the Far East. The ordinary time of a journey from Cairo to Baghdad is two or three weeks. General Salmond's flight occupied 12 hours thirty-five minutes.

The flight seemed, at that time, an astonishing feat, bringing Mesopotamia so much closer to Egypt.

Next day, Geoffrey, Borton and Ross Smith decided to continue the flight to Karachi. They flew from Baghdad to Bussorah, Bussorah to Bushire, then on to Bandara Abbas, Charbah and from Charbah to Karachi. Their average speed was 70 miles an hour and the actual time from Cairo to Karachi was 36 hours. From Karachi they flew on to Delhi, another 480 miles (772 km), where they received a tremendous welcome.

The local Indian paper reported their arrival:

Major General Salmond and Brigadier General Borton added a new and striking exploit to the wonderful records of the Royal Air Force and established an aerial link with the East that has vastly impressed the imagination of local India. The Viceroy and the Governor of Bengal advanced to receive the Generals as their aeroplane dropped to the ground.

The Times pointed out that

> The flight was not undertaken in an attempt to fly against time, but to place General Salmond in a position to advise the Government of India on the best route to be followed in the future.

Immediately, the possibility of a regular service arose. *The Times* continued:

> The atmosphere conditions are favourable for an uninterrupted service to be maintained all the year round over the route, and it is understood that there are no difficulties in the way of a regular service which cannot be overcome.

Both Geoffrey and Borton were delighted with their success. However, amid all the congratulations and telegrams which reached them in India they both knew that in spite of their successful and dramatic flight, huge obstacles and great difficulties, both practical and political, lay ahead before their vision of the future could come true.

★   ★   ★

In England, after the wild celebrations at the Armistice and the happiness of welcoming the returning soldiers there was, as always, an uphill struggle. Those who had gone to France as boys returned as thin, anxious men. They had been promised 'Homes for Heroes' but for many this never materialized. There was even a strike at Southampton among soldiers who were expecting to be discharged but were ordered abroad again. General Trenchard was home and was asked what he could do. He calmly controlled the strike, listening to every man's anxieties and freeing most of them from all blame. His enormous value as a leader was recognized and was not forgotten by Lloyd George. He was to be knighted in the New Year's Honours list for his services in the Field, but refused to take any credit, saying that the honour belonged to the RAF and was 'entirely due to the exertions of the officers under me'.

Early in December 1918 Lloyd George found himself Prime Minister once more after the 'Coupon Election', with a huge vote of confidence. He immediately sent for Winston Churchill, who had been Minister of Munitions for the past few fateful months, and offered him either the Admiralty or the War Office, but after consideration he asked him to take the War Office adding, almost it seemed as an afterthought, 'And you can take the Air too', a gesture which was to have far-reaching effects. It was extraordinarily fortunate for the Air Force, still under a year old, that Winston Churchill, with his sympathy for everything new and adventurous and in particular for the aeroplane, should be Minister for Air, and perhaps even more fortunate that he admired and trusted General Trenchard.

With stringent economies necessary on all sides and plans to reduce the armed forces dramatically, it would have been quite possible to have agreed with Admiral Beatty, the hero of the Navy, or General Wilson that the RAF should be broken up and the aeroplanes returned to the Army and Navy. The biting remark of General Wilson early in the War, describing the Air Force as 'coming from God knows where, dropping its bombs on God knows what, and going off God knows where' was still quoted, in spite of the glorious record of the pilots. Many Admirals and Generals of the Senior Services felt that now the war was over a separate Air Force was not necessary. All credit must be given to General Smuts' 1917 report and to Trenchard's White Paper, for it was they who really saved the RAF.

General Sykes, the Chief of the Air Staff had, meanwhile, with great vision and foresight, produced a detailed and comprehensive plan for the future of an independent Air Force. However, in the atmosphere of drastic economy and reductions which pervaded Whitehall and Westminster, his plan was not considered feasible immediately, although it held a vision of the future vast expansion of the RAF. A more modest but equally comprehensive plan was put forward by General Trenchard. This recognized the necessity of a much reduced complement, while emphasizing the necessity for training of a high standard. The upshot was that Trenchard followed General Sykes as head of the RAF when Sykes was given the position of Head of Civil Aviation. With great self-sacrifice, he left the Service to take up the position, and was thanked by Winston Churchill in the House of Commons. General Trenchard, later Sir Hugh, was to find his task one which only a man of immensely strong character could carry out. His determination and complete honesty must certainly have appealed to Churchill in the difficult years which followed.

Soon after Christmas Geoffrey was able to return home on leave. All Peggy's plans for going out to Egypt had had to be postponed, for in December Joyce had developed bronchial pneumonia. In those days, before antibiotics and penicillin, pneumonia was a very serious illness and she had to be nursed day and night. Peggy could not leave her side until, in January, she began to recover. 'Flu was still raging in the country when Geoffrey arrived and Peggy went up to London to meet him. Both caught the virus and brought it down to Ditchingham. In their weakened state of health so soon after the war, the whole household, with the possible exception of Mr. Carr, then went down with it. The three children were nursed by Peggy's sister Dorothy as soon as she herself had recovered, as their nurse was desperately ill. Fortunately her own sister appeared to look after her. All the servants were nursed by Peggy's sister Joyce. After an anxious time for everyone at Ditchingham, Geoff had to return to Egypt in February, by which time the family was more or less convalescent.

As soon as he returned to Egypt, Geoffrey began work on the desert route which he was planning for the Middle East. After his own record flight to India he visualized the flight of commercial aircraft to distant parts of the world, taking mail and passengers, even drawing people of all nations closer together. He envisaged a mail service from Cairo to Baghdad, a route which could be flown at the first sign of any disturbance in Mesopotamia and by which aircraft could fly safely and swiftly to India. At the same time he had been asked to lay out an air route from Cairo to the Cape, which he had, in fact, begun planning even before his flight to India. The main difficulty was the enormous swamp near Gondokoro – the Sudd – which had defeated many explorers. If an aircraft should be unlucky enough to crash into it, the result could only prove fatal. With a gigantic map of Africa on the wall of his office, Geoffrey was constantly at work plotting alternative routes.

On 12 March he submitted his scheme recommending air routes to the Middle East and Africa to General Sykes, as Head of Civil Aviation. Sykes took him to see Winston Churchill who expressed approval of Geoffrey's plan, saying that the proposed organization was an Imperial project and he wanted further details. At this time Churchill was going with Lloyd George to the Peace Conference in Paris, and, just at first, it seemed as if Geoffrey's project for the Middle East might be delayed indefinitely. Disappointed by the slow response, he wrote to General Trenchard. In his letter, a copy of which, in Geoffrey's own handwriting, is kept in the RAF Museum at Hendon, he wrote:

> Air Ministry, April 10th, 1919. Dear General, I have been very anxious to see you for some time, as I felt that you would want to know when I proposed returning, and also I wanted to let you know what I have been working at all this time and obtain your views. Actually I have brought this question of the future organisation of commercial flying in the Middle East and India up to the point which, provided it goes through, will I feel sure be of the greatest assistance to the Air Arm in the Middle East in all its dealings with them and also to the future of commercial flying in these parts and to the aircraft industry in general.

He also told Trenchard of his visit to Winston Churchill and went on:

> I have advocated the formation of an Imperial Air Transport Company, backed by a Royal Charter, to run the route from Cairo to India and thence to Australia, and the Cairo/Cape route. This company [is] also to be responsible for commercial development in Mesopotamia up to the Caspian, Persia and Afghanistan and also for the Imperial development of India. It could also be responsible for development in the various countries on the Cairo-Cape route.

In recommending this Imperial Company Geoffrey was once again showing his remarkable vision of the future, for Imperial Airways, which was to take over all these routes, was not officially formed until 1924. He went on:

At first I thought this company might be found by amalgamating Holt Thomas Aircraft Manufacturing Company, Handley-Page, Bristol and Vickers for Air Transport work. However, after talking to Holt Thomas and Handley-Page it became quite clear that they would not amalgamate, although Holt Thomas said he might amalgamate with Sopwith and the Bristol people. But the more I discussed this question with these people, the more I saw that they were out for their own particular show . . . and since the Company that obtains the Cairo-Karachi contract will practically secure the monopoly, it was easy to see that in the end probably only one firm would survive, and that would probably be the Aircraft Manufacturing Company. This would stifle all the aircraft industries in the country and be bad for England's aviation. This led to the conclusion, and I feel sure it is correct, that the Board of Directors of this great Imperial Air Transport Company should not be individuals actually interested in aircraft construction firms. There are so many Imperial and other interests involved. They should be big, sound well-known business men in a position to give their orders for aircraft to all and sundry, provided they, the firms, could supply the machines they require.

Geoffrey visualized the Company as becoming immensely powerful. He thought it would be necessary that members of the controlling board should have no business interests in aircraft construction if competition and progress were to flourish in the aircraft industry. He felt most strongly that there should be no small firms competing with each other in Egypt and India. He wrote:

> I feel most crashes, loss of life and an inevitable set-back to aviation for a good many years would take place.... I look on strong maintenance service under a common policy as the key to success. A large organisation can ensure this, a small organisation never can. And that is why I am so anxious to see the policy settled before I return.

Although he advocated the Imperial Company so strongly, he also sent in a report which included the comparative expenses incurred by a large company or by the Government, and it was quite clear that if the RAF itself was to run the desert route it would be far less expensive than financing a large company. The bases would already be there, the personnel would be Royal Air Force officers and mechanics, the Handley-Page could be used to start the service and the advantages would be very great. The journey from Cairo to Karachi was expected to take only 36 flying hours, and a total journey from London to Karachi only nine days, while it took three weeks by ship. It was this second plan which Trenchard was to put forward to the Treasury in May.

Meanwhile Trenchard himself had been seriously ill with 'flu and pneumonia. At first he refused to confess that he was ill and was cared for anxiously by Maurice Baring, but eventually he was nursed back to health by Katherine Boyle, the widow of one of his great friends. During the summer all his friends who, of course, included Geoffrey and Peggy, were delighted to observe that he was actually falling in love, and in fact he was married on 17 July at St. Margaret's, Westminster. Lady Trenchard was tall and beautiful and amusing, a marvellous help to him in all the difficult days ahead when he had to fight and fight again to preserve the independence of the Royal Air Force.

Knighthood. Planning The Desert Route

While Geoffrey was planning the route from Cairo to Karachi, the Peace Conference in Paris was occupying everyone's thoughts. Lawrence, determined to do his best for the Arabs to whom he had promised so much, translated for the Emir Feisal at the Conference, wearing an Arab head-dress with his khaki uniform and medals, standing beside the tall, dignified figure of Hussein's second son and looking like a figure out of the Arabian Nights.

Immediately after the Armistice, and following the signature of the Sykes-Picot agreement, Mesopotamia – soon to be called Iraq – had been declared independent by Britain and France. This Franco-British Declaration was followed at the Peace Conference by arrangements that Syria, Palestine and Iraq should become 'Mandated Territories' under the newly-formed League of Nations. France was to be responsible for Syria and the Lebanon. However, it was not until 1920 that Iraq was properly established. A National Government was formed in that year and in October Sir Percy Cox was appointed High Commissioner. In the meantime, the country had been the scene of rioting and unrest.

★　　★　　★

The spring and early summer of 1919 had been very happy months for Geoff and Peggy. Geoff was home on leave and Jack was back from the Army of Occupation to command the Inland Area. As always, the brothers met and discussed everything, especially the future of the RAF. It was at this time that the ranks and titles of RAF officers were settled, and Peggy always remembered the discussions. 'Wing Commander' and 'Squadron Leader' seemed to come quite naturally, but when 'Air Commodore' was suggested it caused some anxiety on the part of the Navy, while the title of 'Air Marshal' was hotly opposed as being too close to the French 'Mareschal.' Sir Henry Wilson, always a critic of the RAF, considered that 'the ridiculous title of Marshal of the Air would bring the rank of Field Marshal into disrepute'. Even the King gently remarked that 'Marshal of the Air' might seem to poach on the preserve of the Almighty. He suggested simply 'Marshal of the Royal Air Force' and this title was, of course, adopted.

His Majesty also praised the RAF Ensign. The red, white and blue roundels which had been so gallantly borne on the wings of the wartime RFC and RAF aircraft were permanently adopted. To General Trenchard and all those in the RAF who had served in the war they were a badge of courage.

Honours had been showered upon Jack for his brilliant command of the Air Force in France. The French had awarded him the Legion d'Honneur and the Croix de Guerre. On his return to England he was created a Knight Commander of the Order of the Bath (KCB). Meanwhile, Geoff had been given a bar to his DSO in January and in the June Birthday Honours was made a Knight Commander of the Order of St Michael and St George (KCMG), in recognition of his outstanding work in the Middle East and especially in support of Allenby's triumphant operations in which Geoff's squadrons had frequently been decisive.

It was a time of great happiness. Even the children felt the relief and joy after the depression of the war years. Their grandfather put up a marquee in the park at Ditchingham Hall to celebrate the peace with his volunteers and all those soldiers from Ditchingham and Hedenham who had come home from the war. Joyce remembered an amusing scene in the nursery at Ditchingham. As a rule, the old butler, Baker, never mounted the steep back stairs to the nursery, but when the knighthood was announced he appeared in the doorway, to the surprise and amusement of the nurse and nursery-maid. 'From now on,' he announced solemnly, 'you must call Mrs Salmond Your Ladyship.' There was delighted amusement from his audience and he added, 'You may call her Your Ladyship when you first speak, but later on in the conversation you may call her My Lady.' Great hilarity followed his slow departure down the stairs.

Trenchard asked Geoffrey to return to Egypt on 6 June to train many more recruits in Cairo, to replace those demobilized. He was to organize the necessary expansion of his training establishment and establish a new facility to replace the old Eastern Aircraft Factory. The Aeroplane Supply Depot was to be divided by Geoff into two parts: a construction branch in which aeroplanes would be built and a supply branch.

Letters from Sir Hugh Trenchard to Geoffrey followed in quick succession. Sir Hugh had not forgotten the Desert Route, and was tremendously enthusiastic, although economy was always stressed in his letters. One of the first requirements was, of course, a grant from the Treasury, and Geoffrey said that he wanted full authority to spend £100,000. While he felt his greatest headache would be a solution to the overheating of engines in the hot months, he needed the necessary hangars and transport before he could even start the route. Trenchard stressed that the route should be primarily for military purposes 'as owing to the unsettled state of affairs in India, it will be in continual use'. In May a rising in Afghanistan was put down by the RAF, which dropped a bomb on the enemy headquarters at Kabul, suitably impressing the Indian Government with this manner of subduing small frontier risings. They became very interested in Geoffrey's project, but Geoffrey's hopes were dashed by Trenchard in his next letter, for he wrote:

> 10 June, 1919. Trenchard to Salmond. The letter has gone to the Foreign Office, enclosing a copy of the scheme of the Cairo-Karachi route. I am pushing the Government but have received no answer yet, and I am pushing the Treasury but no answer yet. Yours H.T.

Geoffrey wrote from Egypt in June:

> As regards the Cairo-Karachi Air Route, Major Baily will be leaving for Damascus in a very few days to blaze the route across the desert from Damascus via Gabut to Abu Kemal. The Deraa-Gabut sector is very disturbed at present and I am despatching the teams via Damascus to start with. The route will be marked every twenty miles and should be completed by the beginning of August.

He had not yet decided whether the Central Air Communications should be at Bushire or Basra but felt Bushire might be best and would decide when he went out. He was also establishing Security Posts at Damascus and Abu Kamal. He wrote:

> As soon as the desert has been marked they will listen in when machines are known to be travelling across the desert and should anything happen to an aircraft, they will receive news of this by wireless.

In July 1919 Geoffrey went to India, for he hoped that the Government there would be able to support part of his programme. Later in the year he was able to assure General Trenchard that the Indian Government had indeed agreed to be responsible for the upkeep of the stations and buildings in the Persian Gulf – Bushire, Bunda Abbas and Charbar – while the RAF would be responsible for the supply of personnel. There was to be a Central Communications Station at Shaiba (near Basra) which would provide for the maintenance and repair of any aircraft along the route. However, owing to the heat and lack of amenities it would be important that RAF personnel should be changed frequently.

In October Trenchard sent Geoffrey in India the good news that the Cabinet had finally sanctioned the Cairo-Karachi Route and would support it. On 4 November he wrote:

> Find a means of sending whole squadrons, if necessary, by the Cairo-Karachi route. It is vital for us to keep our Air Force for service purposes

in the three storm centres – Egypt, India and Mesopotamia. We have to use happy-go-lucky methods at present, until we can get the personnel trained, which will be in a year or 18 months. It is no good drawing up great schemes of what could be done when there are no men available.

Sir Hugh was still dogged by the necessity for strict economy and felt it was impossible to support the Cape-Cairo Route financially at the moment. 'I can do nothing until I have swept away the war wreckage,' he said.

But in spite of everything, by the end of 1919, the Desert Route was no longer a dream. The Cabinet supported Trenchard and India had become responsible for the buildings and maintenance of the stations on the Gulf. Plans were being made for no less than ten O/400s to take part, supported by DH.9As. It was a most exciting prospect.

It was not only Geoffrey Salmond and General Borton who seized the opportunity to become pioneers of an air route so soon after the war. As 1919 dawned it seemed almost as though aircraft designers and pilots all over the world felt a new sense of freedom and refused to be tied down by the pervading deprivation and poverty. The RAF was drastically reduced in Britain, but the great aircraft firms, Handley-Page, the creator of the O/400, Vickers, A.V. Roe and Tommy Sopwith all continued to produce new aircraft designs, at whatever cost to themselves.

The first airline passenger flights between Paris and London were inaugurated on 8 February 1919 by a Farman F.60 Goliath, owned by the Farman brothers, Maurice and Henri, and piloted by Lucien Bossontrot. Civilian flying was still not recognized in England, so the payload had consisted mainly of military passengers, and it was not until 22 March that the first sustained regular service for commercial passengers was opened once more by the Farman brothers between Paris and Brussels. Civil flying in Britain was not actually restarted until 1 May, after the publication of Air Navigation Regulations. It is interesting to note that the first Certificate of Airworthiness was issued on that date to a Handley-Page O/400, one of which had completed the Cairo-Karachi flight so magnificently only six months previously. That machine, left in India with General Borton and the pilot, Captain Ross Smith, was taking part in an examination and exploration of the route which was to result in Ross Smith's brilliant flight to Australia later in the year.

Quite surprisingly, even though so much had been done to promote the popularity of air travel, those who attended the Peace Conference in Paris almost always preferred to travel by steamer and train rather than face the adventure of a flight across the Channel, which was still considered rather risky. Perhaps they were right, for General Sir Frederick Sykes, always courageous, when returning from the Peace Conference with his pilot, Knott, in an open DH.4 crashed on landing. Despite being badly hurt, he pulled his dying pilot free. He was temporarily blinded and in hospital for two weeks. However, when he recovered, he continued to attend the Aeronautical Commission with Seely, as British representatives. He announced that Britain intended laying out airways to India, South Africa and Australia and in July, 1919, produced a Memorandum to the Air Ministry, proposing flights from England to Australia via Egypt and India and the East Indian archipelago. He also recommended the Cairo to Cape route, but his vision was always frustrated by the lack of Government financial support for civil aviation.

A short time earlier two brave British Officers, Captain John Alcock and Lieutenant Arthur Whitton Brown, had made their historic first non-stop flight across the Atlantic in just under 16 hours. This achievement must have brought great joy to Geoff as proof positive of the immense possibilities of long-range flight. It could surely now be only a matter of time before such crossings became commercially viable and permanent traffic across the oceans by air commonplace.

Regular civil air services were now springing up in England. A.V. Roe started one between Manchester, Southport and Blackpool on 10 May with three Avro aircraft, although it was to be discontinued in September. The first practical light aircraft to be produced after the war for civilian use was the Avro 534 Baby. Although the prototype crashed on take-off on 10 May, its 35hp. Green water-cooled engine was salvaged and restored in the second aircraft, which was to win its class in the Aerial Derby on 21 June.

It was as though the pre-war pioneering spirit was back. While Alcock and Brown had shown that it was possible to fly the Atlantic in only a few hours, A.V. Roe, Sopwith, Handley-Page and Vickers captured the public imagination by providing air routes not only to France and Belgium but to Egypt, India and beyond.

Trenchard's White Paper

While Geoffrey Salmond and Brigadier General Borton had been blazing the first trail by air across the desert to Baghdad and Geoff was planning the route from Cairo to the Cape, Sir Hugh Trenchard was reshaping and reforming his plan for the future of the Royal Air Force.

He persuaded Winston Churchill to support him, writing a long report dated 11 September 1919, in which he wrote that there were only two alternatives for the future of the RAF – either it was to be used 'simply as a means of conveyance, captained by chauffeurs' for the two senior Services, or there could be an 'Air Service which will encourage and develop airmanship – and to make a force that will profoundly alter the strategy of the future'. The result was that Churchill gave his blessing to Trenchard's vision and presented the report to the Cabinet at the end of October. In an accompanying paper Churchill exploited the difference between true airmen and 'sky-borne chauffeurs'.

With his foreword, Trenchard's Paper was to become the famous White Paper which was to form the foundation of the Royal Air Force and which would play such an important part in the lives of both Jack and Geoffrey Salmond. Trenchard's well-founded confidence in them would lead to their appointment to positions within the Royal Air Force of the utmost importance and, ultimately, to each becoming Chief of the Air Staff.

It was to be the guiding vision for many years to come and when Sir Hugh Trenchard retired in 1929 he was to say

> I have laid the foundations of a castle, and if nobody wants to build anything bigger on it than a cottage, it will at least be a very good cottage.

Ten years later C. G. Grey wrote: 'Today a castle has been built on his foundations, far bigger than ever he visualised when he laid them.'

In his report Trenchard wrote: 'The problem confronting us, the problem of forming the Royal Air Force on a peace basis, differs in many essentials from that which confronts the older Services.'

First of all, he planned a smaller and yet effective force, the regular officers to be joined by those with short service commissions, entirely independent of the Army and Navy. He jettisoned any idea of training his men with the Army, for he wanted to build up an entirely new Service, inspired and led by the daring spirit which his pilots and observers had shown in the war, and yet based on a firm and enduring foundation. Although he visualized a small active force, he was to concentrate above all on training. He wrote:

> We now come to that on which the whole future of the Royal Air Force depends, namely the training of its officers and men. The present need is not, under existing conditions, the creation of the full number of Squadrons we may eventually require to meet strategic needs, but it is first and foremost the making of a sound framework on which to build a Service. First, we must create an Air Force spirit, or rather foster this spirit which undoubtedly existed in high degree during the war, by every means in our power.

He recommended the creation of an Air Force College for Officers, to be built at Cranwell in Lincolnshire, where Naval officers had been trained during the war and, just as important in his eyes, a training school at Halton for boys who wanted to join the engineering and mechanical branches, for this side of the RAF was always considered as important as the pilots who flew the aircraft. The engineers who kept the aircraft flying had shown themselves as self-sacrificing as the pilots and aircrew during the war, and Trenchard was determined to preserve their unique spirit. There were to be other 'foundations'. Five experimental stations were to be created – a navigation school, a wireless and electrical training school, a school of photography, a balloon school and even an airship school. There were to be two aircraft repair depots, one mechanical transport depot, three stores depots and an airship station. One factor he insisted upon was a comprehensive programme of research. He wrote:

> One matter of supreme importance has not yet been mentioned, namely the provision made for research. The Departments of Supply and Research are being transferred from the Ministry of Munitions to the Air Ministry. Steady and uninterrupted progress in research is vital to the efficiency of the Air Force, and to the development of aviation generally, and on it depends both the elimination of accidents and the retention of the leading position we have established at such heavy cost during the war.

Geoffrey himself, on his return from Egypt three years later, would be the first Officer to fill the position of Air Member for Supply and Research in London.

It was inevitable that the launch of the new Service, at a time when all the emphasis in Whitehall and Westminster was on massive disarmament and swingeing economies, should have had to be conducted in the face of extensive cuts in manpower and aircraft. There were many other frustrations, not the least of which was fierce inter-Service rivalry. Nevertheless, thanks to Trenchard's visionary but eminently practical White Paper, the future of the Royal Air Force seemed to be on a more hopeful and stable footing than had seemed possible only a few months previously, and another great long-distance flight was to take place before the end of the year.

In September 1919 the Commonwealth Government of Australia offered a prize of £10,000 to anyone who could fly from England to Australia. To Geoff, who had long dreamed of such a venture, the news must have seemed too good to be true. He swiftly set about organizing an attempt on the prize. He chose Captain Ross Smith, who had flown with him and General Borton to India in 1918, to make a survey of the route. Ross Smith recommended that from Calcutta the route should be: across the Bay of Bengal to Rangoon and then across Thailand and the Gulf of Siam to Penang and Singapore, then Batavia (Surabuya in Java), Kupang and then after crossing the Timor Sea, to Darwin in Australia. Thence, via Thursday Island and the Queensland ports, to Sydney and Melbourne.

It would be a wonderfully romantic and exciting adventure and Ross Smith at once volunteered to make the attempt provided he could fly the magnificent Vickers Vimy bomber.

With Geoff's blessing, Ross Smith wrote to Vickers, describing the route and adding, quite calmly: 'The longest distance is roughly 16,000 miles to Sydney by this route.' He finally put it to the firm that:

As an advertisement both in Australia and throughout the world, this accomplishment would be tremendous, especially in view of the fact that Aerial Transport Companies being formed in Australia are now approaching the stage at which they are looking for a suitable type of machine. As far as my own capabilities are concerned, I have been flying since 1915, on all types of machines, and with all types of engines including Rolls-Royce, both in England and France . . . and I have had no crashes since I graduated as a pilot, except on two occasions when my controls were shot away while flying in France.

Vickers did indeed offer him the Vimy, only asking that on arrival he should fly to Sydney and Melbourne, and then present the machine to the Australian Government. Needless to say, Geoff was wholeheartedly behind him and copies of letters and telegrams to Geoff and to General Caddell of Vickers are still treasured in the Salmond family.

Ross chose his brother, Lieutenant Keith Smith, as Navigator and two mechanics, Sergeants Bennet and Shiers to accompany him.

The Vimy took off from Hounslow on 12 November and despite ten days of trying weather conditions (freezing his sandwiches in the open cockpit) he made good progress to Basra. Reaching Dehli on 26 November, the Vimy had established a new record from London to Delhi – a welcome first dividend for Vickers! Ross was full of praise for his mechanics. He wrote: 'They are doing splendid work . . . I can hardly get them to eat and sleep when we stop at a place.' Only twelve days after leaving India, where General McEwen, the Air Officer Commanding-in-Chief, and his staff had given invaluable support, they were in Surabaya. The end was almost in sight.

Only twenty-eight days after leaving Hounslow, the Vimy touched down safely in Darwin to the wild delight of the local population. There Ross and Keith learned they were to be knighted. Ross wrote to Geoff:

The honour I have received does not worry me very much. I had always wanted to do the flight and my own self-satisfaction would have been ample reward without the KBE and the £10,000. However, I shall always be eternally grateful to you and Vickers for helping me to carry out what was then my dearest wish.

The care with which that flight had been planned and the wholehearted support that he had given to the project was typical of Geoff. It had been for the good of the Royal Air Force and for the British aviation industry and another step forward in his vision for the spread of long-distance flight throughout the world. That the flight had brought such credit to his own officers and NCOs would have delighted him above all.

The Mad Mullah

1920, the first real year of peace, dawned with high hopes for the development of the RAF and civilian flying, in spite of the tremendous reductions in men and machines which had been felt necessary. In the Middle East Geoffrey continued to help the Army to keep order in India, Palestine and Mesopotamia. Early in January, a short sharp operation threw light on the power of the Air Force to put down a rebellion with far less loss of life and disruption than the Army could hope to achieve.

In the summer of 1919 British Somaliland had become of pressing importance to the British Government. For many years the Somali Chieftain, Mohammed Abdullah Hasan, often called the 'Mad Mullah', had been a thorn in the side of the British administration. During the war he had terrorized and threatened his whole country, pillaging the villages and taking prisoners, forcing them to join as recruits for his army. Huge stone forts had been built to guard the passes into the hills and his armed bands were now roaming the land, robbing and killing all who stood in their way. Early in 1919 Lord Milner, the Colonial Secretary, had already begun to review the situation with anxiety. The only possibility seemed to be to send a military expedition, but Sir Henry Wilson informed him that at least two divisions would have to be sent, as the campaign might take many months in that inhospitable country, probably costing several million pounds. In the atmosphere of strict economy after the war this seemed a near impossibility, and yet the alternative was to leave the ruthless bandit to roam the country at will.

With great foresight Lord Milner sent for Sir Hugh Trenchard at the end of May and asked him if he could suggest a solution. At once Trenchard suggested that the RAF should take charge of the whole operation. A meeting was arranged between Winston Churchill, Leopold Amery (the Colonial Under-Secretary), Sir Hugh Trenchard and Sir Henry Wilson, the CIGS. Wilson at first objected most strongly, not at all approving of the RAF taking over, and objecting to the idea of initiating a military operation without War Office consent. He wrote in his diary:

> This evening Winston Churchill, Amery and I had a meeting about the coming campaign in Somaliland, to be conducted by the Colonial Office and the Air Ministry. I had put in a strong objection; but this afternoon both Amery and Trenchard said that under no conceivable circumstances would they ask for troops, so I withdrew my objection and gave my blessing.

Six months later, after due preparations, Geoffrey ordered a single bomber squadron of twelve DH.9s to leave Cairo for Somaliland, under the command of Group Captain R. Gordon. Gordon's staff officer was a red-haired young man, Wing Commander Frederick Bowhill, who had learnt to fly at Upavon in 1913, and who would later join the highest ranks of the RAF. Also with them was Squadron Leader John Grey, who had recently transferred from the Navy and was to be awarded the DFC for his part in the operation. The bombers were to be supported by a small camel force and a single battalion of the King's African Rifles.

As soon as the squadron arrived in Somaliland on 21 January 1920 the Mullah's main camp at Medistie and his fort at Jideli were bombed. The arrival of the aircraft was terrifying to the wild followers of the Mullah, many of whom had never seen one before, and they fled into the hills. On 28 January Jideli was occupied by the Camel Corps, whereupon the Mullah himself fled and took refuge in his main fort at Tali, but on 9 February Tali was captured. The power of the dreaded 'Mad Mullah' had been completely broken and his army scattered. He escaped with only four followers to Ethiopia, where he died soon afterwards. The operation, which had lasted only three weeks, was so successful that twenty years of peace were to follow in Somaliland.

This swift success astonished the British public and Parliament, who had been accustomed to hear about fruitless military expeditions against the Mullah almost every year since 1905. To add to the victory, the cost had been only £77,000, which was described by Amery, the Colonial Under Secretary, as the cheapest war in history! To Sir Hugh Trenchard, fighting so gallantly for the very existence of the RAF as a separate Service, the victory over the 'Mad Mullah' was the greatest encouragement. A single squadron of RAF bombers from Cairo, with little support on the ground, had demonstrated quite clearly that the Royal Air Force, if called upon, could bring about an astonishing victory in an amazingly short time with far less loss of life than a military expedition would entail. Trenchard had written in 1919: 'An Air Force cannot be built on dreams, but it cannot live without them either, and mine will be realised sooner than you think.' Perhaps the victory over the 'Mad Mullah' might have been the first of those dreams which actually came true, for Air Control had been born.

★   ★   ★

Meanwhile, there was great happiness at home in the Salmond family. Peggy and Geoff had rented a house in London soon after Christmas, at 2 Cambridge Square, and it was there on Sunday 8 February, 1920, while Geoffrey was at home on a short leave, that their son was born. Congratulations poured in, including a telegram from Trenchard, letters and messages from all Geoffrey and Peggy's friends. The girls heard the news at Ditchingham and were told that they had a baby brother. He was called John after his uncle, and the RAF was to be his life.

Almost as soon as Geoffrey arrived, Peggy began making plans to go out to

Egypt, for he had to return almost at once. There was still unrest in Mesopotamia and a rising in the Euphrates Valley, and the flight from Cairo to the Cape to be finalized. Besides these considerations, the project dearest to his heart, the Desert Route from Cairo to Baghdad and Karachi, was at last taking shape. Perhaps this was Geoff's most imaginative plan, the highly original way in which he proposed to cross the 500 miles of waterless desert between Amman and Baghdad. He had seen on his own first flight over the route that the camel caravans left ruts in the sand which were not blown away; rather, when the hot desert wind blew over them, the tracks grew clearer, for the sand piled up against the ruts, making a long shadow across the desert. Geoffrey hoped to make a track which would be visible across the wide desert from the air, and which could lead aircraft to their destination. Could he have guessed that the 'True Furrow' that he was to create would still be visible at the beginning of the next century?

★   ★   ★

There were two attempts to fly from Cairo to the Cape in early 1920. The first, organized by Lord Northcliffe and *The Times* newspaper, met with disaster, but the second flight, by Lieutenant Pierre van Ryneveldt, was more success- ful. He and his co-pilot Quintin Brand, followed the route mapped out by Geoffrey.

Two telegrams exist in the family which show the difficulties they might meet. The first reads:

> Cairo to Cape Flight. Are all aerodromes marked with circle? Attempt may be made to fly at night. At what aerodrome can arrangements be made to light signal fires, visible long distance? Have arrangements [been] made for lighting smoke fires for showing wind direction at each aerodrome? These fires should be kept constantly lighted after prearranged notice – Cable answer to these points urgently.

The second reads:

> Cairo to Cape Flight. Are arrangements reported for transfer of petrol and oil to Broken Hill, Bulawayo, Johannesburg and Victoria West at seven days notice, still in force?

An article in *The Times* of 4 February, 1920, read:

> Africa is not yet surveyed. One cannot see far through elephant grass twenty feet high or in a forest into which the sunlight cannot penetrate. The enterprise about to be undertaken is . . . a very great adventure. Then

comes the Sudd area, where masses of water plants and papyrus form floating islands . . . Sometimes these floating obstacles are of sufficient thickness to support the weight of men or of hippopotamus, at others they open and engulf the wanderer – who can neither walk upon them nor swim through them.

The article ends with a warning of even more formidable dangers:

Volcanoes are likely to cause atmospheric disturbances, which in their turn might bring about a forced landing among tribes addicted to canni- balism and inhabiting a country of dense forests wherein even scientific observers might be overwhelmed by both flora and fauna, even if they eluded the attentions of the dwarfs and the Balekes.

It was altogether a daunting prospect, but the second expedition, undeterred, set out on the same day as the article was published. They flew from Brooklands in a Vickers Vimy bomber. Unfortunately, whilst attempting an emergency landing at Wadi Halfa in the Sudan, they crashed, but the South African Government provided another Vimy and, after eleven days, they set off again. They crashed once more at Bulawayo in Southern Rhodesia on 6 March. Once again the South African Government provided a replacement aircraft, a war-surplus DH.9, and on 17 March they set off again. Three days later they reached Wynberg Aerodrome at Cape Town, where they were greeted with great enthusiasm. They had completed the first flight ever from Britain to South Africa. Pierre and Brand were both knighted by King George V and received £5,000 in prize money.

★   ★   ★

And so, in spite of criticism from the two senior Services, Trenchard felt he had much of which to be proud. He had shown the world that a few aeroplanes could not only defeat the enemy, but could keep the peace afterwards. There had been the example of Kabul in 1919 when one strategically placed bomb virtually ended the rising and there was now the adventure of the 'Mad Mullah' in Somaliland. Both Geoffrey and Trenchard felt that at last air power could be recognized as an instrument of peace as well as war.

A rising in May in the valley of the Euphrates led to the despatch of another squadron to Iraq and, as unrest was spreading, Winston Churchill consulted Trenchard on the possibility of actually policing Iraq by air. He realized, he said, that Egypt was the watershed of the Middle East. No one had contributed more to this than Geoffrey. He had created his 'city' of airfields, workshops, training grounds and repair depots to support his aeroplanes, and in Egypt a stream of young cadets were being trained to join the RAF. Record flights had been made, to Baghdad and India from Egypt, and now from Cairo to the Cape. When, in July, Sir Hugh Trenchard spoke to the officers who had served with him at Nancy, he told them he had grounds for optimism, and that he was confident in the future of the Royal Air Force.

★   ★   ★

As Peggy was determined to go out to Egypt, passports were arranged, a nurse for Penelope and the baby was engaged and a governess found for Joyce and Anne. Peggy's sister Dorothy was persuaded to travel out a few weeks in advance, to prepare the house which Geoffrey had chosen. She was to travel with Eleanor Fellowes, the young wife of Peregrine Fellowes, who was later the first officer to fly over Mount Everest. Finally, the moment came for the family to embark and, with John Geoffrey packed into a large wicker basket, they were driven to Tilbury and were soon at sea, bound at last for Egypt.

It was a long but uneventful journey. At last they arrived and the family were together again. It must have been a wonderful reunion for Geoff and Peggy, after the long years of separation in the war. He was at last able to show her all the things he had described so vividly in his letters — the 'city by the sea', the aircraft which had been constructed in Egypt, and all the sights and sounds of life in Cairo.

Always light-hearted, and very pretty, Peggy was able to slip into the social life of Cairo quite easily and was greeted with open arms by all the families of the army and air force officers stationed there, for Geoffrey was very popular.

6

THE CAIRO CONFERENCE

Winston Churchill, having been Minister for War and the Air since January 1919, succeeded Lord Milner as Secretary of State for the Colonies in November 1920, and decided at once that one of his first priorities was to settle the unrest in the Mandated Territories. Up to that time the affairs of Palestine and the newly created Transjordan had been in the charge of the Foreign Office, while those of Mesopotamia were under the India Office. Winston Churchill decided to create a new Middle East Department of the Colonial Office to unite these departments into one.

It was obvious that a Conference would have to be arranged and during the first week of February, Churchill decided that it should be held in Cairo. Perhaps the RAF's success against the 'Mad Mullah' had helped to convince him that it was indeed possible to establish air control without involving the expense of a huge military operation, for he knew that Geoffrey Salmond had built up an air force in Egypt where none had existed before. He had also been in consultation with Lawrence and other experts on the problems of the Middle East. Allenby's historic victory had driven the Turks back in a masterly campaign but now, to his distress, he saw riots and rival factions beginning to spring up in almost all the territories for which Great Britain was responsible. He felt, with Lawrence, that it was essential that Arab confidence should be restored. Even before the Conference he had been determined to suggest that Feisal should become King in Mesopotamia, now to be renamed Iraq. He had already consulted Trenchard on the possibility of policing the country by air. It was a revolutionary idea, but Churchill felt sure it could be done. Trenchard wrote to Geoffrey at the end of the month:

> The Secretary of State for the Colonies, Mr. Churchill, is probably going out early in March to Egypt to confer with the Palestinian and Mesopotamian authorities. The chief point will be the running of

Palestine and Mesopotamia. He (Churchill) is very much in favour of the Air taking control, I believe. (Keep to yourself). Broadly speaking, I am in favour of risking a good deal to Egypt and Palestine to equip Mesopotamia early. I am very keen on taking over Mesopotamia next cold weather, if not before.

An enormous hotel in Cairo, the Semiramis, was taken over for the distinguished gathering of soldiers, airmen and politicians, and for Churchill's private suite. Lawrence, who had been persuaded by Churchill to leave the quiet of All Souls College, Oxford, described it as 'very expensive and luxurious, a horrible place', but was determined to bear anything, and was at his most charming and helpful, for the sake of the Arabs.

The work of the Conference was unremitting. Sir Hugh Trenchard defined his plans, supported by his Chief of Staff, Wing Commander G. L. Gossage DSO MC. General Ironside came over from Persia, Sir Percy Cox from Mesopotamia, with Gertrude Bell, who was at that time his administrative adviser and who knew more about the various tribes and was more loved and respected by them, both in Kurdistan and Mesopotamia, than anyone else. There were Consuls and pro-Consuls, including Sir Herbert Samuel as High Commissioner for Palestine. The Conference, which had been so carefully prepared beforehand, was to take only a fortnight, in spite of the enormous amount of work which it entailed, and was to include a visit by Churchill to Jerusalem. On only the second day Churchill was able to telegraph to Lloyd George in London saying that the Conference had agreed to choose the Emir Feisal as King of Mesopotamia. It only awaited the election by the people of the country themselves to confirm his appointment. Feisal had thus at last been rewarded for his support all through Allenby's advance. His unhappy months at Damascus were at an end and he was soon to be crowned King in Baghdad. It was, to Lawrence and all his supporters, a happy result of months of preparation.

The most important decision as far as Trenchard and Geoffrey were concerned was the adoption of Trenchard's plan to use air power to enforce law and order in Iraq, as Churchill had postulated. After putting his reasons in a long report, Trenchard wrote:

> To render the Air Force scheme of control a success after the conditions enumerated above have been realised, it is absolutely essential that the command of all the forces in Mesopotamia is vested in an Air Officer, who should serve under the superior political authority. Given the best will in the world, it cannot be possible for the instructions of an Air Officer to be carried out through an intermediary Military Commander. In an essentially Air Scheme, which has been propounded above, the lack of knowledge of the Military Commander in Air matters could only

tend to produce serious arguments as to the nature of any operations which might be required for any purpose, and also with regard to the actual means of carrying out the operations themselves. Should a Military Commander prove to be very strong-willed, with an overpowering personality, there is no doubt that he would direct the plans and decisions of the Air Officer serving under him. This, of course, would only tend to produce entire confusion, and foredoom the scheme to failure.

This was a broadside across the bows of the Army, but was approved in principle by the Conference. If the scheme was brought into operation the Imperial garrison in Mesopotamia would be reduced to one brigade and one pack battery instead of the alternative military complement of twelve battalions of infantry, one cavalry regiment, one field battery, one pack battery, one sapper and miner company and five squadrons of the RAF.

In Trenchard's scheme, with a local Arab army, properly equipped and trained, the element would consist of four squadrons of single-engined two-seat DH.9s; one squadron of single-seat Snipes; one Corps reconnaissance squadron of Bristol Fighters; and two squadrons of twin-engined Vimy bombers converted to take ten or twelve armed men, and capable of carrying a load of cargo for the purpose of supplying posts of troops by air. A further reconnaissance squadron might also be necessary. This was obviously a far more economical method of exercising control than mobilizing the army. The only difficulty was over the supply of armoured cars, which Trenchard hoped the Army would at first be able to supply.

Geoffrey was present at almost all the meetings of the Conference. The matter of greatest interest to him, of course, was the Desert Route, which was also discussed with considerable enthusiasm. According to the Report of the Conference:

> The Secretary of State impressed upon the Conference the necessity for carrying out a far-sighted policy of Imperial air development in the future. One of the main air routes of the Empire would undoubtedly be that connecting Egypt with Mesopotamia and India, which would shorten the distance to Australia and New Zealand by eight or ten days. He directed that the Committee should examine the possibilities of opening up a route across the desert from Palestine to Iraq.

Geoffrey was to preside over this committee. He recommended that the route should run via Amman, Azrak and Ramadi. He arranged that at intervals there would be dumps of petrol so that pilots could refuel, and large white arrows should be marked across the rocky outcrops of the desert. Landing grounds could be marked by large circles drawn by Crossley tenders.

It had been a source of great encouragement to Geoffrey that, at the Conference, he was able to discuss the route informally and at first hand with Trenchard, who was almost as enthusiastic as himself. They were often seen poring over large-scale maps both at the Hotel and at Aboukir. Lawrence was often with them.

On the whole the Conference was a great success. Lawrence wrote afterwards: 'I felt I had gained every point I wanted', and of Churchill:

'His was the imagination and courage to take a fresh departure and enough skill and knowledge of political procedure to put his political revolution into operation in the Middle East, and in London, peacefully.'

Lord Trenchard's biographer, Andrew Boyle, emphasizing the importance of the air control of Iraq, wrote 'Not only did it save the Arab world from sinking into the anarchy of the pre-war Balkans, it also saved the RAF from possible extinction the next year'.

Although the Cairo Conference was in full session and Committees and Sub-Committees were thrashing out the details in so short a space of time, there was still an afternoon when Winston Churchill found time to sketch the pyramids, and there were evenings when the various delegates would meet for dinner.

One of the members of the Conference, sitting on the Palestine Political and Military Committee with Geoffrey, had been Colonel C. R. 'Jack' Newman, a tall, charming soldier who was also a frequent visitor at Ghezira Place. He and Dorothy, Peggy's sister, often rode together in the morning before breakfast, and it was not long before they became engaged.

With the Conference behind him, Geoffrey decided that no time should be lost in completing his vision of the air route to Baghdad. Now that the Conference had decided that the Air Force should be responsible for the control of all military units in Iraq, the route across the desert had become of vital importance and was to be completed in only three months. Hinaidi had already been chosen by Geoff as the central airfield, with the main Repair Park and advance stores also sited there. In Iraq the base airfield was to be at Shaiba, ten miles (16 km) from Basra, while the principal airfield in the north was to be at Mosul.

Unfortunately the ancient caravan route lay partly outside the sphere of British influence, which was why Geoff had suggested a route via Amman, Asrak and Ramadi at the Conference. Just as he had planned, the RAF was even then making a track across the wide and waterless desert, dividing it into sections, equipped with the landing grounds marked with a circle, and the re-fuelling points where the fuel was almost buried in the sand in huge containers, to which only pilots would hold the key. After a time the tribes took little notice of these dumps, showing very little interest in them or in the tracks across their desert.

Immediately after the Conference two convoys set out, one from the east and the other from the west, from Ziza to Baghdad, marking the desert between the oasis of Ziza and the Euphrates with a furrow nearly 500 miles (800 km) in length. Although experience had shown that the best track on which the sand would pile up was that made by the wheels of cars, over some portion of the route a Fordson tractor with an attached plough was also used. Every twenty miles (32 km) a circle was ploughed on level ground and marked with a letter or a number to show that it could be used as an emergency landing ground. The scientist who helped Geoffrey and the RAF in surveying the route was a Dr. Bull. He fixed his position by the stars and set up a small wireless station from which he listened every evening to the Eiffel Tower time signal. At that time it seemed almost a miracle that the French operator in Paris could send his message 2,000 miles (3200 km) to a British scientist wanting to locate his position in the far-off desert.

Photographs survive of the Fordson tractors ploughing their way across the desert from both directions, showing the airmen, stripped to the waist in the shimmering heat, often rescuing their lorries from the sand, and still determined to complete the track in less than three months after the Cairo Conference. There are pictures of the long white arrows marking the black basalt rocks that seemed to burst from all sides of the desert. At last the meeting between the two convoys was achieved and the track was finished. There is a picture of a white-robed Feisal, now chosen King of Iraq, standing with Geoffrey on the airfield at Hinaidi, outside the city of Baghdad, to welcome their return. Last but not least is a photograph of the gallant airmen who took part, plunging into the oasis at El Azrak for a bathe after days in the blazing heat of the desert.

The airmail route between Cairo and Baghdad was finally opened on 23 June 1921, on which day the three aircraft accompanying the first Desert Route survey party reached Baghdad from Amman. On 30 June Wing Commander Fellowes flew from Baghdad to Cairo over the route in one day, his flying time being eleven hours, an average speed of 79 miles an hour (127 kph). On 1 July, not to be outdone, Geoff himself also flew from Cairo to Baghdad in one day. It was the triumphant ending to all his plans. Civil airmail, after considerable negotiation with the Postmaster General, was flown by the RAF almost from the first. By sea a letter from London to Baghdad had, because of unrest in the region, to travel via the Suez Canal, the Red Sea, Karachi and the Persian Gulf and Basra, taking about a month. The airmail altered all that and telescoped twenty-eight days to nine, or even less.

In November Wing Commander Roderick Hill wrote an account of his first journey across the route, carrying the Baghdad Air Mail. It was obviously still an adventurous if not a dangerous flight, even though the landing grounds were marked by letters from the alphabet, e.g. Ziza to landing ground F, and landing ground F to landing ground V and so on. Hill wrote:

I was a bit heavily loaded leaving Ziza and I hardly climbed at all. I turned into wind, found an up current and shot up about 300 ft. Saunby followed about fifteen minutes later. I made across the hills, past Kasr Kharana, south of C and the blue pools of Azrak, across the plain to D, over the D mud flats and into the basalt country. The sun was getting low and flooding the desert with a warm orange light, and the track was terribly difficult to see. Before F I lost it and circled. Meanwhile Saunby passed me. He wirelessed saying he thought we could just make H before sundown, but Roche advised landing at F, so I signalled I was going to do so. I did not land on the mud flat, as Roche said it might be wet, but just on the edge, where F is ploughed. I landed alright but nearly ran into a bad basalt heap. Saunby followed, struck a bad boulder with his tail-skid (which I had missed by a fluke) and smashed the skid. I taxied 'Valkyrie' round and drew up by 'Morpheus'. The red sun had dipped below the horizon and I saw almost the most vivid colouring I have ever seen. Landing ground F to Landing ground V: I taxied across the mud flat to take off, as we had found by walking on it that it was quite hard. As soon as we got going, I found that we had a following wind, and the weather report from Ramadi by W/T said it was strongest at 1,000 ft. We made a very good run. I flew the aeroplane as far as El Gid, and then had a second breakfast of tea out of my Thermos, ham, rolls and chocolate. As we were approaching the avenue through the hills at L.G.IX I could see afar off two hills, one triangular and one flat-topped, through which the track passes, and we more or less cut straight towards them. The visibility was wonderful and we could see for miles and miles.

He went on:

I landed at LG V to refuel, dropping a smoke candle. The great thing was to find an avenue through the camelthorn, which is so bad at LG V that no tyre is proof against it. I did a wriggle after I touched the ground and managed to keep out of it. The final stage of my 1,720 mile trip to Egypt and back. There was a good wind with me, and we arrived at Hinaidi at 15.05 hours local time. The last bit of the way, after I had passed Baghdad West and the Tigris, I put my nose down and came in low over the cantonment. I then turned round into wind at the far end of the aero-drome and made quite a decent landing. The total flying time of the trip was 24 hours, 57 minutes; and during that time over hills and desert, from morn to pale evening, the engines ran with a steady murmur like the surge of the sea heard afar off. I felt an extraordinary affection well up in me for the craft which had borne me so faithfully and well over the gaunt hills and vast silent spaces of the desert. Anyone who can look unmoved at an aeroplane after it has been on a long run must indeed be insensitive to romance. An aeroplane home at last, with the oil dripping gently off her, has something extraordinarily grand. She is the symbol of conquest, the earnest of fresh conquests to be.

At the end of July Geoffrey received the following letter from Trenchard's private secretary at the Air Ministry. It read:

22 July, 1921. My dear Air Vice Marshal, Sir Hugh Trenchard wishes me to forward you the attached letter which he thinks will be of interest to you. The opening of the Desert Route has been magnificent and has been a source of very great pride and satisfaction to everybody here. Many congratulations. I hope that you are fit and well and that I shall be seeing you here again shortly. We have got a very nice room ready for you. Yours sincerely, T. B. Marson, Captain.

The enclosed letter read:

Buckingham Palace. 22 July, 1921. My dear Trenchard, The King read with much interest your letter of the 21st July with the enclosed account of Salmond's latest achievements in the Middle East, and of the historical meeting in the desert between Mesopotamia and Egypt.
Yours sincerely, Clive Wigram.

The next year, which was to be Geoffrey's last in Egypt, was to contain the fulfilment of all his hopes. The route to Baghdad and India was established; an air mail service was regularly carried out by RAF aircraft between Cairo and Baghdad, and his 'City by the Sea' was thriving. There were workshops, repair shops and, above all, a huge training unit for RAF cadets, both men and women, by the summer of 1922.

On 14 June 1921 Winston Churchill had explained to Parliament the vital conclusions he had reached with General Trenchard on policing the Near East. He said: 'Arrangements are being made for aeroplanes to fly regularly to and fro across the desert between Baghdad and Cairo. Once the route has been marked the whole Air Force in Mesopotamia can be speedily transferred to Palestine or Egypt, and vice versa.'

It had been decided at the Cairo Conference that Iraq should be controlled by the RAF. The Arab rebellion in 1920 had cost some 2,000 casualties and had involved bringing in troops from India. It still seemed impossible to many people that the RAF should replace the Army in control. Sir Percy Cox, the High Commissioner in Iraq, had at first been violently opposed to the plan of 'control without occupation', but in a few months he began to realize the enormous saving in soldiers' lives which would result from the new method of 'Air Control'. The whole vast organization of a military campaign was unnecessary when, as had been shown in Somaliland, a few bombers could fly over enemy territory and, after dropping leaflets warning the tribes, would next day fly over and drop a few bombs on crops and herds to cause disruption. This usually brought the tribes in before any loss of life was involved. Sometimes even the sight of an aeroplane would so alarm the warriors that they would at once give in.

General Borton was put in charge of the RAF in Iraq during the first few months of RAF control, and was supported by four RAF squadrons from England, under Group Captain Hugh Dowding. The same 'umbrella' was extended to Transjordan and Palestine. Geoffrey himself was to explain his method of control in a lecture given to the Army in 1922:

> If a political officer is dissatisfied with the state of affairs, he can by procla-mation, which should always be held in readiness, inform the tribesmen that they must comply with his demands or suffer the penalties as announced, in increasing severity, and only at the last resort would he sanction the bombing of human life.

He also spoke of the attacks made by tribes on merchants crossing the plains:

> If raids take place on the caravans going, say, from Samarra to Mosul, the tribe which carried out the raid is invariably known immediately, but hitherto it has not been possible to take any effective action owing to the speed with which the raiders disappear into the desert. It is hoped, however, by the combined effect of the Intelligence and the Air Services to bring the whole of this business under organised control and to largely stop these raids, which have been the terror of the wretched merchants plying between Baghdad and Mosul for countless ages.

He also emphasized the role of aircraft in conveying troops at short notice to any area, saying:

> The sudden appearance, in response to a wireless call, of fifty to a hundred British troops would generally have a very steadying effect on not only any faint-hearted Arab troops, but also on the tribesmen them-selves. Rumour spreads in the East, and fifty men could very soon be exaggerated into 500 or 1,000. Machines exist, such as the Vickers Vernon, capable of carrying ten armed men, or rations for, or an equiv-alent amount of ammunition. They could be rationed and supplied with ammunition from the air. That this is no imaginary statement, I would remind you that in January, 1921, the Royal Air Force Middle East, rationed with food, water and petrol, thirty men who were constructing the Desert Route, from Amman to Baghdad, for a fortnight. In Iraq a

> mobile column . . . need be concerned about its water supply only. The development of this form of supply will, I feel sure, have a great value in the hill country to the North/North East and East of Mosul.

He ended his lecture by saying, 'The mule and the lorry were born and bred into us, but the new generation will accept the air just as we accepted the car.'

The wild tribes in the hills were not to be thought of always as disruptive. On one occasion, when a Chieftain was taken ill with acute appendicitis, an RAF pilot saved his life by flying him to the nearest hospital. His whole tribe were so grateful that they became entirely loyal to the government.

The conversion of Sir Percy Cox, too, was probably largely due to the influence of his adviser, Gertrude Bell, the intrepid Englishwoman who had made her home in Baghdad and who knew almost all the leading tribes in Iraq. She could speak their language and had lived and worked among them for so long. She had also attended almost every meeting of the Cairo Conference.

Geoffrey was very conscious of the fact that the Turks, in spite of Allenby's great victory, had managed to revive their warlike spirit under a new leader, Kemal Ataturk, who, courageous and popular, had become a real threat to Greece and even to Northern Iraq. Inspired by his leadership, the Turks had already begun to infiltrate the wild mountainous regions of north-east Iraq, Kurdistan, and Geoffrey and General Borton were only too aware of the possible danger to the Kurds and the city of Mosul. Geoffrey was delighted that his brother, Sir John Salmond, was to succeed General Borton as Commander of the British Forces in Iraq in September 1922.

Meanwhile, inspecting his wide-flung command, Geoffrey flew everywhere in his own Bristol Fighter, named 'The Burgate', or drove in his white Rolls–Royce. He was always friendly, infinitely approachable and his care and thoughtfulness for all ranks under his command became proverbial, and all ranks were devoted to him. It was said that he encouraged those whom others would have passed over, bringing out their best qualities by his sympathy and understanding.

Geoff was utterly absorbed by his work and the furtherance of the many projects which he had initiated, covering every facet of his extensive responsibilities, but Peggy was with him at last and after those long years of separation during the war, she was a source of immense joy. He made time to be with her and the children and, taking leave, travelled with her to Jerusalem to show her the city which had so impressed him and about which he had so often written in his letters home.

Sir Hugh Trenchard's request to the Army at the Cairo Conference to provide armoured cars to help in the defence of Iraq was refused by Sir Henry Wilson, who had never approved of the RAF as a separate Service. He said that Trenchard should not order army weapons without consulting the War Office as to their tactical worth. Trenchard was furious and replied that the RAF would provide them themselves. A few were sent from England, but the vast majority were made in Geoffrey's aircraft factory in Cairo. When General Wilson retired and was succeeded by the Earl of Cavan, he showed a much more co-operative attitude and offered to provide them, but by then Trenchard could proudly refuse, saying 'We are quite self-sufficient now'.

With his Command growing ever more interesting and Peggy at last with him, Geoffrey was quite unprepared for a family crisis later in the year. He was travelling for once by train when he suddenly felt a tremendous sense of impending disaster. He had never thought of himself as psychic, but would always pray for his airmen when they were in danger or if, as sometimes happened, they were lost in the desert. Now he felt he must pray. The carriage was crowded with people and he quietly left the compartment and shut himself in the washroom, where he prayed that whatever the disaster was, it could be lessened. His prayers were answered. On arrival at the station he learnt that Jack Newman had been involved in a terrible aircraft crash, at just the time when Geoff had been travelling, and that he was unconscious but so far had survived. Geoffrey gave up everything and rushed to his bedside. He knew he had to help Jack and although he was unconscious, Geoff talked to him, especially of Dorothy, hoping to give him the will to live and to fight for his life. In a few days, after a major heart operation, he survived by a miracle and, although he always afterwards walked with a limp, he made a complete recovery. News of the accident had been cabled to Dorothy at Ditchingham, and she and her mother decided to return to Egypt by the first possible boat. In those days the journey took at least two weeks, and with no wireless on board one can imagine their anxiety as the ship steamed through the Mediterranean. At last they were in sight of Port Said, where they would hear the news and they hoped that Geoffrey might meet them. Suddenly, on the quay they saw a tiny figure in the distance, dancing, leaping, and throwing his hat in the air. As they drew nearer they saw it was Geoff, and with a rush of relief they knew that, although out of earshot, he was telling them that Jack had survived. Geoffrey never cared what others thought of him, and this was something which everyone who knew him loved. The family were moved to a cottage by the sea at Alexandria in the hot weather, but Mrs. Carr and little Penelope developed dysentery. It was a very anxious time, but both had recovered by the time they were to return home to England.

Among Geoffrey's many inventions, including ground-to-air co-operation and the smoke screen, was the minor invention of the weighted canvas message bag. When the Royal Air Force was created in 1918, these message bags were coloured dark blue, light blue and red, the RAF colours. Where there was no wireless communication they could be dropped from an aircraft and also picked up by an aircraft in flight, when hung between two poles. At the end of their time in Egypt Geoff and Peggy went to a fancy dress dance, Peggy as a message bag with real RAF message bags hung round her waist.

After six years of brilliant achievements, the time had come to leave the great Middle East Command which he had built. Geoff was intensely proud of the officers and men who had served so loyally and gallantly. The most modest of men, Geoff would always give credit for the command's success to them. Between them they had not only created a magnificent fighting force with a swift and far reach and an enviable reputation, but they had set an example which had done so much to secure the survival of the RAF. The RAF owed much to the Middle East Command and no one knew that better than their great master and mentor, Sir Hugh Trenchard.

To leave his brainchild behind was naturally a terrible wrench for Geoffrey. However, he must have been feeling the excitement of the prospect of the new challenge that awaited him in London as the first holder of the new post of Air Member for Supply and Research.

As the children left the house at Ghezira Place for the last time their little friend, the small boy with the goats, held up a white kid to give them. They had given him a few toys, but he was offering them his greatest treasure. They were seen off at the station by all their friends. Peregrine Fellowes' small son Michael presented them with a huge box of chocolates on behalf of all the officers and their wives and Peggy was showered with bouquets of flowers. As the train steamed slowly between Cairo and Port Said, there were groups of airmen standing beside the line, and at every stop they were drawn up cheering their General. Geoff and Peggy stood on the platform at the end of the carriage, waving. It must have been very moving for them. When they finally embarked, again having said goodbye to many friends, an aircraft appeared overhead and swept down to drop a message bag on the deck and, as the ship drew slowly away from the shore, it was followed by another, and another. It did not matter that the messages all fell into the sea — Geoffrey knew what they all meant. Gradually the ship sailed further and further away. The coast of his beloved Egypt faded into the mist, and Geoff and Peggy turned to set sail for home and a new life together.

Air Member for Supply and Research

When Sir Geoffrey Salmond and his family arrived home on a cold February morning in 1922 they had no idea of the warm welcome which awaited them. Geoffrey was to find that at the Air Ministry he was surrounded by many of his oldest friends. Air Vice Marshal Oliver Swann, who had been one of the first Naval officers to experiment with seaplanes at Barrow-in-Furness and who had been with him in Egypt, was now Air Member for Personnel. Air Commodore Brooke-Popham (later Air Chief Marshal Sir Robert Brooke-Popham, GCVO, KCB, CB, CMG, DSO, AFC) was working with him in research and Group Captain Arthur Longmore (later Air Marshal Sir Arthur

Longmore, GCB, KCB, DSO, his great friend from early days) also gave him a great welcome. He was working at Adastral House under the shadow of the great Trenchard, whom they all knew was fighting for them and for the very existence of the Royal Air Force.

It was true that Sir Hugh Trenchard's White Paper of 1919 had established the RAF as a separate Service but, even so, Admiral Beatty, who had never lost a battle in his life, remained a very real opponent and had not given up the struggle to claim a Naval Air Arm. Had he succeeded there was a very real danger that the RAF would have become so weak and depleted that, as a separate service, it would have soon ceased to exist. A few months later, giving evidence to the Balfour Subcommittee, Geoffrey himself, speaking on behalf of the Air Ministry, put the situation clearly before his audience. He disclosed the true extent of the extra cost involved in any major change when it became clear that if a wholly Naval Air Arm was allowed, it would inevitably result not only in the duplication of operational organization but in completely separate supply and research departments, stemming from the axiom that the producer must be under the control of the user, particularly in the case of aircraft when the user's life was at stake. Meanwhile, on the grounds of economy alone, Churchill supported the independent RAF in Parliament, quoting the success of the operations in the Middle East and in Somaliland.

Geoffrey was literally 'thrown in at the deep end'. He accompanied the Secretary of State for Air on a visit to the aircraft carrier HMS *Eagle* at Portsmouth, to see for himself how the RAF was working with the Navy. The result was that they were seen to be on excellent terms and were working very well together, without the necessity of creating a separate Naval Air Arm. In the end, after much debate, it was decided that the RAF should train all pilots and personnel but when at sea they should be under the command of the Captain in whose ship they were serving. It was, however, not until the Salisbury Committee met in 1923 that the RAF felt it was really safe as a separate Service.

In the winter of 1922 a political crisis swept the country. For some time the Conservatives in the Coalition had become disillusioned with Lloyd George. A vote went against Lloyd George in the House and within a week he had lost his leadership. In the General Election that followed, the Conservatives romped home and Bonar Law took up the reins of Government. Samuel Hoare, who had helped in the crisis, waited anxiously to see if he had an appointment. At last the telephone rang asking him to come to Bonar Law's house in Onslow Gardens. He was offered Minister for Air, but without a seat in the Cabinet. Perhaps influenced by his father-in-law, Frederick Sykes, Bonar Law added 'But before you answer, I must tell you that the post may be abolished in a few weeks.' There was to be yet another inquiry by the Committee of Imperial Defence and the Cabinet.

In spite of the warning, these words did not unduly depress Samuel Hoare, who immediately went to see Trenchard. On their very first meeting he was overcome by Trenchard's sincerity, his driving force and his vision of the Third Service. He thought of him at once as a prophet and it was as such that he afterwards regarded him. Sir Samuel Hoare as Minister and Air Chief Marshal Sir Hugh Trenchard as head of the RAF made a formidable combination which was to guide the RAF for many years to come.

One of the first things Geoffrey did on taking over his new job was to separate the two departments of Research & Development. He had hoped to enlist the help of Mr. (later Sir) Henry Tizard, an aeronautical expert as well as an airman, who at that time was Assistant Secretary at the Department of Scientific and Industrial Research under Lord Curzon. Tizard felt he could not make the financial sacrifice involved if he were to accept. When the Treasury raised the proposed salary to £2,000, Curzon refused to part with him. Meanwhile a deputy director had been appointed, Mr H.E. Wimperis – the inventor, among other things, of the course-setting bomb sight – who until then had been in charge of the Scientific Laboratory at the Imperial College. It was a splendid choice as Wimperis was not only a brilliant inventor but an able administrator as well. Sir Samuel Hoare was to write of him: 'Wimperis and his Directorate were time after time proved invaluable.' He later played an important part in the development of Radar.

Initially, Geoffrey had three principal aims: he determined to give encouragement to all those firms trying so hard to keep their inventions and the production of aeroplanes going, in spite of the fierce economy cuts of the 'Geddes Axe'. The aircraft companies were all desperately in need of help. In spite of financial hardship, Sopwith, de Havilland, Bristol and A.V. Roe were struggling to produce new or reconditioned aircraft. Secondly, he hoped to encourage the use of metal airframes rather than the wooden frames which he knew from experience suffered so much in the heat of the Middle East. Thirdly, he hoped to stimulate flying clubs throughout the country. Tommy Sopwith had wound up his company while still solvent in 1921, owing to lack of supplies and financial support, but almost immediately he had started the Hawker Aeroplane Co. with Sigrist and Harry Hawker, and this was now going from strength to strength. De Havilland was making headway with their Aircraft Disposal Company, and also managing to produce new versions of the DH.9 and DH.9A.

In contrast, the Royal Air Force Pageant, started by Sir John Salmond in 1920, had now become one of the highlights of the social summer season, and was literally 'bringing the Air to the People'. During the struggle for the independent RAF it seemed essential that the enormous potential of the air should be recognized by everyone, and the idea of an Air Pageant was born. Jack made it a summer event as exciting as the Royal Tournament or Ranelagh. The King himself gallantly attended, and in 1921 Queen Alexandra graced it with her presence. In that year the *Aeroplane* magazine commented:

It was to Hendon that all roads seemed to lead on 2nd July when the great RAF Air Pageant was presented for the second year. Excitement had been stirred by the promise of aerial fighting of the most realistic character in which machines would be 'shot down' in flames. Two great Handley-Page bombers will be attacked by Scout machines and destroyed.

Air Commodore (later Air Chief Marshal Sir Robert) Brooke-Popham, Group Captain Dowding, T. C. Higgins and Arthur Longmore were all present, names which were to become illustrious in the RAF in years to come.

There were, however, some sad gaps among Geoffrey's friends whom he had hoped to meet on his return. General Henderson, who had led the Headquarters to France in August 1914, and who was so much admired and beloved, had died in Geneva in 1920 while organizing the Red Cross. He had had no personal ambition, but had so often smoothed the way for others on his staff. The greatest tribute was that paid by C. G. Grey in the *Aeroplane* when he wrote: 'He was a very perfect gentleman.' The other loss, felt no less keenly, was of Geoffrey's pilot in Egypt, Ross Smith. Hoping to fly round the world in the summer of 1922, he had been testing his Viking IV at Brooklands on 13 April. Suddenly, after climbing to 1,500 feet, it developed a spin, and both Ross Smith and his passenger lost their lives. His was the greatest personal loss to Geoffrey and to the whole of the Royal Air Force. Another loss, in the summer of 1922, was Harry Hawker, considered the best of all British pilots, who lost his life while testing the Goshawk at Hendon. 'If ever there was a trier, Hawker was one,' wrote C. G. Grey. 'Once he made up his mind to do a thing, he would try, try and try again. He loved things that were worthwhile, and did them for the sake of doing, not for gain.'

In his support of metal airframes, Geoffrey was not alone. The great German inventor, Professor Hugo Junkers, had written of his Duralumin frames:

As far back as 1910 I was well aware that the main goal of aeroplane construction must be greatly diminished parasite resistance. The streaming, or fairing or covering, must be shaped as a hollow space producing minimum drag with maximum lift. This is the nucleus of my patent.

However, although France and Germany were very much in advance, English inventors were still slow to recognize the value of steel and aluminium. Handley-Page came out strongly in support of wooden airframes and, even in 1924, current advance in engineering design was rarely more than a cautious replacement of wooden structures by light gauge high-tensile steel. Shorts, however, with their monocoque fuselages, kept pace with their competitors in Germany and France producing metal airframes. An amusing story was told by Oswald

Short. Having been refused his tender for an all-metal twin Condor-powered flying boat, he decided to take his design to Geoffrey Salmond himself:

> I then telephoned to Sir Geoffrey Salmond and said, "You know that we have lost the order for the Singapore?" He replied, "Yes, Short, I am very sorry that you have." I replied, "Well, I am going to build it if I bankrupt the firm." He answered cheerily, "Good fellow. I will come and see you tomorrow morning." Next day I showed him the plans and he immediately said, "Why have I not seen these?" He said he liked the appearance of the machine and asked how much I wanted in that financial year if he gave an order. I replied that with such an order no doubt the bank would grant a larger overdraft . . . He would not hear of borrowing more, and said he would give the order, but in that financial year the Air Council had only £10,000 left and the balance would be paid the next year.

This quotation not only shows Oswald Short's courage in his convictions, but also the vision which Geoffrey showed in encouraging him. Later, Lancaster Parker was to say, 'I have no hesitation in saying that the pre-eminent position which Great Britain achieved in flying-boat design in later years was a direct result of Oswald's foresight and courageous decision.' The quotation, however, also shows the financial difficulty under which Geoffrey had to act, but his support of good design was unfailing. After the Condor, it was the Supermarine Southampton which was to appeal to so many RAF pilots. Designed by Reginald Mitchell, Supermarine's brilliant young designer, six were immediately ordered by the Air Ministry, showing their faith in Mitchell's exceptional talent, which was to be so well rewarded in the years to come.

Steel and Duralumin were gradually adopted in aircraft production, and in 1929 the victorious Schneider Trophy aeroplane would be built entirely of these materials.

In the difficult post-war period there was nothing which seemed to lift the spirits of all those interested in aviation more than the Schneider Trophy races, later to be known as the Schneider Cup. This international competition had been inaugurated by Albert Schneider in December 1912. Its rules laid down that any country, club, or individual that won the Cup three times in five years could hold it in perpetuity. Howard Pixton, flying a Sopwith Tabloid, had won it for Britain at 86.78 mph in 1914, but the race was suspended during the war years. Restarted in 1919, the Italians should have won, but were disqualified, although they subsequently won in 1920 and 1921. However, in the following year, Henry Baird, Supermarine's chief test pilot, flying the Supermarine Sea Lion II and with a 450 hp Napier Lion engine, won the race at Naples averaging 134.7 mph. This was in 1922, just after Geoffrey returned from Egypt. The Americans, however, won in 1923 at Cowes.

That night, at the Royal Aero Club banquet, Geoff's old colleague and friend Air Vice Marshall Sir Sefton Brancker said:

> Our glorious defeat is likely to do us good; moreover had we won despite our great handicap [lack of government support], the Admiralty would have said they were right in not assisting, and that everything was splendid. They now have something to worry about, though there are plenty of millionaires who now have the chance of being patriotic enough to provide funds to bring back the Cup from America next year.

However, America was to win again in 1925, but the Italians, on Mussolini's express order, won at Hampton Roads in 1926.

Meanwhile the Air Ministry had been studying new ideas for high-speed seaplanes, and Geoffrey was much in favour of a British entry that would win the Schneider Trophy – preferably outright. He carried out a review of the 1925 race and came to two conclusions: firstly that our design and performance were close enough to the American team to give us confidence to take part in the 1927 race, and, secondly, as all other entrants were military teams he felt that this was not something to be left to private firms, but that a special High Speed Flight should be established by the RAF. Winning the trophy would have the dual benefit of a gain in leading technology and in British prestige. At first Trenchard demurred, feeling that the building up of the RAF at home was all-important. To Sir Samuel Hoare he wrote: 'Frankly, I am against this contest. I can see no value in it.' However, after consultation, he not only agreed but supported the Air Council in their approach to Winston Churchill, then Chancellor of the Exchequer, asking the Government for support. At length the Treasury agreed to an extra grant of £100,000 for the special High Speed Flight, which was to be based at Felixstowe. As a result, Reginald Mitchell designed the Supermarine S5 which, with an 875 h.p. Napier Lion engine, won the Schneider Trophy at Venice on 26 September 1926, with an average speed of 281.65 mph, piloted by Sidney Webster. Second was Flight Lieutenant O. E. Worsley, also flying an S5, fully justifying the entry of the RAF into the contest. It was a tremendous victory, but Trenchard still had reservations. However, Sir Samuel Hoare and the Cabinet were enthusiastic and, early in 1928, the Air Ministry was able to prepare to win once more.

By this time Geoffrey was coming to the end of his tour in India. Without his staunch support for the High Speed Flight and his interest in the techno-logical genius of Mitchell, which he had done so much to encourage, the whole history of the Schneider Trophy might have been different. As it was, Britain won the race in 1929 at Calshot, near Spithead, when Flying Officer H.R.D. Waghorn achieved a speed of 328.63 mph, and another member of the Flight, Squadron Leader Orlebar, set up a world speed record of 357.75 miles an hour. These achievements together with the subsequent triumph in winning the Cup outright in 1931, were not only a source of delight to Geoff, but a firm foundation for the combination of Mitchell's airframe design and Sir Henry Royce's engines which were to lead to the Spitfire and the Hurricane. Sir Samuel Hoare was to write later:

> The Mercury and the Merlin were in later years the outward and visible signs of the research work on the engines, and the evolution of the Spitfire can be traced directly to the building of the Schneider Cup monoplanes between 1927 and 1931.*

Although it was a notion on the Continent that British aircraft of the 1920s were mostly developed from original wartime aeroplanes, despite the necessity for economy, aeroplanes and their engines were being designed in Britain which could easily match those developed abroad. It was not only the High Speed Flight's success in the Schneider Cup Race which demonstrated the progress of British design. There were also the long-distance flights by Alan Cobham, by the Australian Bert Hinkler and, in 1930, Amy Johnson, all of which demonstrated progress in aircraft design as well as the courage and adventurous spirit of the pilots themselves. When Alan Cobham decided to fly from London to Cape Town in 1925 he was following Von Rhyneveldt, who had flown over the route first planned by Geoffrey Salmond in 1918. Cobham had already flown with Air Vice Marshal Sir Sefton Brancker on a survey flight for Imperial Airways from London to Rangoon and back. On that occasion he flew a DH.50, which was only the second of its type to be built. Now he decided to fly the same aircraft to the Cape and back, only changing the 230 hp Siddeley Puma engine for a 385 hp Siddeley Jaguar, which, being air-cooled, would give him another 160 hp for exactly the same weight. This biplane, with an open cockpit for the pilot and a small cabin immediately in front of him, covered the route without any serious danger through dust storms, blinding wind and rain, over mountains and across deserts in nine days and returned to Croydon on 13 March, 1926, having covered 16,000 miles.

Only three months later, on 30 June, Cobham and his mechanic Elliott took off once more, this time to fly to Australia and back. He was piloting the same aircraft, converted into a seaplane for the largely over-water flight. On 1 October a large crowd gathered outside the Houses of Parliament to watch him land gracefully on the Thames just outside the Palace of Westminster. The success of the flight was, however, marred by the death of Elliott, who had been killed by a stray bullet fired by a Bedouin while flying over the desert between Baghdad and Basra on the outward flight. Cobham was knighted for these flights, which pioneered future Empire routes around the world and brought Geoff's dreams of global air traffic several steps nearer to fruition.

---

* See *Empire of the Air* by Viscount Templewood.

Geoffrey's third interest was one which he felt could be shared by every air-minded person in the country — flying clubs using small aircraft which almost any keen aviator could buy. There had been a meeting near Lewes in 1922, but the first important meeting arranged by Geoff was at Lympne. It was very well organized and many small aircraft took part, giving it a feeling of light-hearted competition, very like the meetings at Brooklands before the war.

Terence Broughton remarked: 'It was a meeting of enthusiasts, of men who were in aviation not for the material reward it offered, but simply because its unique blend of subtle theory and practical engineering, of mental agility and physical skill, of eccentricity and adventure, made it the one life they really cared about.' Geoffrey had persuaded the Air Ministry to put up valuable prizes for the various races and events and he interested himself in composing many of the regulations.

Within a fortnight another meeting was held for light aircraft at Hendon. It was again a great success, although a sad event was the crash in which Maneyrol died, due to a failure of the light tubular bracing struts in his aeroplane. Fatalities through crashes were becoming all too frequent in the 1920s, and at length parachutes were provided. Until the mid-twenties there had been an extraordinary prejudice against parachutes and all through the war the only RAF personnel to be provided with them had been those manning observation balloons. There was some controversy as the American-style parachute was accepted as the safest, and Geoffrey was determined that if he were to expect his pilots to use them he should have tested them himself. Without telling their wives, he and Peregrine Fellowes decided to use examples of the first para-chutes to be ordered. In those days they had to climb out on the wing of the aircraft when in flight and be pulled off when the parachute opened. Peregrine and Geoff planned to come down at the same time. After climbing out on the wing, Geoffrey was lifted off successfully and was able to talk politics with Peregrine as they drifted down. They had no instructions on how to land and Geoffrey came down rather heavily in a beet field. He always said his worst moment was actually watching the ambulance following them below. Jack also decided to test a parachute and narrowly missed a railing as he landed.

Light aeroplane meetings became a feature of every summer in the 1920s. New clubs were formed, and by 1926 there were fourteen of them in England. It was from these small aircraft that the whole race of British light aircraft sprang, and they were agreed at the time to be superior to anything of the sort in the world. The de Havilland Moth made its first appearance in 1925, and the prototype, G-EBKT, became the centre of interest for every flying club, as the first really practical dual-control light aircraft. The Tiger Moth and the Puss Moth were to follow, and it was in a Moth that Amy Johnson herself was to make her record-breaking solo flight from England to Australia some four years later. Because of his initiative and sympathetic encouragement, Geoff has been called the 'Father of the Light Aeroplane'.

There occurred at this time an amusing interlude, but one which could have been very serious. An inventor, Grindell Mathews, claimed that he had invented a 'Death Ray' capable of killing troops at a distance, and even bringing down aircraft, and considered that it was the weapon of the future. There were questions in the House, and Sir Samuel Hoare said 'The Service Departments have been put in a difficult position in dealing with Grindell Mathews, partly because of the vigorous press campaign on his behalf, and partly because this is not the first occasion on which the inventor has put forward schemes in which extravagant claims have been made.' He had already been paid £25,000 by the Admiralty for an invention to direct vessels by wireless, but with no result. Geoffrey decided to test the apparatus. A canary was put in a cage fifteen yards from Mathews and his 'Death Ray'. There was absolutely no result and the canary was still chirping happily at the end of the experiment. The Government then suggested that if he could stop a small petrol engine at the same distance he would be paid £1,000 provided he allowed the Government fourteen days to consider further financial arrangements for developing the invention. But no more was heard from Mr Mathews.

*　　*　　*

oh dear!

Peggy, meanwhile, had become one of the prettiest hostesses in London and had many friends. It was a time of dances and dinner parties, but at the same time she made all her children's dresses and also joined a crèche in the East End, where she made dresses for less well-off children. On one occasion, she was measuring a little girl for a dress and noticed her swollen face. Within two weeks Peggy had developed mumps. As it was just before Christmas it was not possible for the family to go to Ditchingham as usual, but Geoff decided to make the best of things. First, he took all the children to the circus, and then, on Christmas Day, he gave them all whistles and, with him leading, they marched all over the house, round Peggy's bedroom and downstairs to the kitchen where the cook threw her apron over her head in amazement. Finally, following their father, they all rushed out of the front door into Regents Park. There the real fun began, as Geoff led his ragged line of children, from Joyce who was eleven years old down to John who was only three, all round the Park, jumping on to seats and over railings, blowing their whistles all the time. An astonished elderly gentleman, in regulation Sunday top hat and frock coat, taking a dignified Christmas walk in the Park, stopped in astonishment when he saw the line of children following their father as he ran round the Park, throwing his hat in the air. To the children that Christmas was one of the most exciting they had ever had. It was typical of Geoffrey, who could always make everyone laugh and turn a sad situation into a happy one.

of course!

Crisis in Iraq and Visits to Clouds Hill

In the Autumn of 1922 Jack Salmond flew to Iraq and Gertrude Bell wrote:

> A new planet has arisen in the shape of Sir John Salmond, Air Marshal,
> who takes over command of all British Forces in Iraq on October 1st . . .
> He is alert, forcible, amazingly quick in the uptake, a man who means to
> understand Iraq and all dealings with its people. He dined with me last
> night . . . he is delightful to talk to on any subject.

This was the first time that an RAF commander had taken over a whole theatre,
commanding the Army as well as the RAF, and it was treated as a test case to
determine whether Air Control could indeed reduce casualties and carry out
effective operations, including the support for all flying units in Iraq.

On arrival, Jack found the Turkish troops were already threatening the
province of Mosul and occupying the outlying villages, more especially in the
town of Rowanduz. In the south of Iraq was the treacherous Sheik Mahmoud,
who, after being given the governorship of the province of Sulaimaniya, had
gone over to the Turks. The situation in Iraq was growing worse day by day.
At home the Cabinet was anxious and alarmed, feeling that the country could
not face another war. The Air Officer Commanding the forces in Iraq was told
to retreat if the Turks advanced towards Mosul. Jack cabled to Trenchard:

> I note the policy indicated to me is that of continuous retirement in the
> face of a superior enemy. As you know that is a most difficult manoeuvre
> once we become engaged, as I do not anticipate the possibility of retiring
> continuously even in the face of a superior enemy, without firing a shot.

It was said that Trenchard was delighted, and stated that he had complete
confidence in his officer commanding in Iraq and would stand or fall by his
decisions.

Retreat was not a word in Jack Salmond's vocabulary. The airman who had
carried out daring and successful operations in France carried out a masterly
campaign in which the Turks were virtually cut off and so effectively
bombarded from the air that at last they retreated in disorder. One small incident during the 'war' showed Jack at his most gallant. When three aircraft were
flying home after an engagement, the engine of one failed and the pilot was
forced to land almost within rifle fire of the enemy's fort. Jack, in one of the
two remaining aircraft, ordered his pilot to land alongside and the crashed pilot
had to sit on his knee all the way back to Baghdad. The campaign was entirely
successful and Trenchard's trust was rewarded. The case for air control had
again been made, this time on a substantial scale.

In January 1923 Jack returned home and was immediately promoted to Air

Marshal. He was then appointed AOC-in-C Air Defence of Great Britain, at the age of forty-one. In 1925 he was appointed ADC to King George V and in that year, too, he married again. His bride was Monica Grenfell. It was described as the wedding of the year – the war hero and the beautiful daughter of Lord and Lady Desborough, who themselves had shown a great interest in flying.

of course

*   *   *

In the 1920s there was great public interest in the development of the airship, despite the alarming accident rate with these great machines. There were those who saw this as the best hope for the creation of long-distance Imperial communication. However, the politicians of the Coalition Government were distinctly luke-warm about it – probably due to a reluctance to embark upon costly new ventures at the expense of the Exchequer and the apparent un-reliability of the concept. Nevertheless, the Admiralty pressed hard for recognition of the military potential of these lighter-than-air craft and a well-known retired naval officer, Commander Dennison Burney produced a plan to restart airship construction on an ambitious scale and even for a regular trans-Atlantic service between Britain and the United States.

Finally, in 1924, the short-lived Labour Government supported a plan for the building of two great airships, one by the Air Ministry and the other by private enterprise. Of course, in his capacity as AMSR, Geoff had a consider-able professional interest in the project.

In 1924 and 1925 Geoff was spending as much time as possible with the children. Their grandfather, William Carr, had died suddenly and Geoffrey was often at Ditchingham when his onerous duties made this possible. The telephone was a primitive affair in those days and shared lines were common. At Ditchingham one ring was for the post office, two rings for Sir Rider Haggard who lived nearby, and three rings for Ditchingham Hall. In April 1925 the phone rang three times; the call was from the Air Ministry to tell Geoff that the latest small airship, the *R33*, had broken away from her masthead at Pulham in Norfolk, where she had been left with a skeleton crew. The nose had torn completely away. Luckily, the top fabric had folded over the gaping hole and the airship was just steerable. A 30-knot wind had drifted her towards Holland, but the Air Ministry message was that she was floating back towards the mast at Pulham. Immediately the whole family were flung into the old Overland motor car and set off for Pulham. The huge airship eventually appeared, with an enormous and terrifying hole in her envelope, and drifted towards the mast. A gigantic metal chain hanging from her bows suddenly swept down from the trees as she descended, scattering the onlookers, but soon, miraculously, she was once again attached to her mooring mast and the crisis was temporarily over. Her first officer, Flight Lieutenant Booth, had navigated magnificently during the flight. The children were always to remember that day, and how near the airship was to disaster.

★   ★   ★

Quite often Geoffrey would take the children to play in Richmond Park at the weekend and there they would meet their little cousin Joy. They all spent many of their summer holidays together, now that Jack was at home. On some occasions they drove a little farther, to the New Forest, and from there they once or twice called on Lawrence at his cottage, Clouds Hill. It was a tiny house, smothered in rhododendron bushes, and the children were told to stay outside, as Lawrence's manuscript of *Seven Pillars of Wisdom* was spread out round the room. Geoff took the opportunity of talking to Lawrence, especially about the fact that he had had to leave the RAF. He had been frustrated by the publicity which Lowell Thomas' film *Lawrence and the Arabs* had given him. The Press had discovered 'Aircraftman Ross' and his position had become impossible. He had been forced to leave, and was now a private in the Royal Tank Corps, using the name of T. E. Shaw to hide his real identity. He had apparently chosen it at random from the telephone book on the day he joined. But he was now doing all he could to be transferred back to the RAF. Afterwards Lawrence played hide-and-seek with the children in the bracken, and, of course, it was always impossible to find him.

On one of these occasions Lawrence had asked Geoffrey to have his portrait painted for inclusion in his book, and the children remember walking across the Park to Stanley Spencer's studio in St. John's Wood. It was a very small room at the top of a high house, overlooking the roof tops, and round the walls were pictures of the Last Judgment, and Cookham. A sketch for the portrait was made, but the family thought it made Geoff look too old, so it was never included in *Seven Pillars of Wisdom* after all.

On yet another occasion, when Jack and Geoff were on holiday together, Lawrence told them with his impish humour of an excellent beach nearby, where they could have a birthday picnic. He declined to come with them. Geoff and Jack drove to the beach with their families, and as they all gathered round for the picnic and had just lit the candles on Geoff's birthday cake a furious figure was seen striding along the lonely beach towards them. The children were horrified, but Geoff and Jack still sat nonchalantly on the sand. When he came near enough he started shouting at them, saying it was his private beach. When he paused for breath Jack said calmly, 'Have some cake!' The man's face grew purple with rage and he shouted 'I'd rather have your blood!' Jack, very tall and elegant, got slowly to his feet and opened his coat. 'Take it then,' he said in his most charming voice. The old man stamped off, muttering 'I'm too old! I'm too old!' Of course the children adored their uncle after that. Peggy always felt, however, that Lawrence had sent them there on purpose.

Geoffrey always supported Lawrence, and he told Joyce at the time that anything that Lawrence wanted, anything at all, he should have. He had done so much for his country. Soon afterwards, Trenchard arranged for Lawrence to rejoin the RAF, still under the name of Shaw, and at last he felt once more at peace with himself and once more out of the limelight.

Much later, Lawrence wrote to Trenchard:

> Do please credit your most experienced aircraftman who has in his time been a man of action, and even made a tiny fighting Service out of nothing, when he assures you that the RAF is the finest individual effort in British history . . . that the RAF is your single work, that every one of us, in so far as he is moulded to type, is moulded after your image, and it is thanks to your being head and shoulders greater in character than ordinary men that your force, even in its childhood, surpasses the immemorial Army and Navy. No man in the three or four continents I know could have done what you have done. The RAF is 30,000 strong, too huge for you to have personal contact with many of us, but there is not a barrack room in which your trumpet does not regularly sound; and these thousands of your champions find no opponents. We grouse and grumble at everything and everybody, except you; and all but one per cent of ignorant airmen know you are our exemplar and creator and try (does it frighten you? It would me) to be better copies.

Perhaps this tribute is all that the great Trenchard could ever have wished for.

In 1926 Geoffrey was created a Knight Commander of the Order of the Bath, in recognition of his service in many capacities in the Empire and, in December of that year, he was appointed to command the Air Force in India.

7

BY IMPERIAL AIRWAYS TO INDIA

The first civil airline flight to India was to be undertaken by Imperial Airways. This long-awaited company had been launched in 1924, as a result of the decision of the Hambling Committee, whose task had been to find the best way of encouraging commercial aviation. By this agreement the company had to guarantee subscription of half the shares of the operating company, which would purchase, on approved terms, Handley-Page Transport Ltd., Instone Airlines Ltd., Daimler Airways and the British Marine Air Navigation Company Ltd. During the ten years of subsidy a yearly average of one million miles must be completed, for which payment would be made in diminishing instalments. Every pilot had to pass a course of instrument flying, and all pilots had to be in the Air Force Reserve or the Auxiliary Air Force. The huge Imperial Transport firm was thus very similar to the company visualized by Geoffrey himself in his report to Winston Churchill in 1919, especially as it was debarred from holding shares in any aircraft or aero-engine construction firm. As Imperial Airways it was to become the most important civil airline to fly in the decade.

At first the aircraft confined their flights to the Continent, but in 1926 it was hoped that the very first civilian airline, flown by Hercules aircraft, could inaugurate a regular service to India. The route they were to follow was the same route which had been originally flown by Geoffrey and General Borton in 1918. Sir Samuel Hoare, as Minister for Air, was determined to take part in the flight and to be accompanied by his wife, Lady Maud Hoare. Sir Samuel had decided that, in order to publicize the air and to demonstrate the safety of flying, the Minister should fly to all his engagements abroad, rather than travelling by ship and train. Already he and Lady Maud Hoare had flown to Brussels, and then, venturing further, had flown in stages to an engagement in Sweden. His only anxious moment, he said, was when he saw the small pocket-handkerchief sized airfield on which they were to land outside Stockholm, with the King and his entourage looking on. In order not to 'push his luck too far' he had returned by ship and train. Now he felt he should take part in the first historic Imperial Airways flight to India, and Geoffrey, on taking up his new Command, was determined to go with him.

It was still dark in the early morning of 26 December 1926 when a small party drove through the quiet streets of London towards Croydon, and still almost dark when the huge outline of the de Havilland Hercules was just discernible in the dim light of dawn. Five of these aircraft, each equipped with three 450 hp Jupiter engines, had been ordered for Imperial Airways. A group of well-wishers had gallantly come to wish the travellers 'Bon Voyage', and the small party 'emplaned' (Geoffrey's own expression), at just after 7 am.

Unfortunately it was the very worst time to go, as regards weather, but Sir Samuel Hoare felt that he could only go in the Parliamentary recess. Many of his friends thought it wrong for a Cabinet Minister to go at all. 'Remember Huskisson,' somebody said. Huskisson was the Cabinet Minister who, travelling on the first train journey of the Liverpool & Manchester Railway almost a hundred years previously, had lost his life in an accident. Surely it was foolhardy for the Minister for Air to travel to India on the very first civilian flight? It was even more astonishing that Lady Hoare was to accompany him, for no woman had ever flown to India before. While listening politely to all their advice, Sir Samuel had not the least intention of altering his plans, and Lady Maud was determined to go with him. The flight was of special interest to Geoff as they were to take the route from Cairo to India, which he himself had planned and flown eight years before. Christopher Bullock, Sir Samuel's invaluable private secretary, was to be the fourth member of the party.

At last they were off and as they left the ground and rose into the air above London they knew that they were the pioneers of a route which was to become a great Imperial highway from England to India. Everything had been done to make the cabin in which they were to travel for the next 10,000 miles as comfortable as possible. There were basket chairs and a window from which they could see the ever-changing scene below them. In those days it was still considered dangerous and almost impossible to fly at night, and they were to land at various places for lunch, so that the journey was broken up in a most interesting way. Sir Samuel Hoare had chosen a route across France to Marseilles, and then on to Pisa and Naples, and across the Mediterranean to North Africa as the start of their journey, the only anxiety being that a landplane was to cross 600 miles (960 km) of open sea. The First Lord of the Admiralty kindly offered a chain of destroyers to look out for them, in case of accident, and so they light-heartedly dismissed the gloomy forecasts of their friends that, even if they escaped from drowning, they would probably meet death by freezing. Lady Maud Hoare wrote: 'We had equipped ourselves with the latest pattern of life-saving waistcoats, made of hydrogenated rubber. During the flight provision had to be made for sun and rain, heat and cold, deserts and drawing-rooms, all within the limits of a suitcase and a dressing-case.'. She was very particular about her dress in the aircraft, as space and weight were limited. She continued: 'My actual wardrobe consisted of a stockinet coat and skirt, with crêpe-de-chine jumper worn most days, and a woollen jumper and tweed skirt as a change. Then, in layers according to temperature, woollen cardigan, leather coat and fur coat.' Two felt hats were also taken, as no lady could arrive hatless in those days, and a black lace dress for the evening receptions they were bound to attend en route. As they flew, they all made pencilled notes, and Geoffrey's notes are still treasured in the family.

The first part of the journey was exceedingly bumpy in the gusty December weather over France, and they had to pull themselves together to face the reception committees which invariably greeted them at every landing stage across Europe. They were always met by dignitaries and sometimes even greeted by a band. Sir Samuel and Lady Maud Hoare, being inveterate sight-seers, were fascinated by Vesuvius and Pompeii and asked, when over Naples, if they could circle round the volcano. Sir Samuel wrote that they 'almost penetrated the chocolate clouds of smoke that were emerging from it'. When they finally crossed the Mediterranean safely and landed, first at Benghazi and afterwards at Sollum, they were met by RAF aircraft which had flown from Cairo, and were escorted by the RAF to Hinaidi in Iraq. Here their pilot, Captain Barnard, left them and Captain Wolley Dod took over for their flight across the desert route to India.

Geoffrey, meanwhile, smart and unruffled in his uniform, inspected RAF contingents whenever they landed, and when they eventually reached Cairo safely, he must have felt he was in his element once more, at home with the Middle East Air Force. Their route, passing the Suez Canal and flying over Jerusalem, was to fly from Aboukir to Ziza and from there over the desert and the oil wells at Rutbah to Baghdad. From Baghdad they were to fly to Basra, then down the Persian Gulf to Bushire and Jask, and at length via Parni to Karachi.

Sir Samuel paid Sir Geoffrey a great tribute in describing the success of the Desert Route:

> For five years in succession Air Force machines have flown safely over this route, carrying mails and official passengers with an almost unbroken regularity, and maintaining a quick and constant communication between Iraq and the West. A desert that was once one of the world's greatest barriers is now crossed with ease and comfort in the space of a few hours, and Arab Sheikhs who have never lived in a house or seen a railway, accept the passing of aeroplanes as one of the ordinary features of their daily life. Henceforth the machine that will chiefly use it will be civil and not military. Henceforth the military air route will become a thoroughfare for civil passengers and freight. At the moment when this

transformation is taking place, let us remember the enterprise and perseverance of the pioneers who marked it out, and of the Air Force pilots who, week after week, and year after year, flew with such courage and precision. It might be thought that the winds and shifting sands of the desert would soon obliterate the thin line of the track. This is not the case. The scars and furrows of the desert, even the ghostly signs of ancient civilisations, seem to last for ever. The line of the track was as easy for us to distinguish as the lay-out of the submerged cities over which we were to pass the following day. A flash of blue water showed that we were over the oasis of El Azrak. At length there was Lake Habbaniya, looking more like a mirage than a real sheet of water, and the Euphrates curling in circles, like a cat trying to eat its tail.

At Baghdad they were greeted by King Feisal, who was extremely interested in their journey, and a reception was held in the evening by Sir Henry Dobbs, who had succeeded Sir Percy Cox as High Commissioner. Next day they flew low over the ancient city of Ur, over the excavations which Professor Woolley was carrying out, this time without the help of Lawrence, exposing amazing outlines of ancient streets and buildings. Finally, they landed near Basra, at RAF Shaibah.

Next day Bushire on the Persian Gulf was reached, and it was here that they first met two tiny Moths, flown by two young men, Stack and Leeke, who were also lightheartedly flying to India. When asked what they took with them in their extremely small cockpits, they answered 'An attaché case each, and a ukulele between us!' Amazingly, these two young adventurers reached India successfully, only carrying a packet of biscuits as an emergency ration in case of a forced landing.

As the Hercules flew down the Persian Gulf over desolate country, Sir Samuel wrote: 'From time to time Sir Geoffrey Salmond pointed out the emergency landing grounds that he and Air Commodore Borton had marked out ten years ago for the first flight to India.' Eventually, after leaving Bushire and Lingeh, they arrived at Jask, where they were due to spend the night at an isolated telegraph station. The landing ground proved to be some miles away in the desert, and the only means of transport was by camel. There still exists a delightful photograph of Sir Samuel Hoare and Geoffrey on camels, setting out towards the telegraph station, with the Hercules parked behind them. They stayed the night with the Janes, of the telegraph company, and the next morning they left on the camels at 06.00 in order to continue their flight. Then, to their consternation, they found that the weather had changed. A thick mist and fog surrounded the Hercules when they reached the airstrip. Leeke and Stack decided not to risk it in their Moths but, relying on the greater range of the Hercules, Sir Samuel Hoare and his party took off and rose to a height of 2,000 feet. The mist soon turned to a violent dust storm, and it became clear that conditions were worsening. The altimeter began to fall from the 2000 foot mark to the 200 mark and finally from 200 to only 20. They were forced to fly close to the sea, and see the dark waves only twelve feet below them. Visibility was nil. The following notes were pencilled by Geoffrey during the flight:

Left at 7.10 local time in fog. Went off in fog and climbed through to avoid it. When we get the height, we can see nothing below us. 9.20-9.30. For some reason we have come down to a few feet off the sea. Suddenly we see the land – on the wrong side. I don't know why. Bullock made a joke, saying 'Where are we going to?

The notes here break off abruptly, but the next day Geoffrey continued his account of the adventure:

Jask. We came back yesterday, owing to a sandstorm. Our pilot, Wolley Dod and Johnson, the navigator, made a very wise decision, after ten minutes flying. They ran into a sandstorm at 4,000 feet. Possibly the ground mist at Jask was its precursor. Anyhow Wolley Dod, who had been in a sandstorm 200 miles long across the Red Sea, thought it wiser to turn back. We turned and came down to within twenty feet of the sea, and flying like this and navigated by Johnson, we made the coast about the Bay of Bechiz – then flying along it he thought he saw a hut which is near Jask aerodrome. He then turned in. I did not know what he was doing until I saw the telegraph line. He made a very good landing. It was really a very fine performance. We were all very pleased . . . The wisdom of Wolley Dod's decision was shown later, as the sandstorm grew worse, it was clear it was raging at Chahbar and Pasni. We decided to wait until Friday. Had Wolley Dod gone on, we would have been in Queer Street.

Once more they mounted their camels and returned through the blinding dust storm to the telegraph office. Next day the weather improved very slightly and Geoffrey Salmond continued his notes in the morning while in flight:

9.35 visibility is not too good. Sandstorm. Country as before – barren. 9.55 at 5,000 feet. 10.25 9,000 feet. Visibility on Port side still not too good – and lots of sand hanging about. On Starboard side, not bad. We passed the Indian Border at 11.37. We have just done it.

Later, after a reception at Karachi and a night at Jodhpur, they were approaching the end of their great adventure. Geoffrey wrote:

In the air 1800 feet. speed 110 mph. We are now on our last lap between Jodhpur and Delhi, where we hope to arrive at 12.30. The machine is flying low in order to go as fast as possible, as we want to have a quarter of an hour in hand when we sight Delhi, so as to arrive absolutely punctually. The result is she is rolling about a bit, and my writing suffers accordingly . . . We have had a most thrilling journey, all the way. It is Saturday today and we left Croydon on Monday a week ago. We have been in France, Italy, Sicily, Malta, Tripoli, Benghazi, Egypt, Palestine and Transjordan, Iraq, Persia, India. The engines have been wonderful. Lady Maud Hoare has been wonderful. But this is an 'air express', and, as you sit in the comfortable chair, looking out on the country beneath you, it feels like one.

Exactly on time, at 12.30 pm, the large crowd which had gathered to receive them at the Raisina Aerodrome at Delhi saw the Hercules, its wings flashing in the sunlight, flying towards them, circle and land. Sir Samuel Hoare, Lady Maud Hoare and Sir Geoffrey Salmond had arrived in India.

⋆   ⋆   ⋆

Although in those days it was not considered wise for children to remain in India after the age of seven, Geoffrey was determined to take all his family with him, and so Peggy, all the children, a governess and a nurse set out from Tilbury in March to travel to India by sea. It was a leisurely journey, and the P & O liner was to become their home for the next three weeks.

For the children the most exciting thing was the arrival at Bombay at 4 o'clock in the morning, when the throb of the engines died away and they could hear the Lascars shouting at each other, and the chains clanking noisily as they secured the ship. Then there was the slow journey by train to Delhi which took a day and a night. At every station mangoes and oranges were for sale, and the train became more and more crowded, many Indians clutching onto the roof. As the heat was very great in the plains they were to go straight to Simla, in the Himalayas, so they joined the Darjeeling Himalayan Railway, which wound its way up through rhododendron trees and dark firs. Each new view grew more and more beautiful as the snow-capped mountains appeared between the trees, Kanchenjunga and even, in the distance, the outline of Everest and the peaks of snow-covered Makalu.

Simla is 7,000 feet above sea-level, and the air was cool and clear when at last they reached the station. No cars were allowed except for the Viceroy and Commander-in-Chief, so they were swiftly transported by rickshaw out of the town, through the bazaar, and at last reached Elysium Hill. There they found they were to live at the very top of the mountain, in a large grey wooden house, which had the imposing name of 'Stirling Castle', given to it by the rajah who had lived there.

And so began their two years in India, a time of great happiness for the whole family. In Simla, when they arrived, they found snow still lying on the hillside, and clouds often rolling down the valley below them, but it soon became sunny summer weather, with cosmos and pansies in their garden, and their apricot tree covered in blossom.

Geoffrey found it difficult to convince the generals in India that the RAF was now the most important service for keeping peace on the frontier with Afghanistan. For so long soldiers had been sent to the frontier on military punitive expeditions, which had often ended in loss of life and bloody battles with the wild tribesmen, with enormous expenditure and doubtful victory. Even so, it was difficult for the Army to forget these traditional methods and accept the fact that aircraft could keep the peace far more effectively. It was especially difficult for Geoffrey as he was himself younger than many of the generals with whom he came in contact, but luckily his time in the Royal Artillery stood him in good stead.

In England, due to the single-minded struggle by Sir Hugh Trenchard, the RAF had been recognized as a separate service, and had been granted an annual sum by Parliament, but in India the RAF was still accepted very much on sufferance. Even as late as 1927 it was exceedingly short of spares and equipment. In 1922 Jack had visited India with the express purpose of examining the post-war position. He had expected to find some reduction in aircraft after the war, but was astonished to find all the equipment in such poor condition. At a hill station he found that the pilots were nothing if not inventive. When he had noticed a large hole in the wing of the aircraft in which he was to fly, the young pilot apologized and said that no material was available for repairs. Canvas could usually be bought in the bazaars, but when this was not possible they had to do without. Even tyres were in short supply. Sir John had sent a startling report to the Viceroy, then Lord Reading. 'With regret,' he wrote, 'I have to inform you that the Royal Air Force in India is to all intents and purposes non-existent as a fighting force at this date.' He recommended a number of changes, including the addition of two more squadrons, and also that fifty engines should be sent to England to enable the aircraft to be repaired. He also recommended an extensive building programme, to provide accommodation for aircraft, personnel and equipment. In spite of this report, often known in India as 'The Bible', and the efforts of succeeding RAF Officers Commanding in India, Air Vice Marshals Adrian Chamier and Sir Philip Game, the increase in new machines was slow, and it was only in 1928 that the two additional squadrons would at last arrive.

Meanwhile, during 1927 and 1928, Geoffrey reorganized the available strength of the RAF, putting all squadrons in the North-West Frontier Province under the command of Group Captain Mills at Peshawar. The two squadrons, 11 and 39, to be equipped with Westland Wapitis Mk.IIA, were anxiously awaited by No. 2 Indian Wing at Kohat and were the first post-1918-designed aircraft, with the exception of the Hinaidi, to be introduced to India. The Hinaidi, the first machine of its type ever built, a huge twin-engined heavy transport machine, was to be assembled at Lahore and was still undergoing trials in the summer of 1928. In contrast to some of the Army criticism, nobody could have been kinder or more sympathetic than the Viceroy, Lord Irwin, and the Commander-in-Chief, Sir William Birdwood, of Anzac fame.

Perhaps the most inspiring approach to the young Service in India was Sir Hugh Trenchard's vision, in which Geoffrey shared – the vision that one day the vast continent of India would be linked by civil and military air routes to China, Hong Kong, Singapore and Trincomalee, and that the RAF in India, through its closer relationship with the other Commands and with the Chief of Air Staff personally, would become a lifesaving force, not only in war but in peacetime as well. Such a link was to be found far sooner than anyone had expected, in the situation which was developing in the remote fastness of Kabul, the capital of Afghanistan. Less than a month after Group Captain Mills had been given command of all squadrons in the North-West Frontier Province, Geoffrey received a message from Sir Francis Humphrys, the British Minister in Kabul, on 5 December 1928, asking that arrangements should be made to evacuate all women and children from the British Legation in Kabul by air.

Crisis in Kabul; Rescue over the Mountains

At this time the Viceroy and his staff and all their families had moved from Simla down to Delhi for the winter months. Until the message arrived life had seemed very relaxed. There were race meetings and picnics, and the Salmond children would ride their ponies before breakfast in the cool early morning. Their father was, however, immensely busy, travelling to all RAF Stations in his India Command and making every effort to improve them. He had been especially conscious of the situation on the North-West Frontier, for news was spreading that the tribes in Afghanistan, and especially the Pathans and Shinwaris, were about to rise against their king, King Amanullah, whose attitude, for several years since his accession in 1922, had been quite out of tune with his own followers. Having travelled to Europe with his beautiful young bride and been fêted and spoilt, he had determined to introduce reforms in his own country. With some courage he had gathered the leaders together, lecturing them himself on the ways of the West. But it was all too much for his followers. He went too far, especially in insisting that his tribal leaders should all wear Western dress and adopt Western customs, which were entirely foreign to the Afghan tradition. Their country, remote and mysterious, a country of high mountains and deep valleys in which each tribe lived according to its own

of course!

rules, was quite unsuited to the King's new regulations. When he insisted that they should send a proportion of their daughters to a modern school, either in Kabul or to Western universities, and that they should wear short skirts and cut their hair, the Shinwaris were the first to rise against him. Other tribes flocked to their banner, as they advanced towards Kabul. Very soon they invaded Jalalabad, led by a rebel, Bacha-i-Saquo, the son of a water-carrier, and the road from Kabul to Kandahar also became unsafe. At this time, too, the vital road from Peshawar to Kabul became impassable. Bridges were blown up and the British Legation was cut off by road and land line, the Afghan wireless station in Kabul becoming their only communication with the outside world. Years before, in 1841, there had been a rising against the British in Kabul, and unwisely the Army had decided to retreat across the mountains towards India. It was bitterly cold, and the Army, together with wives and daughters, women and children, 'camp followers' and tradesmen, set out without proper organization to retreat through the Khoord Kaul Pass. They were fired on continuously by snipers from the heights surrounding the pass, and many died from exposure after sleeping in the snow. The only survivor was a Doctor Brydon who had ridden, tired and exhausted, into Jalalabad on his worn-out horse. The memory of his story was engraved on the hearts of the British in India. No such retreat through the mountains and the bitter weather would be possible.

As the rebels under Bacha-i-Saquo advanced on Kabul, and the Government forces under King Amanullah prepared to meet them, the British Minister had to make a quick decision. The Embassy, an imposing white building some five miles from the city centre, was surrounded by gardens and a high wall. He knew he was temporarily out of danger, but realized that the Embassy was in the direct path of the rebels. Already gunfire could be heard. There were women and children whom he had swiftly gathered into the 'Big House'. Desperately, he decided to send a last message through the Afghan radio out to Delhi, requesting that the women and children be rescued by air. Geoff received the message while on manoeuvres. Sir William Birdwood, the Commander-in-Chief, was with him and at once gave him his blessing. It was necessary to assemble aircraft which could fly over mountains some 10,000 feet high in one of the coldest winters on record. He was determined they should be prepared, not only to rescue the women and children from the British Embassy, but all the other residents, perhaps up to 500, who were at that time in danger in the Italian and German embassies in the capital. From the time of the minister's last message no more communication was possible. The lines were all dead.

The RAF deployment on the frontier consisted of 1 (India) Group, commanded by Group Captain Mills, MC, DFC, 1 (Indian) Wing stationed at Kohat, 2 (Indian) Wing stationed at Risalpur, 27 (Bomber) Squadron at Risalpur and 60 (Bomber) Squadron at Kohat. There were no aircraft large enough to carry passengers except the Hinaidi, which at that time was in

Baghdad waiting to bring the new Foreign Secretary, Sir Denis Bray, to India. Geoff immediately got in touch with Sir Hugh Trenchard at home, asking permission to be lent Victorias from Baghdad in which to mount an evacuation operation. Sir Hugh gave his permission, and eight Victorias, with the Hinaidi, piloted by Squadron Leader Maxwell, were to be sent to Peshawar as soon as possible.

Vickers Victorias were the latest developments of the famous Vimy, which had been the first aeroplane to fly the Atlantic in 1919, powered by Napier Lion engines. Geoffrey had seen the first Vimy aircraft when on leave in 1919, and in 1922 he had developed the idea of troop-carrying by air which had resulted in the development of Vernons and Victorias. Before the evacuation could begin, tests had to be carried out to see if the Victorias, without their bomb racks, wireless and other heavy equipment, could fly above the high mountains. These tests at Quetta were successful. None of the crew was to be armed, even with a revolver, as it was necessary that the mission was to be seen as peaceful, especially if the aircraft had to make a forced landing or was shot down. This was very hard for the pilots to bear, but they realized the importance of the decision.

They now only awaited permission to land at Sherpur, the Kabul airfield, but no message came. Geoffrey decided to send one of his DH.9A aircraft over the mountains to the British Legation to see what was really happening, and to drop a 'Popham Panel', a method of signalling developed by Sir Robert Brooke-Popham, who was then in command at Baghdad. The aircraft succeeded in flying over the mountains, and at length approached the Legation, which they quickly saw was now almost surrounded by rebels. Gunfire could be heard in all directions. Inside the Legation Sir Francis Humphrys had already counted 400 bullet holes and, although realizing that the Embassy was not the target of the guns, could see that the wild rebel tribesmen were shooting indiscriminately and were advancing towards the King's Palace. A house in the grounds belonging to Basil Gould was destroyed by fire just after he, his wife, two small children and their governess, Miss Pulford, had moved into the 'Big House'.

The pilot of the DH.9A, Flying Officer Trusk, and his observer and radio operator, Leading Aircraftsman Donaldson, saw the Legation apparently silent and deserted, but they dropped the 'Popham Panel', coming down very low to do so. The next few minutes are described in Donaldson's own words:

> I turned round to speak to Trusk and he was covered in black oil. He said 'We've been hit! I'll have to land.' I said, 'Get some height – I want voltage!' In those days we used to have a generator on the wing. So up he went, and took her as high as he could, until the engine conked . . . and while he was climbing I rapped out this message and Peshawar picked it up. When we got down on Sherpur aerodrome we didn't realize our

tyres were shot away – we just turned over, and we just sat there, and I saw a car coming over the aerodrome. All we could see were rifles pointing over the side of it, and half a dozen chaps in Balaclava helmets and rifles came up and took us prisoner. We certainly did have fourteen bullet holes. I had a hole in my Sidcot suit.'

In the evening they were taken to a room in the town. Fortunately, the door was locked, for the next morning they found the guard standing at their door had been murdered. They managed, at last, to slip through their captors guided by a bearer sent from Sir Francis, and reached the British Legation. Again, Donaldson's words are the most vivid. The Legation stood the other side of a long lawn in the cross-fire of the two armies. He wrote:

> We waited till the firing had died down a bit, and the bearer said, 'Do you see those French windows in the house over there? I'm going to make for those.' If there's firing when I cross the lawn, wait till the firing stops, and then the next one go!' So he went off. And then Trusk went off, and then I went off, and we all made it! One Army on one side, one on the other, taking pot shots at us on the way. It felt like a hundred and fifty miles, you rather dreamed you had been running for ever, and going backwards. As we got to the French windows they opened the doors, and I fell in. It was the library or billiard room and I looked up, from thinking I was going to be shot at any minute, to find three or four kiddies playing with their toys on the floor. If you told anyone about it, they wouldn't believe it had happened.

As a wireless expert Donaldson suggested that he should slip through the lines once more, remove the wireless set from his aircraft at night and fix up an aerial on the roof. This, with great courage, he at last managed to accomplish, hoping that he could at last send a message from the Legation to Peshawar.

Meanwhile, Lady Humphrys had thought of a brilliant idea. She set all the ladies to work tearing up large white sheets and the bearers were kind enough to lend some of their long white turbans. Miss Pulford, the children's governess, continues the story:

> We put out a message on the lawn, we cut it out in sheets. They were six feet long, and the bearers cut stakes to measure them out. Sir Francis had said, 'They will put an aeroplane up'. And they did. We put 'Do not land. Fly High. All's well'. We were day and night on it, because we thought any moment the aeroplanes might come. And they did come.

The white sheets, spelling out their message, lay out on the grass in the moonlight of 17/18 December and from time to time Sir Francis and Lady

Humphrys, and those anxious men and women in the Legation, would glance through the shattered windows at the grey mountains between themselves and safety and wonder if their message had got through and if help would come.

On the next day Geoffrey wrote to Trenchard:

> Another machine was sent up at 13.00 hours, Flight Lieutenant Prendergast being the pilot, with instructions to drop a Popham Panel on the Legation, as we could not be certain that the original Popham Panel had been dropped by Trusk.

When Prendergast arrived over the Legation the signals were laid out in white letters: 'Don't land. All's well'. He was heavily fired at. Clearly, therefore, the idea of evacuation had been abandoned for the time.' Geoff continued in his report:

> It is as well here to state the enormous relief which the appearance of the Royal Air Force over the British Legation on the 18th gave to the Legation personnel in Kabul. When Flying Officer Trusk and later Flight Lieutenant Prendergast appeared, they realised they were not forgotten.

For several days the operation was repeated. DH.9As flew over the Embassy and always the same message was put out. 'Fly high. Do not land'. Quite suddenly Donaldson, the wireless operator, found he could get through to Peshawar.

It was evening in the Salmond bungalow in Delhi, their parents were both out and the little ones were in bed. Joyce and Anne were in their dressing-gowns when, at about 9 o'clock the telephone rang. Joyce, who was now fifteen and understood the emergency, rushed to answer it. She heard a very faint voice, asking for her father, and recognized it as Group Captain Mills from Peshawar. When she told him her father was out, he said that the message was very, very important, and asked her to tell her father that a message had just come through that evening from Sir Francis Humphrys to say he would like the women and children evacuated the next day. Joyce did not hesitate. She telephoned her father's office, but he had already left. Then she telephoned Sir Denys Bray, the Foreign Secretary, who had just arrived from Baghdad. Lady Bray was surprised that Joyce was telephoning so late in the evening, but Joyce said she must speak to Sir Denys at once. When he heard the message he congratulated her on her prompt behaviour, and asked where her father was. Joyce told him what she had done, and added, 'He's very elusive.' Years later she told her sister that the book she was reading, *The Elusive Pimpernel*, was under her pillow at the time. She had just put the telephone down when she and Anne heard the scrunch of their father's car wheels on the gravel outside. He just said, 'Well done', put his arm round Joyce for a moment, and was gone into the night.*

It seemed that in Kabul, at about noon on 22 December, the King's troops had made a determined move against Bacha-i-Saquo, forcing him to retreat temporarily and for the moment the airfield was in the hands of the King's troops. Thus Sir Francis had felt he could send the emergency message from the roof of his Legation at last. Geoffrey wrote to Trenchard afterwards:

> You can imagine my feelings when, in the absence of the telegram itself, I thought that the evacuation now asked for by Humphrys had to be a forced evacuation . . . However, in a very short time I received Humphrys' telegram which was to the effect that that afternoon two Afghan officials had been to see him and informed him that he could evacuate the women and children as soon as arrangements could be made, from Sherpur aerodrome.

During the hours of darkness which followed, plans which had been made so carefully by Geoffrey and his staff were put into motion. One Wapiti, piloted by Squadron Leader Nicholas, followed by one Victoria piloted by Squadron Leader Maxwell, would fly with three DH.9As over the mountains to Sherpur at dawn. The women and children of the Legation were collected at 4 am on 23 December and, just before dawn, the gates of the British Legation were quietly opened. A small party of twenty-three women and children, escorted by a few Afghan soldiers, slipped silently through on foot and walked noise-lessly into the darkness. Sir Francis Humphrys himself escorted them for half a mile, until they were through the battle-line. Desultory fire had already started round the Legation. The children were wrapped in as many clothes as possible because of the intense cold and snow and the women were wrapped in long scarves and shawls. They carried the children who were too small to walk – a silent but gallant band. In an hour they had reached the Italian Legation, which was near the airfield. Soon they saw the huge Victorias approaching over the mountains.

Lady Humphrys wrote in her diary:

> We are driven down to the aeroplane at once. The Vickers is a glorious sight, and our splendid airmen, amongst the crowd of Russian and Afghan airmen, make one thrill with pride. The Legation becomes a tiny white speck among the grim hills. Since we have left it has become possible for the British Legation to move about the garden, and fifty-nine

* It is of pleasant significance that Geoffrey's great-granddaughter, Melanie Baker, acted the part of Joyce in the BBC production of 'The Evacuation of Kabul' produced by Alfred Shaughnessy at Christmas, 1975.

shells had been identified on the building alone, many more in the gardens, bullets everywhere.

Just an hour after landing at Sherpur, the Victoria was airborne once more and flying Lady Humphrys and the women and children to Peshawar and safety. But for Lady Humphrys and the wives of those men left behind it had been a heart-rending order, for the British Legation was still under fire and they did not know if or when they would see those dear to them again. There was no flying on Christmas Day, and for two days afterwards it snowed so hard that no aircraft could fly. However, on the 27th the rescue was resumed.

Gradually the relief force was assembling and Sir Geoffrey wrote: 'The following aircraft, therefore, were available on the frontier on December 29 1928: 3 Victorias, 1 Hinaidi, 2 Wapiti machines, two Squadrons of DH.9As.' It now became easier to visualize a mass evacuation. On 29 December Sir Francis Humphrys again wired that the evacuation could continue. It was even rumoured that he had employed combatants from either side to clear the snow from the airfield at Sherpur. In any case Squadron Leader Maxwell landed safely in his Victoria, while Flight Lieutenant Anderson landed in the Hinaidi. Thirty-one Italian, German, Indian, Turk and Syrian women and children were evacuated. Next day twenty-three more flew to safety. On 4 January Trenchard received a telegram from Francis Humphrys in Kabul:

First January. Best wishes for New Year to Lady Trenchard and yourself. We are all filled with admiration for achievements of RAF in evacuating 132 women and children to Peshawar since December 23rd. Francis Humphrys. Kabul.

Geoffrey wrote:

Thus ended the second phase of the operation. Instead of a situation of acute anxiety as to the safety of the women and children in Kabul, events have come about, through the operations of the Royal Air Force, whereby a great load of responsibility was removed from the Legation . . . It is also striking testimony to the efficiency of the officers and men of No. 70 (Bombing) Squadron, under the command of Squadron Leader R. S. Maxwell MC DFC, and of the Victoria aircraft that these machines were operated with unfailing regularity, some thousands of miles from their base, with practically no workshop facilities and only a handful of stores and spare parts, whilst the maintenance was carried out by the crews of the machines themselves almost without assistance. No shed accommodation was available at Risalpur aerodrome and all the work of maintenance was carried out in the open and a great proportion of it after dark, often throughout the night.

He also paid tribute to Sir Robert Brooke-Popham, the AOC in Iraq, for the rapidity with which he had managed to send the aircraft.

Only one shadow hung over the swift decisions and eventual success of the Kabul operation, one situation which was regretted by both Trenchard, Geoffrey and by all who knew Lawrence. That was the departure, on 8 January, from Miranshar of an unusual serviceman, known as Aircraftman Shaw. For Lawrence, who had sought peace and sanctuary in the ranks of the RAF, had thought that in the remote and isolated station of Miranshar, under the command of Sir Geoffrey Salmond who knew him so well, and far up in the Himalayan mountains, that he would be able to carry out his duties as an airman clerk without being followed and without the persecution of the Press. He translated Homer's *Odyssey* in his spare time, sitting by a rough table with the light of a candle, and was meticulous in carrying out his duties. However, in December, he found himself in the glare of publicity once more. It came as a shock not only to his friends but to the whole world when in a newspaper article dated 5 January 1929 appeared: 'The Afghan authorities have ordered the arrest of Colonel Lawrence on the grounds that he is believed to be assisting the Afghan rebels to cross the frontier.' Wild accusations followed from the German and Italian press. It was rumoured that Lawrence was travelling in disguise, but nothing could have been further from the truth. Under these circumstances, Sir Francis Humphreys, trying hard to preserve a neutral and unbiased front in his bullet-torn Legation, asked for Aircraftman Shaw's withdrawal to some place far from the frontier. At first Geoffrey refused to send him home, but after receiving a letter from Trenchard he was forced to agree. Two letters from Lawrence, passionately denying the accusations, were sent to Geoffrey, who wrote to Sir Hugh Trenchard: 'Poor Lawrence! The whole thing is a tragedy. Directly I received your telegram I ordered him down by air to Lahore, and sent up Colonel Turner with a personal letter from me explaining the circumstances.' Trenchard had written to ask if Lawrence would like to go to Aden, or to Somaliland or even Singapore. He wrote: 'I am ready to do anything I can to help Lawrence. Please wire me where Lawrence wants to go.' But Lawrence wrote passionately to Geoffrey, saying he would be hounded wherever he went by the Press, and asked to be sent home. Geoffrey wrote to Trenchard: 'He was very much upset. However, he understood the necessity. He felt it was no good going to Singapore as, as soon as there was some row there it would be put down to him. He said he would always be hounded about wherever he went. He had therefore decided to come home. I am sending him on as soon as possible.'

On arrival at Karachi from Lahore Lawrence wrote to Sir Geoffrey:

Your letter was exceedingly kind; I am very grateful – I didn't answer it then and there because I was a bit dizzy after a rough flight and the news in your letter wasn't good. How far I had expected it may be shown by my having left all my Indian kit and drill at Miranshah and came away just with my English stuff. I voted for England of the alternatives given me, since to have entered another colony with the 'chit' of political deportee from India would have been only asking for trouble. You told me to see the funny side of it: well, perhaps, but not just yet. Everybody will believe that there must have been something up for me to have been slung out so suddenly. However, perhaps it does not matter what everybody believes. Three times now the reputation I most undeservedly possess has got me into trouble. The good thing to hold onto, for the moment, is a memory of eight very happy months in Miranshah. It is the sort of place in which P. C. Wren's Legionnaires could go cafard and shoot their officers, and commit suicide. The four of us permanently there were always volunteering to stay on and on, and there was competition, lately from the squadrons, to get on detachment there. I think this was partly my doing, for I did all I could to make it a decent place, and I feel that I have run away and deserted the ship. They are three very good fellows, the survivors of the Miranshah permanent staff. I would have been glad to do something for them, if I could, but I'm perhaps the most in need of help now. I now have just enough money (four pounds) to take me comfortably home. Thanks for your telegram to Depot here, all the same. As I said before, I'm exceedingly sorry to have given trouble. What gives trouble is my wanting to be in the RAF. Yet the year or two of civil life which I tried was worse many times over than the ranks. In the ranks my past only crops up once a year or so and hits me, as now. In normal life I used to meet it every day. It's a horrid lesson not to do unusual things: otherwise you get a tin-can of a reputation tied to your tail and are driven mad by it. The car will be here soon to take me to the boat; so here ends my India effort. I do wish it hadn't ended this way. Yours, T. E. Shaw. p.s. That last long fly-down, from Lahore here, was lovely. I wish I were a Secretary of State, to fly all day.

Geoffrey gave Lawrence permission to wear civilian clothes for the journey, and a second class passage was booked on the SS *Rajputana*. Geoffrey wrote to Lawrence saying the whole of the RAF in India regretted his departure. When the *Rajputana* put in at Plymouth, Lawrence was met, on Trenchard's instructions, by Wing Commander Sydney Smith, whose flying boat squadron at Cattwater (soon afterwards to be named Mountbatten), was nearby. After a few days leave in which he was invited to stay with Trenchard at his country house, Dancer's Hill, Lawrence joined the Flying Boat Squadron and here perhaps he was able to find something of the peace of mind and contentment which had been denied him on the North-West Frontier of India.

During January 1929 the Victorias and the Hinaidi flew regularly over the mountains to rescue not only the women and children but all the members of the different Legations who wanted to leave. Bacha-i-Saquo, though wounded and in the hills, was still attracting more and more followers, and the situation was growing very grave. Sir Samuel Hoare wrote to Sir Francis Humphrys, suggesting that he should leave, but he replied that he was unwilling to leave until not only his staff but all the staffs of the other Embassies had been given the opportunity to go. Sir Francis also received a request from the government of King Amanullah, asking that he should move further into the city for his own safety. It seemed strange that the Cafe Wali Hotel, from which Trusk and Donaldson had so fortunately escaped, should be suggested as a suitable Headquarters for the Staff of the British Legation. Sir Francis replied in a digni-fied note: 'It is not the practice of His Britannic Majesty's ministers to quit their Legations without orders from their own Government.'

The weather was now so bitterly cold that pilots were given orders to keep their aircraft engines running after they landed. On 14 January King Amanullah issued a proclamation saying he withdrew all his reforms. But it was too late, and he seemed to realize this, for at 04.00 that day a fleet of seven cars headed through the gates of his Palace and set off at high speed down the road to Kandahar. The King, some say disguised as a Mullah, had abdicated. Sir Francis Humphrys was later to describe the King's abdication:

> It seemed very surprising that a man of Amanullah's courage did not place himself at the head of his troops and risk everything in a final counter-attack. He would probably have taken this desperate course if his antagonist had been a person of Royal Blood. What he could not face was the enduring disgrace to his house of being tied to a tree and shot like a bandit. There is no doubt, however, that in a country where personal bravery counts for almost everything, this hasty flight made it inconceiv-able that he would ever be able to return to Kabul again.

Amanullah chose his brother to succeed him, but the palace was now surrounded and he was only king for three days. Sir Francis somehow persuaded the rebels to let him go free, as long as he left Afghanistan for ever. He was flown out safely three days later by Squadron Leader Maxwell and Flight Lieutenant Ronald Ivelaw-Chapman. Everything seemed proceeding almost better than had been hoped when, on 31 January Trenchard received a cable from Geoffrey: 'I am very sorry to have to report to you that Chapman's Victoria was missing on the 29 January. We searched all yesterday, and also on the afternoon of the 29th. but so far have been unable to locate him.'

There was great anxiety in India during the next few days, for it was thought Chapman and Davies, his observer, could not possibly have survived a crash in the fearful mountains of the Hindu Kush. Suddenly Maxwell, when flying his Victoria to Kabul, spotted the aircraft far below him, perched on a narrow ledge only 60 feet (18 m) long and less in width, with a drop of 200 feet (61m) on three sides, but there was no sign of the crew. Those who knew

Ivelaw-Chapman, or 'Chaps' as he preferred to be called, had great confidence in his cool courage and resource under any circumstances. He had obviously brought the Victoria down with immense skill but now, without arms, without anything other than the clothes he stood up in, he had to persuade the wild tribesmen that both he and Davies were not enemies. This was especially difficult as Russian pilots had been flying ancient DH.9s over the rebels and bombing their troops. 'Chaps' wrote later:

> From the air we had seen not a soul, but we were soon surrounded by a mob of heavily armed and wildly shouting Afghan tribesmen. They were speaking in Pushtu. I could speak a little Urdu but no Pushtu. Davies spoke neither, so we could not communicate by speech at all.

Eventually a so-called 'General' arrived and they were taken prisoner, but with his undoubted charm and confidence Ronald Ivelaw–Chapman persuaded the 'General' to take him back to his aircraft the next day. He found that water had frozen in the fuel, and this had been the cause of both engines dying at once. Clearly the aircraft could not be moved, and Chaps began to devise other means of escape. This was even more difficult as Davies had injured his knee badly in the landing. He was eventually taken to see a Holy Man, a religious leader, who lived in a fort not far from Jalalabad. Although about eighty years old, he held great influence over the warring tribes and through an interpreter it was found that he had originally lived in Baghdad. This created a bond between them, and the Pir Sahib not only offered Chaps his guest tent, but also gave him permission to make an airstrip not far from his summer camp.

The ground was rough and stony, but the Pir Sahib granted him many helpers from the tribes to flatten the ground. Chaps then sent a message by foot in the care of a tribesman who knew secret ways into India, to Peshawar, asking that a Victoria be sent to rescue them. In a few days a Bristol fighter appeared and landed. Unfortunately in landing it broke a tailskid, but in a few hours, with the help of the leg of a broken chair and much luck, the tail was repaired and Davies, whose knee was still giving him pain, was the first to be rescued. Chaps followed a week later and on 18 February he wrote that he was once more back in the Peshawar Club, having a drink with Squadron Leader Maxwell and all his friends.

Meanwhile, as diplomatic telegrams were passing urgently between London and the Legation at Kabul, Geoffrey continued to organize almost daily rescue flights to Sherpur whenever the weather made landing possible. However, it was becoming colder every day and there was continued anxiety after Chaps had made his report. Geoffrey wrote to Trenchard:

> In order to minimise the possibility of further catastrophes from this cause (i.e. water in the Benzole mixture), refuelling and storage arrange-

ments at Risalpur were immediately overhauled, and the following precautions taken: a) All fuel was filtered twice before being passed into the tanks; b) On completion of the day's flying, all petrol filters were cleaned and tanks filled overnight; c) Before proceeding to Kabul, each aeroplane carried out a short test flight, flying for a few minutes on each tank, then landed and all petrol filters were cleaned. These precautions proved successful.

One can imagine the intense cold of filtering the petrol twice in icy weather, and one cannot but admire the devotion of the crews. As another precaution an interpreter was also carried on every flight after Ivelaw-Chapman's forced landing. During the last week of January and up to 15 February six more Victorias arrived from Baghdad to take part in the evacuation and in spite of the bitter weather, the rescue continued. Mr G. A. Copping, the rigger of Anness's Victoria, wrote later:

> I made three trips to Kabul and back. We had seen some pretty rugged country on our way down the Persian Gulf and the Gulf of Oman, but the terrain between the Khyber Pass and Kabul is awe-inspiring in its rugged grandeur, rank upon rank of jagged peaks, most of them snow-covered as far as one could see, in any direction, and now and again a valley so deep it appeared quite dark at the bottom, it may have been a trick of light and shade but I was fascinated . . . I was cold – I remember the cold more than anything – it seemed to penetrate to the bone, in spite of extra woollies and our 'Sidcot' suits.

And so, all through those weeks of ice and snow, battling against the intense cold, the pilots of the Victorias continued to fly almost every day. By 20 February members of all the legations, with their women and children, were flown to safety. However, on 22 February Flight Lieutenant Anderson reported that he was unable to take off in the Hinaidi as the snow was too deep on the airfield at Sherpur, and the Victorias following him were instructed to turn back. Sir Francis, well aware of the acute political situation developing, organized every available means of clearing a runway. Camels and even the few elephants in Kabul were mobilized and the whole population seemed inspired by Sir Francis to clear a track of snow. Two days later Anderson reported that a track 600 yards long by twenty yards (550m by 18m) had been cleared and was fit for the Victorias. Four Victorias therefore took off that day from Risalpur and rescued a total of twenty-seven passengers. This completed the rescue of the entire French and Italian Legations, and many civilians, including Germans. There now only remained the Minister and staff of the British Legation, and it was decided that the operation should be concluded in one day.

It was the morning of 25 February. One by one the seven Victorias, accompanied by the Hinaidi, roared over the Legation, making their journey over the mountains to Kabul for the last time, after taking off at intervals from Risalpur at 07.45. One by one they landed, keeping their engines running, on the airstrip so carefully prepared and guarded, whilst firing had already begun in the city. Already Shinwari and Khogianis were advancing from Jalalabad towards Kabul, with the intention of attacking the city. Sir Francis, while preserving complete neutrality and thus commanding respect from both sides, had seen the clouds gathering and he knew that, if Kabul were once again engulfed in conflict, it would be impossible for members of any of the Legations to escape. Now he was satisfied that all those who wished to go had been rescued, and he was determined that he would be the last to leave. Members of the Legation gathered on the lawn for the last time that morning included Flying Officer Trusk and LAC Donaldson, who had so gallantly organized the telegraph throughout the rescue. Beside them were the long French windows of the billiard room through which Donaldson had flung himself on 22 December, just two months before, and in front of them the scarred white walls and shattered windows of the Legation stood bare and grim in the morning sunlight. Suddenly those anxiously watching saw that Sir Francis himself was not with them. Time was running out for Habibullah Khan. The rebel leader, so precariously upon the throne, was no longer in control of his army and already the sounds of shots and gunfire were beginning once more to shake the city.

Every moment seemed precious; the members of the Legation looked at one another anxiously. In a few minutes Sir Francis appeared again on the steps, carrying under his arm the Union Jack which had flown over the British Legation. The gates were opened for the last time, and the small party, led by Sir Francis Humphrys, walked to the airfield. They were only just in time. As Donaldson looked back he saw the city behind them already engulfed in flames. But the aircraft engines were running, and Sir Geoffrey wrote in his report: 'The last aeroplane conveyed Sir Francis Humphrys, Flying Officer Trusk, and LAC Donaldson.' It was a proud moment for Donaldson, who was just twenty-two years old when he and his pilot were chosen to be the last to leave, with Sir Francis Humphrys. When the Minister finally stepped on to the airfield at Peshawar, to be greeted by Sir Norman Bolton and Group Captain Mills, he still carried the Union Jack under his arm.

The massive mountains and valleys of the lower Hindu Kush range and the Khyber Pass had been daringly faced and conquered by a handful of young pilots and airmen during the worst winter on record. Not one life of crew or passengers had been lost. The aircraft they flew had none of the equipment now thought essential for flying, and all had gone totally unarmed to a city on the brink of revolution. In one month 586 passengers of all nationalities, including 153 women and 165 children, had been rescued in 84 sorties through the mountains. In all, 57,438 miles had been flown, if all journeys were included, over mountains averaging 10,000 feet, and over country which afforded very few opportunities of making a successful forced landing.

Perhaps the story should end here, but this would be entirely out of character with those early days of the RAF. For it was not only the pilots who deserved honour, but every member of the crews, every mechanic, rigger or 'erk' – all those who had battled with the elements, defying rest and comfort, to keep their machines in the air.

Geoffrey flew to Risalpur on 26 February to inspect 70 Squadron. Telegrams had already been pouring in to congratulate all taking part. In particular one from Sir Francis Humphrys to Hugh Trenchard: 'We owe everything to magnificent achievements of RAF. Francis Humphrys Peshawar.'

Geoffrey received a signal ordering the Victorias back to Iraq, where they were urgently needed. There was not much time to lose. He wrote to Trenchard:

> On the evening of the 26th, after the Inspection, the Royal Air Force gave a dinner to No. 70 Squadron, at which Sir Francis Humphrys, Sir Norman Bolton and various members of the British Legation, Kabul, attended. I had Humphrys on my left, and it really was a unique occasion. I wish you had been present. Oratory flowed, and it was a fitting conclusion to the whole show.

Neither was Geoffrey going to let the magnificent 70 Squadron and the pilot of the Hinaidi go without due recognition from Headquarters at Delhi. He wanted the Viceroy, Lord Irwin, to meet them and the Commander-in-Chief, Sir William Birdwood, who had helped so much in the swift transport of supplies with every sort of support.

And so, on 27 February, only two days after the gates of the Legation at Kabul had closed for the last time, an inspection and celebration for all those members of the RAF who had taken part in the evacuation was planned in Delhi, the Headquarters of the RAF in India, over 600 miles away. Donaldson described the thrill and rush of the preparations. Not only had the aircraft themselves to be serviced, but every member of the crews had to check his kit for inspection. But all knew that, however they appeared at such short notice, they were the heroes of the hour. Even so their first thought was for their aircraft, and the second for their smart appearance, to do credit to the Service.

Sir Geoffrey wrote:

> I had arranged for the machines to fly line ahead at a comparatively low height over Delhi. This they did twice, and I am told by everybody that it was a most impressive sight.

Four o'clock at Delhi was perhaps the loveliest time of a spring day. The heat of the sun was over and the gardens were full of bougainvillea, canna lilies and spring flowers. The huge aircraft appeared at exactly 16.00 over the sun-washed capital and were indeed a magnificent sight. The Legislative Assembly was in full session, but hearing the roar of the Victorias' engines overhead, all members stopped their debate to stand outside to watch them. They landed exactly on time, in perfect formation, on the airfield at Raisina. Treasured photographs taken by members of the Squadron record the proud moment of their arrival at Delhi, and the Inspection the next morning, when, at exactly 11.45 the Hinaidi, the DH.9As, the Wapitis and the 'glorious' Victorias stood proudly in brilliant sunshine, their crews beside them, as smartly as on a parade ground after weeks of preparation. In the photograph we can see the Commander-in-Chief, Lord Birdwood, walking from man to man, shaking hands and having a word with every man of the crews. The Viceroy, Lord Irwin, made a short and amusing speech. Group Captain Maxwell is seen talking to the Viceroy, and Geoffrey walks proudly behind the Commander-in-Chief with Sir Denys Bray the Foreign Secretary.

That night there was a dinner and dance for all those who had taken part in the evacuation, and their guests. Needless to say, on the menu was 'Salmond Mayonnaise'. Squadron Leader Anderson sat next to Sir Geoffrey's eldest daughter, Joyce, at the dinner and the young pilots drank her health, as in Sir Denys Bray's words, she had been 'her father's best Staff Officer'. To overcome the difficulty of finding enough partners for the sudden arrival of so many young airmen for the dance which followed, Donaldson was told that the order had gone out that before the ladies danced with anyone else they should be sure that every airman who had taken part in the evacuation of Kabul had a partner. And so the brilliant tropical night ended with a typical celebration by the RAF, far from their home base, in the heat of New Delhi and under myriads of stars.

*   *   *

Soon after the evacuation of Kabul the Salmond family returned to England. John was to go to a preparatory school, Sandroyd School at Cobham, and Geoffrey took three months of his leave to join them. The family returned from Bombay by P & O ship, while Geoff was to follow by air.

On his return to England, Geoff was asked to give a report to the Prince of Wales on the evacuation of Kabul. He was most impressed by the Prince's knowledge of events in Afghanistan and his very real interest in the outstanding achievements of the Royal Air Force. Geoffrey himself was promoted to Air Marshal that summer.

It was an exciting time to be at home. Jack was now an Air Chief Marshal and principal ADC to the King. Once more the brothers were able to consult each other, and as Jack had recently returned from Australia, where he had been asked to help organize the Australian Air Force, long-distance air routes were also discussed, as was the future of air power, both in India and the Far East. Nearer home, there were the preparations for the 1929 Schneider Trophy race, and for the first long-distance flight of the Rl00 airship, which was to take place the following year.

To his delight, Geoffrey was also to find that light aircraft, and especially the Moth, were growing ever more popular. Several private Moths and Avians were fitted with slots by Handley-Page, and in the election campaign in May a number of candidates used light aircraft, including Captain Balfour, standing for Thanet, and the Marquess of Clydesdale in the Govan district of Glasgow.*
As a result of the General Election Sir Samuel Hoare was succeeded as Minister for Air by Lord Thompson, himself passionately interested in flying, and especially in the huge airship, the *R101*, now nearing completion at Cardington. When he was elevated to the peerage, he chose the name Lord Thompson of Cardington in honour of the airship.

⋆   ⋆   ⋆

All too soon Geoff had to return to India, leaving the family at home and John at school. During the next two years, Geoff was to encourage an interest in the air throughout India, hoping that the Government of India itself would support long-distance flights, and that shorter civilian flights would be supported locally. It seems astonishing that up to 1927 no Indian had yet learnt to fly. The situation is best described in Geoffrey's own words a year later:

> As a result of Sir Victor Sassoon's very active support, the Light Aeroplane Movement was started in this country. The movement provides a means by which Indians can prove that they can fly as well as anybody else. The scheme of the Government was to establish light aeroplane clubs in Delhi, Karachi, Calcutta, Bombay, Madras and Lahore. The result was that Indians like Messrs. Chawla, and Manmichan Singh very soon proved that they were as skilled aviators as those of any other country.

The first actual flight by an Indian pilot was by R. N. Chawla between 25 April and 1 May 1930, flying a Moth. As a result of the Light Aeroplane Clubs, the Indian Princes began to take a keen interest in aviation. The Maharajas of Khalsa and Jodhpur learnt to fly, and their interest led to much more enthusiasm in the Indian States. It was due to Geoffrey's inspiration and

---

* The Marquess of Clydesdale was later to lead the first flight over Everest.

encouragement that the clubs were started, on the same pattern as those he had so successfully promoted in England.

Meanwhile, on 1 January 1930, the great Sir Hugh Trenchard resigned as Chief of Air Staff and was succeeded by Sir John Salmond. Sir Hugh had guided and inspired and fought for the Royal Air Force for just over ten years, and now he wanted to hand over to a younger man. Sir Samuel Hoare had paid a great tribute to him in Parliament, saying:

> I do not suppose that any Service had ever been so closely identified with its Chief of Staff as has the Air Force with Sir Hugh Trenchard. What it owes to his wise guidance, his consistent foresight and his resolute purpose I have had perhaps a better opportunity of judging than anyone else. Trenchard was beloved throughout the Service and has been called 'The Father of the Royal Air Force'.

Jack was only forty-nine when he took over as Chief of the Air Staff.

★   ★   ★

Early in 1930, Peggy and Joyce were able to sail out to India once more to join Geoffrey. The other children were to stay with their grandmother at Ditchingham Hall and John would join them for his holidays.

While Geoffrey and Peggy were together in India the first flight of the two great airships was due to take place. In the summer of 1930 the *R100* left the huge hangar at Hendon and flew successfully across the Atlantic. After flying over Ottawa, Toronto and Niagara, the gigantic airship made the return journey across the Atlantic in only three days to arrive at Cardington on 16 August. Her flight was the greatest encouragement to those working on the *R101*.

Sir Samuel Hoare, who had often visited Hendon and Cardington when Minister for Air, said that the team working in the vast hangar at Cardington which contained the *R101* were all his personal friends. He wrote:

> There, beneath the huge shed, at that time the largest building in the world, under the shadow of the towering landing mast, and face to face with the monster of silk and steel, they lived and worked like a religious community, intent upon their single purpose.

The airship had taken far longer to complete than Sir Samuel Hoare and Parliament had hoped, and it was partly due to the impatience of the public and of Lord Thompson himself that she set off on 4 October with a last-minute Certificate of Airworthiness, and with real doubts on the part of Sir Sefton Brancker unanswered. Lord Thompson had said:

So long as the *R101* is ready to go to India by the last week in September, this further delay in getting her altered may pass. I must insist on the programme for the India flight being adhered to, as I have made my plans accordingly.

Landing masts had been erected at Cardington, in the Suez Canal Zone and at Karachi, to which the giant airship could be attached without having to enter a hangar. Geoffrey, the Viceroy and Sir William Birdwood were all ready to welcome the *R101* on her arrival at Karachi, and to greet Sir Sefton Brancker and Lord Thompson.

The night of 4 October, when the *R101* set off, was rough and windy. At that time helium was considered too expensive, and so the huge gasbags lined with gold-beaters' skin contained hydrogen, a far more inflammable gas. On the other hand, the diesel engines, though heavier than the petrol engines of the *R100*, were considered safer. The huge airship sailed safely over London and disappeared into the night. Early in the morning of 5 October the terrible news reached England that the *R101* had crashed near Beauvais in France, with the loss of all but eight of those on board. The exact cause of the accident would never be known.

An inquiry led by Sir John Simon took many months and concluded that nobody was to blame for the accident. All work on airships was ended. The *R100* was scrapped. It was especially disappointing to Barnes Wallis, who had designed the airship, and all those who had worked on her for so many months and seen her cross the Atlantic so successfully. The greatest tragedy was the loss of so many lives, all those brilliant men who had set off with such high hopes on that October evening, and who had given up so much to work and live with the *R101* for so many months. To Geoffrey the loss of Sir Sefton Brancker, one of his greatest friends, must have been devastating.

Meanwhile, in India in 1930, an opportunity arose for Geoffrey to make a long-distance flight himself, an official RAF flight to Rangoon and Bangkok to visit the Siamese Government, which had visited India in 1929. He was to carry messages from the Viceroy to the King of Siam, on the occasion of his birthday. Geoffrey was to fly in the Hinaidi, accompanied by two Wapitis. As the country over which they had to fly was uninhabited, with vast jungle and swamps between Rangoon and Bangkok, they took hatchets and emergency supplies with them in case of a forced landing in the jungle. The Minister for War in Siam, Prince Bovaradej, went by train to meet them at Dom Muang airfield. Sir Cecil Dormer, the British Ambassador, wrote:

Shortly before noon two Bristol Bulldog machines went up to meet them. A telegram despatched from Rangoon announcing that the flight would not arrive before 2 pm missed me, and as the flying conditions seemed anything but favourable and the country between Rangoon and here consists of mountains, jungle and swamps, we had a somewhat anxious time waiting. However, all was well. The Air Marshal was cordially welcomed by Prince Bovaradej on behalf of the Government, and he then presented the officers of the Flight. . . . In the afternoon I accompanied them to the Palace and had the honour of presenting Sir Geoffrey Salmond to the King. The Air Marshal handed to His Majesty the message from the Viceroy of India, and presented the members of his staff. The audience lasted a quarter of an hour and was of a most friendly nature.

In the evening there was an official dinner and the Ambassador wrote again:

Prince Bovaradej welcomed the Air Force visit, in which he expressed the gratification of the Government that the flight should have been led by so distinguished a personage as the Officer Commanding the Royal Air Force in India with whom, he said incidentally, he had served as a cadet at Woolwich.

Altogether the visit was a great success and Sir Cecil Dormer wrote:

Up to the last moment, owing to the situation on the North-West Frontier, there had been a doubt whether the visit could take place, and the fact that it did take place and coincided, as had been hoped, with the King's birthday celebrations was, I feel sure, duly appreciated here; above all, the fact that Sir Geoffrey Salmond came in person. To his personality and affability in conversing with those whom he met much of the success of the visit is due, and I would pay a similar tribute to Colonel Turner and the other officers. The visit, too, gave no less pleasure to the British community, not to mention His Majesty's Legation, and I think it has contributed in no small degree to the promotion of friendly relations with the Siamese Government.

It had been an unforgettable experience for Geoffrey, especially as so very few visitors had reached Siam from India in those days.

*   *   *

All too soon Geoffrey's tour in India was drawing to a close. At this time Dorothy and Jack Newman were stationed in Bangalore, where General Newman was in command. Their family of three children were with them. In April 1931 Peggy and Joyce heard that Dorothy's eldest little boy, Jimmy, who was seven years old, was very ill. A few days later he died of peritonitis. Geoffrey had saved up his leave and they decided to leave for Bangalore almost at once to be with Dorothy and Jack at such a sad time, saying goodbye to all their friends in Simla and Delhi.

There were many expressions of sadness at their departure. An article in the *Illustrated Weekly of India* reported: 'All the Air Force, which Sir Geoffrey has commanded, have loved him and there has been no jollier house to be invited to, either in Delhi or Simla, than theirs.'

Whilst in Bangalore, Geoffrey gave his views on civil aviation and ended his interview by saying:

> Quite apart from the necessity of developing air communications, India's geographical position is of enormous importance because she lies on the direct route between Europe and Australia, and she is likely in future to become the focal point, as it were, of aviation in Central Asia, for in time many lines will radiate from India in different directions. The future of India is very much bound up with the development of air communications. It is a country of enormous distances, trade centres like Bombay and Madras being very widely separated from one another. By rail it takes about twenty-seven hours to travel from Bombay to Madras. By air this could be done in comfort in about seven hours.

After a few weeks in Bangalore with Dorothy and Jack, Geoffrey, Peggy and Joyce continued their journey home by way of southern India and Ceylon.

8

AIR DEFENCE OF GREAT BRITAIN

One morning in July, 1931, Anne and Penelope were told that they could travel down to Tilbury Docks with their uncle's ADC to meet the boat bringing Geoff, Peggy and Joyce home from India. It was an exciting journey, and as they drew nearer to the jetty Anne asked the ADC if he thought it would be possible for her to take off her hat, so that her father could see her red hair. He said he thought it would be quite all right. Soon they saw the liner draw near and at last Geoff, Peggy and Joyce leaning over the rail.

Geoff was to become Air Officer Commanding-in-Chief, Air Defence of Great Britain which included three other commands, Bombing Area, Fighting Area and Special Reserve, and the Auxiliary Air Force. It was a command which his brother had held for five years. He was to be stationed at Uxbridge and the family would live at nearby Stoke Poges. Geoff was delighted to be home again, and at once found himself involved in preparations for the Schneider Trophy race in September.

For reasons of economy, the Government had refused to support the Schneider Trophy Race in 1931, although the team under Squadron Leader Orlebar had won in 1929. It was particularly hard on the High Speed Flight as they had only to win once again for Great Britain to keep the trophy for ever. As Orlebar had said: 'A race like this is a very great incentive to rapid advance in design, and a definitely fixed date does lend a spur to the process of bringing theory to construction, and construction to test.' In 1930 the refusal of the Government to support the contest which was due to be held in England, would mean that no date could be fixed in the future. Many people throughout the country were in despair. At length the Government said that if any firm could put up £100,000 the contest could go ahead.

Help came from a quite unexpected quarter. Lady Houston, the widow of a rich shipowner, immediately came to the rescue, saying:

When the Socialist Government gave the paltry excuse that they could not afford the expenses necessary for England's airmen to participate in the race for the Schneider Trophy, my blood boiled with indignation, for I know that every true Briton would rather sell his last shirt than admit that England could not afford to defend herself against all comers.

Quite undaunted by any thought of losing the race, she gave the Government £100,000 and it was her proudest moment when she saw the team win in September. Perhaps understandably, she needed constant visits from RAF officers to bring her up to date on the Flight's progress. One of these officers was Geoffrey, who, with his charm and tact, was able to explain the progress of preparations for the race. He told his family afterwards of her immense loyalty to Britain, and of his reception at her house in London where she lay on a couch, covered by a Union Jack. He was tremendously impressed by her magnificent gesture and he was particularly delighted with her enthusiasm, as he himself was convinced that the development of the High Speed Flight was all important, not only to the race but to the whole future of the RAF.

On 13 September 1931 the final Schneider Race was flown at Spithead. The RAF High Speed Flight took part, using a new version of the Supermarine seaplane, the S-6B, also designed by Mitchell, with a further improved Rolls-Royce 'R' engine of 2350 horsepower. Flight Lieutenant Boothman won the Trophy outright for Britain, with an average speed of 340.08 miles per hour. On the same day Flight Lieutenant G. H. Stainforth in the S-6B put the World Absolute Speed Record up to 379.05 m.p.h., and a fortnight later broke even that record, reaching 407.5 miles per hour. The Schneider Trophy thus belonged to Britain outright, and Lady Houston's faith was justified, for the RAF's great achievement was recognized throughout the world. Mitchell's S6B was to give Britain the Spitfire and the fighting chance to save her and the free world from the terror to come.

*　　*　　*

The next year at Stoke Poges was a very happy one. The family was together again and surrounded by friends. Vi Barrington-Kennet lived nearby with her mother and, of course, with their memory of B.K. his wife became one of their dearest friends. Sir Arthur Longmore, who so long ago had been Geoffrey's instructor at Upavon, was now commandant of Cranwell and, on one occasion, the whole family went there to stay with him and his children.

Although Geoffrey and Peggy were much in demand and often out in the evening, Geoff was determined not to lose touch with Anne and Penelope, who were still in the schoolroom working hard for their exams. Every night before he went out he would come to see them, usually with a book of jokes, and so their evenings were really happy ones. In the summer of 1931, both Joyce and

Anne were presented at Court, and there seemed no cloud on the horizon. But in September, when Peggy and Geoff had taken Joyce to Scotland to stay with some cousins, the Thesigers at Tornasheen, Joyce was badly injured in a shooting accident. Brilliant surgeons did their best to save her eyesight but she lost the sight of one eye. She always remembered her father saying, 'I have been in all these wars and never been wounded, and now you are wounded, my Joyce.' It was a very anxious time, although Joyce was extremely brave and was to recover and look as beautiful as ever afterwards.

Politically, things were far from happy. The recession had led to the formation of a National Government and the need for economy had once more postponed the creation of all the 52 Squadrons promised by the Salisbury Committee in 1923. The peaceful atmosphere of Locarno and the inclusion of Germany in the League of Nations still seemed to justify disarmament, although Germany's acquisition of North Silesia had shocked members of the League. A Disarmament Conference was finally arranged, to take place at Geneva in 1932, and Geoffrey attended, representing the Royal Air Force. He was bitterly disillusioned. The British delegation was led by the Prime Minister, Ramsay MacDonald, and Sir John Simon, the Secretary of State for Foreign Affairs, but it seemed to Geoffrey that all the delegates were working for their own country's advancement and were not prepared to work together. He was afraid that the RAF might be sacrificed and flew to Paris, where he arranged to meet Jack to report urgently on the situation.

Jack hastened to Geneva. He at once asked for an interview with the Prime Minister and found to his horror that the Prime Minister and Anthony Eden were discussing the sacrifice of all bombers and machines capable of bombing, leaving only a 'Metropolitan Force' of fighters in Britain. Hitler had just given notice that he was about to withdraw from the Conference and also the League of Nations. Jack Salmond threw all his strength into saving the RAF, and it is to his great credit that he managed to do so. Soon afterwards he announced that he intended to resign in April 1933, in order to make way for younger officers. The Marquess of Londonderry, then Secretary of State for Air, and the Air Council decided that Geoffrey should succeed him. This decision, for brother to succeed brother, must have been unique in the history of a fighting Service. It was Geoffrey's record, of creating the Middle East Command, of his great victory in support of General Allenby's Army, his encouragement of Imperial Airways and his service in India which must have influenced their decision. Perhaps most of all it was his capacity for leadership, for the devotion which he inspired from all who worked for him and his loyalty to the Service, which led to their choice. They were characteristics which were shared by both the Salmond brothers.

In November, when just back from the Conference at Geneva, Geoffrey made a speech which caused consternation among the politicians. It was in answer to an invitation to a private dinner of the Old Comrades Association of the RAF held on 26 November at Harrods Georgian Restaurant. The dinner was reported in *The Aeroplane* of 30 November, and it is worth quoting the report almost in full, for Geoffrey described in his speech the position of the RAF at that time. It was one of the last speeches he was to make. The Chairman said how very grateful they were to have the Chief of the Air Staff elect with them and recalled Sir Geoffrey's achievements, particularly how the Middle East Command under his control had grown. In fact, Geoffrey had made it. He could not do better than couple the name of Geoffrey Salmond with that of the Royal Air Force.

When Geoff rose to speak he said he felt he knew all the Old Comrades. He spoke of the way in which the Service, quite particularly, was linked together by the manner in which the officer had to rely for his safety on his men, in war on his ground crew, in peace on the proper maintenance of his machine. This link accounted for the spirit of the Royal Air Force, and the Service was extraordinarily fortunate in the vital relationship which existed between officers and men. He went on to say that when the economy axe fell in those bitter years of 1918 – 1920 Britain had been reduced from having the foremost Air Force to having only three squadrons in England, five in Egypt and six or eight in Iraq. We had come back to realities to the extent of having today forty-two squadrons at home, four in Egypt and Palestine, four in Iraq, eight in India and one in Aden, besides the Fleet Air Arm Units and the flying boats. He said the British aircraft industry was the finest in the world, but he recalled the shock when the Americans came over in 1923 and won the Schneider Trophy. That made us pull ourselves together. To show the spirit of the industry, he said that when representatives of Rolls Royce came to him when he was Member of Supply and Research they asked for his support in developing a new engine for the Schneider contest, but when he asked how much it would cost the Government, they replied 'nothing'. This illustrated the spirit which animated the industry.

He went on to summarize the part played by the RAF in recent history: the affair of the 'Mad Mullah', who was defeated in a few weeks by the RAF; how Ibn Saud had been defeated in Transjordan by the RAF and armoured cars; and especially the RAF's achievements in Iraq. He then turned to India and how 586 people had been evacuated by air from Kabul, when the airfield at Peshawar itself was deep in snow. He then mentioned the rising on the North-West Frontier of India in 1930, when the only army available was the RAF. 'The Air Force dealt with the trouble and brought it to nought,' he said. 'The Air Force was the weapon for emergency, and I have never known it fail.'

Up to this point in his speech he had emphasized the enormous help the RAF had been in defending the Empire. He now turned to the future, and it was this part of his speech which was to cause such consternation among some Members of Parliament at the critical moment when disarmament was being discussed at Geneva. 'Whenever disarmament is spoken of, they heard the Air

Forces of the World very clearly mentioned,' he remarked. 'It is a tribute to air power that people should be so fearful of the might of this tremendous force – a somewhat different state of affairs from the days before the war of 1914-18 when a high military authority had referred to the aeroplanes as 'very pretty toys'.' He asked whence this question of the abolition of air forces came, and said to his mind it came from misconception on the part of many people that you could make war humane. This was impossible. War was a business of legalized killing. Air Forces were the greatest deterrent against war. He continued:

> Statesmen and others who contemplate a war in the future know full well that if they have the temerity to take the responsibility of abolishing the Air Force they lay open their country to terrible attacks.

The danger to civilization arose from the prolonging of war. Anything that would shorten war, and air forces were the most potent to do such a thing, should be retained. His hearers must not think that the Royal Air Force had their tails down. On the contrary they were quite cheerful, nor did they believe the outcome of Geneva would be as sentimentalists believed.

Unknown to Geoffrey, a reporter was present at the private dinner, and the following morning the speech was widely reported in the newspapers. Immediately, telegrams and letters of congratulation arrived from many RAF friends, but members of the Labour Party in Parliament were to ask questions in the House. In the atmosphere of Geneva, the publication of Geoffrey's fighting speech was bound to bring out into the open the dangers of disarmament. Mr Mander, Labour MP for Wolverhampton East, asked the Under Secretary for Air if his attention had been called to the speech by Air Marshal Sir Geoffrey Salmond, Commander-in-Chief of the Air Defence of Great Britain, on 26 November, advocating that military Air Forces should not be abolished and, seeing this view was contrary to the declared policy of the Government, what action he proposed to take to restrain such speeches by serving officers. Mr Grenfell, Labour MP for Gower, supported him.

Sir Philip Sassoon had to pour oil on troubled waters. He said:

> I do not think it necessary to correct in detail the somewhat misleading account of the circumstances and their implications contained in these questions, but may say briefly that the officer named, in the course of a speech at a private Service dinner, where he had no reason to think his remarks would be reported, made certain observations which were not, of course, intended for publication in any shape or form. Accordingly, I think it is a matter of regret that those expressions of opinion should have been detached from their context and given a publicity which was very far from the author's intentions. (Ministerial cheers). In the circumstances my noble friend does not consider any special action is called for.

After a few more exchanges, the Speaker said it appeared to him that the question on the paper had been answered already, and to put another question would not be in order. So ended the Questions in the House, but how far Geoffrey's speech influenced the public will never be known, nor how much his words contributed to the survival of the Royal Air Force.

Chief of the Air Staff, 1933

The year 1933 seemed to hold such great hopes for the family. Geoff was to take up his appointment on 1 April and they were to move up to London, to their house at 34 Hyde Park Gardens, overlooking Hyde Park, which had been let during their time in India and Uxbridge. They all had very happy memories of it, for they had moved there from Sussex Place before going to India. No one could have foretold the sadness which was to follow, nor the tragedy that lay ahead.

In February there was an expedition which would have been very dear to Geoffrey's heart. The Marquess of Clydesdale had decided to arrange an expedition to fly for the first time over Mount Everest in the Himalayas. Unable to finance the expedition themselves, the members had appealed to Lady Houston, who after due consideration decided to finance the exploit. Wing Commander Peregrine Fellowes, who had come down in a parachute at the same time as Geoffrey, had been chosen to accompany the party, as with his experience in the RAF he would be a great asset. The tests of the aircraft over, the two Westland machines were packed for shipment to India in the SS *Dalgoma*, due to arrive early in March.

On 16 February Geoff, Peggy, Joyce and Anne were all at Hendon to see the pilots of the expedition off to India. The Marquess of Clydesdale was to pilot a Puss Moth, McIntyre a Gypsy Moth and Peregrine Fellowes a Puss Moth, lent by the Fry's chocolate business. Lady Houston telegraphed to the Viceroy (Lord Willingdon) asking him to receive the expedition and give his blessing, to which he had replied: 'Will gladly receive members of expedition so generously financed by you and wish them God Speed in their great adventure.'

The flight over Everest was the greatest possible success. On 3 April both Westland aircraft braved the weather and flew over the mountain. The crews cabled their thanks to Lady Houston for having 'again been responsible for putting Britain in the forefront of aviation.' Blacker, who flew with Lord Clydesdale, recorded later: 'Suddenly our craft sprang clear of the haze into the wonderful translucence of the upper heights and on our right an amazing view of Kanchenjunga in all its gleaming whiteness opened against the blue. For a few moments there was nothing and then, over the pulsating rocker arms of the engine, far away but level with us, came the naked majesty of Everest.' It was an unforgettable experience for all the pilots.

Sadly, Geoffrey was never to hear the story of their flight at first hand. Early in March he thought perhaps his lumbago was returning, but he did not take it seriously, thinking a few days' rest would cure it, but soon the pain grew worse. It was just at that time that Joyce and Anne had been asked to a dance at the newly formed Oxford University Air Squadron. Their father said they could go, and of course they had no idea how ill he was feeling. As they drove out of the gate, a young airman on a motorbike swept into the drive. Recognizing T. E. Lawrence, Joyce immediately stopped the car. He had come to see her father and they later found him talking quietly and seriously to their mother in the drawing-room.

Perhaps some instinct had told Lawrence to come that day to see Geoffrey. He also asked him if he could be given some more interesting work in the RAF, as although his work on the flying boats had fascinated him, and he had been of great help in the Schneider Trophy races, he had now been offered work he felt was uninteresting. He smiled at the two girls and said, 'Enjoy your dance.' Although he kept in touch with their mother, it was the last time they were ever to see him.

It was typical of Geoffrey that although so ill, he managed over the next few days to recommend Lawrence for far more interesting work in the RAF, telling him also how much the RAF appreciated him and all he had done. It was the last act of kindness that Geoff would make for his friend.

Soon afterwards, it became clear that he had to go into hospital. He insisted that it should be the Royal Air Force Hospital at Uxbridge. There it was found that he was suffering from cancer, and that it was already at an advanced stage. Little could be done. Soon afterwards his condition grew so much worse that he was transferred to King Edward VII, Sister Agnes' Hospital for Officers in London where, for three weeks, he fought gallantly for life, but he knew he was growing weaker.

On 27 April, early in the afternoon, his life slipped away. Both Jack and Peggy were with him when he died. He was only fifty-three. His illness had been so unexpected and so sudden that at first his family and friends felt stunned. An official communiqué was issued that night by the Air Ministry:

> The Air Council deeply regret to announce the death of Air Chief Marshal Sir Geoffrey Salmond, KCB, KCMG, DSO, Chief of the Air Staff, which took place this afternoon in the King Edward the Seventh Hospital for Officers.

The editor of *The Aeroplane*, C.G. Grey wrote:

> The death of Sir Geoffrey Salmond will cause personal sorrow to very many people outside the Air Force as well as in it. Few men have had such a gift of inspiring at the same time personal affection and admira-

tion. And everybody who has served with him, or under him, and those civilians who had the privilege of meeting him either officially or in a private capacity, will feel that they have lost a friend.

Speaking at the Annual Dinner of the Royal Aeronautical Society two days later, Sir Philip Sassoon said:

> Before I deal with the toast which stands in my name I should like, and I know you would wish me, to refer briefly to the great loss which the Royal Air Force and our country has suffered in the most untimely death of Sir Geoffrey Salmond. There is a poignant element of tragedy in the fact that a career so brilliant should have been cut short at the very moment when the top of the ladder had been reached. It is a peculiar misfortune to the Service that a man who had played so large a part in its up-building, and in the creation of the fine spirit which inspires it, should have been taken away just at the very moment when the opportunity had been given to him to put the final touches to his life's work. Great in the field, in the air and in the council chamber, his character was so fine, so lovable. He is indeed an irreparable loss. He will be deeply missed, not only by his personal friends but by all ranks of the Service. I feel sure that you would like to stand for a moment in silence, as a token of our respect for our dead Commander, and of our sympathy with his relatives.

No tribute could express more eloquently what all who knew him felt about Geoff. Mr. Fairey, for the aircraft industry, also said that all who knew Sir Geoffrey and worked with him knew him as a great officer and loved him for his humanity.

After summarizing his life, C.G. Grey wrote:

> Thus all may see, by the death of Geoffrey Salmond we have lost a great leader of men, a great organiser, a true statesman . . . but above and beyond that, many have lost a very dear friend.

Most touching, perhaps, was the tribute written by his friend, Air Vice Marshal Borton, in *The Times* of 29 April:

> The most poignant memories in life are perhaps those of youth, and the Royal Air Force, hardly yet grown-up as one of the fighting services, will grieve over the passing of Air Chief Marshal Sir Geoffrey Salmond, whose name will for ever be a reminder of its early struggles and triumphant development. He it was who, in the early days of the Royal Flying Corps, was a constant source of inspiration, and whose faith, vision and enthusiasm never failed. His wide experience and study of flying in all its

branches had qualified him, as few were qualified before the War, to offer suggestions regarding the development of the new factor in military policy, and nature had endowed him with the grit and determination to see them carried into effect. The War was soon to prove that his visions were practical and his foresight unswerving in the development of air tactics. So it came about that in 1915 he went out, with a handful of aeroplanes, to Egypt, nominally to aid in the protection of the Suez Canal. From this small and unpretentious beginning grew the Command whose importance has not yet been fully recognised, and which eventually comprised Egypt, Salonika, Palestine, Mesopotamia, India and East Africa. In each of these widely separated theatres the inspiration to success was the personality of the commander. Salonika welcomed his visits as those of an encouraging friend. In Palestine, nearer to him geographically, the RFC and Australian Squadrons knew and loved him. In Mesopotamia, India and East Africa the tale was the same. His abiding interest in the personal welfare of all under his command never faltered, and endeared him to officers and men alike. After the Armistice, once again his vision and initiative laid foundation-stones of vital importance to the commercial air routes of the Empire. When asked by cable from England for his views on the possibility of investigating the air route to the Cape, it was typical of the drive and resource of the man that he replied, within a few hours, to the effect that he had despatched expeditions to East and South Africa and to the headwaters of the Nile. Thus was laid the foundation of the present Air Mail Service in Africa. Having sent his cable, he embarked without more ado in a Handley-Page aeroplane on a pioneer flight from Egypt to India, accompanied by the writer of this tribute. He was a matchless companion on such an undertaking, and when some damage was caused to the aeroplane in landing at one of the aerodromes on the Persian Gulf it was his initiative and resource which found a worn-out lathe with which to effect repairs. He was destined later to return to India and write the air epic of the evacuation for Kabul. In all his activities, the same outstanding characteristic predominated, a capacity for arousing the loyal devotion of all who came into contact with him. His almost boyish enthusiasm, his personal knowledge and interest in all who served under him, his unswerving fidelity of purpose, combined to make him an ideal leader, and the most lovable of men. There remains the inspiration to go forward, and to realise those ideals upon the fulfilment of which his heart was set, and his great gifts were concentrated.

There was also a tribute in *The Times* from 'MB', which could not conceal the name of Maurice Baring.

While Geoffrey had been ill, Jack had once more taken over as Chief of the

Air Staff, hoping that he would recover. On 1 May Geoffrey was given a funeral with full military honours. The King was represented by Air Marshal Sir Edward Ellington, and the pall bearers included Marshal of the Royal Air Force Lord Trenchard, Air Marshal Sir Robert Brooke-Popham and Air Marshal H. C. T. Dowding. Lord Londonderry, Secretary of State for Air, Sir Philip Sassoon and Sir Christopher Bullock accompanied the procession by many foreign diplomats. The gun carriage was pulled by six horses and Sir Geoffrey's plumed hat and sword lay on the Union Jack which covered the coffin. The escort was composed of the Central Band of the Royal Air Force and a detachment of thirty officers and five hundred men of the RAF. The band played Chopin's Funeral March and the short route from Hyde Park Gardens to St. John's Church was lined by airmen, standing with their arms reversed. Sir Geoffrey's medals and insignia were carried by his nephew, Flight Lieutenant William Hebden (later Air Commodore). Almost all Geoffrey's friends were able to be there that day, and the Church was full of flowers.

Perhaps the most moving moment of all was the appearance of a single aircraft, which flew above the procession and, as they entered the Church, dipped a wing in salute before disappearing into the summer sky. Next day the newspapers were full of tributes, almost all carrying the headline 'The Man who destroyed an Army'.

But I think Geoffrey would have preferred to be remembered, as his friends remembered him, as one of that 'Happy Band of Brothers' who had, by their inspiration, built and shaped the new Service, the Royal Air Force, and who, not so very long ago, had taken their courage in both hands and learned to fly.

PER ARDUA AD ASTRA

EPILOGUE

One of the most moving moments of my life occurred a few months after my father died.

My godmother had taken me to India, optimistic that, in some way, the life out there would help to make my grief less intense, in the hope that I would enjoy it.

Being only just nineteen, of course I did enjoy myself, but nevertheless, a black cloud seemed to hang over me and my heart was at home with my mother, sisters and brother.

After six months I came home alone. I so well remember how I used to stand at the stern of the ship, looking at the golden light of the setting sun streaming over the darkening water and all the time, wondering what life would be like without him, whom we had all loved so much.

There was a young man on board who appeared to feel that he just could not do enough for me. Knowing that he had a girlfriend, I could not understand his concern. Eventually, as we were crossing the Channel, he asked me if he could send a telegram to my family to say that I was arriving. He would do anything he could to help. When I thanked him but said that I was quite all right and could manage that myself, he burst out that Geoffrey had done so much for him when he was a young airman in Egypt: his mother had been seriously ill and my father had helped him to get home to be with her. My father had been so good to him that he would do anything in the world for me.

I have never forgotten that outburst, it was so genuine and so deeply touching and such tangible proof of how Geoffrey's men had felt about him.

For such an inspired leader with the imagination and vision which he possessed in such great measure and which had given birth to so much innovation, never to have lost the essential human kindness and generosity of spirit for which he was renowned throughout the ranks of the Royal Air Force, made him a very special person in its history.

APPENDIX

HONOURS

1. Order of the Bath (Crimean ribbon. Painted Star)

2. KCMG (Blue-red-blue ribbon)

3. DSO and Bar. 1st January 1919

4. DSO March 3rd 1917

'Citation for conspicuous ability and devotion to duty when personally directing the work of the Royal Flying Corps during the action. The striking success was largely due to his magnificent personal example.' For Operations in Sinai at end of 1916.

MEDALS

1. South African Medal with seven clasps. 2. China Campaign Medal. 3. Mons Star and bar. 4. War Medal 1914-18. 5. Peace Medal. Mentioned in Despatches three times.

FOREIGN ORDERS

1. Russian Order of St. Stanislav. Inaugurated 1915.

2. Order of the Redeemer (Greek). Four-pointed star with Greek Cross on reverse side.

3. 2nd class order of 'The Nahda' conferred on Sir Geoffrey by the King of the Hejaz. (Appeared in the *Aquibla* of 24 November 1919. (White ribbon and white rose)).

4. Order of the Nile
'For those who benefited the country'
'What benefits Egypt owes to the Nile – her source of prosperity and happiness.' (Written on the reverse side of the Order.)

EIGHT TIMES MENTIONED IN DESPATCHES

1. Major W.G.H. Salmond attd. R.F.C. was mentioned in a Despatch from Field Marshal Sir John D.P. French G.C.B., O.M., G.C.V.O., K.C.B. 14 January 1915.
(Signed) Winston Churchill Sec. of State for War.

2. Colonel W.G.H. Salmond R.A.
For gallant and distinguished service in the Field.
(Signed) Winston Churchill.

3. Lieutenant Colonel W.G.H. Salmond R.A. was mentioned in a Despatch from General Sir A.J. Murray K.C.B., K.C.M.G., C.V.O., D.S.O. 1 July 1916 for gallant and distinguished service in the Field.
(Signed) Winston Churchill.

4. Brigadier General W.G.H. Salmond D.S.O., R.A. and R.F.C.
18 March 1917 From Gen. Murray.
(Signed) Winston Churchill.

5. Brigadier General W.G.H. Salmond D.S.O., R.F.C. was mentioned in a despatch from Gen. Sir F.R. Wingate G.C.B., G.C.V.O., G.B.E., K.C.M.G., D.S.O. 25 June 1917 for gallant and distinguished service in the Field. (Signed) Winston Churchill.

6. Brigadier General W.G.H. Salmond D.S.O., R.A. and R.F.C. 7 November 1917
(Signed) Winston Churchill. Mentioned in the *London Gazette*.

7. Major General W.G.H. Salmond D.S.O. (R.A.) 23 October 1918. Mentioned in Despatch from General Sir E.H.H. Allenby. (Signed) Winston Churchill.

8. Major General W.G.H. Salmond C.B., D.S.O. 5 March 1919 was mentioned in a despatch from General Sir E.H.H. Allenby, G.C.B., G.C.M.G.
(Signed) W. Churchill Secretary of State for War.

In every mention:
'I have it in the command from the King to record His Majesty's high appreciation of the services rendered.
(Signed) Winston Churchill.'

BIBLIOGRAPHY

AIR 1/2286/209/75/20. *Organisation of the Middle East Air Force* (The Public Records Office)

AIR 1/523/16/12/14. *Notes for Artillery Observers* (The Public Record Office)

AIR 1/524/16/12/21. *Aircraft Co-operation with Artillery* (The Public Record Office)

Baring, Maurice. *Flying Corps Headquarters 1914-18*

Barker, Ralph. *The Royal Flying Corps in France*

Bell, Lady. *The Letters of Gertrude Bell* (Ernest Bell 1927)

Boyle, Andrew. *Trenchard –Man of Vision* (Collins 1962)

Cobham, Sir Alan. *My Flight to the Cape and Back (A & C Black 1946)*

Cromer, The Earl of. *Modern Egypt* (Macmillan and Co 1937)

Dean, Sir Maurice. *The Royal Air Force in Two World Wars* (Cassells 1979)

Gardner, Brian. *Allenby* (Cassell 1965)

Goodall, H.H. *Flying Start* (Brooklands Museum 1995)

Graves, Robert. *Lawrence and the Arabs* (Jonathan Cape 1927)

Hart, Liddell. *T.E. Lawrence* (Jonathan Cape 1934)

Hyde, Montgomery. *British Policy between the Wars*

Jones, A.H. *The War in the Air Vol 2*

Joubert de la Ferté, Philip. *The Third Service* (Thomas and Hudson 1955)

King, H.F. *Sopwith Aircraft 1912-1920* (Putnam 1980)

Laffin, John. *Swifter than Eagles* (Blackwood 1964)

Lawrence, A.W. *T.E. Lawrence by his Friends* (Alden Press)

Lawrence, T.E. *Revolt in the Desert* (Jonathan Cape 1926)

Lawrence, T.E. *Seven Pillars of Wisdom* (Jonathan Cape 1927, 1935)

Lewis, C.S. *Sagittarius Rising* (Peter David 1936, later Penguin Books)

Longmore, Air Chief Marshal Sir Arthur. *From Sea to Sky* (Geoffrey Bles 1947)

Macmillan, Captain. *The Royal Flying Corps in World War 1*

McGregor, Alan. *Flying the Furrow (Saudi Aremco World 2001)*

Naylor, J.L. and Owen, E. *Aviation of Today* (Frederick Waize and Co. 1930)

Norris, Geoffrey. *The Royal Flying Corps –A History* (Frederick Muller 1965)

Orlebar, Christopher. *The Concorde*

Penrose, Harold. *The Adventuring Years* (British Aviation: H.M. Stationery Office 1979)

Penrose, Harold. *Widening Horizons* (British Aviation: H.M. Stationery Office 1979)

Raleigh, Walter. *The War in the Air Vol 1* (The Clarendon Press Oxford 1922)

Robertson, Bruce. *Sopwith – The Man and his Aircraft*

Salmond, Sir Geoffrey. *Letters and Lectures* (The Royal Air Force Museum)

Saunders, Hilary St George. *'Per Adua'. The Rise of British Air Power 1911-39* (Oxford University Press)

Smuts, J.C. *Jan Christian Smuts* (Cassell & Co 1952)

Steel, Nigel and Hart, Peter. *Tumult in the Clouds* (Hodder and Stoughton 1997)

Swinson, Arthur. *The North West Frontier* (Hutchinson 1967)

Sykes, Sir Frederick. *From Many Angles*

Tabachik, Stephen and Matheson, C. *Images of Lawrence* (Jonathan Cape 1988)

Taylor, John W.R. *C.F.S. Birthplace of Air Power*

Templewood, Viscount. *Empire of the Air* (Collins 1927)

Templewood, Viscount. *To India by Air* (Longmans Green and Co. 1927)

Thomas, Lowell. *With Lawrence in Arabia* (Hutchinson)

Trenchard – Salmond Letters (The Royal Air Force Museum)

Wilson, Jeremy. *Lawrence of Arabia* (Atheneum, New York 1990)

Wingate, Ronald. *Wingate of the Sudan* (John Murray 1955)

The History of the Schneider Trophy Races

The Report on the Middle East Conference in Cairo and Jerusalem March 12th–30th 1921

I am grateful for permission to use many other original letters and articles by Sir Geoffrey Salmond and the hitherto unpublished memoirs of Sir John Salmond.

INDEX

Salmond, Air Chief Marshal Sir [William] Geoffrey [Hanson] (Geoff)